Penguin Books

The Lightman Rep

THE NATIONAL UNION OF MINEWORKERS

REPORT OF GAVIN LIGHTMAN, Q.C.,

TO THE

NATIONAL EXECUTIVE COMMITTEE

3rd July 1990

PENGUIN BOOKS

PENGUIN BOOKS

Published by the Penguin Group
Penguin Books Ltd, 27 Wrights Lane, London W8 5TZ, England
Viking Penguin, a division of Penguin Books USA Inc.
375 Hudson Street, New York, New York 10014, USA
Penguin Books Australia Ltd, Ringwood, Victoria, Australia
Penguin Books Canada Ltd, 2801 John Street, Markham, Ontario, Canada L3R 1B4
Penguin Books (NZ) Ltd, 182–190 Wairau Road, Auckland 10, New Zealand

Penguin Books Ltd, Registered Offices: Harmondsworth, Middlesex, England

First published 1990
1 3 5 7 9 10 8 6 4 2

Printed in England by Clays Ltd, St Ives plc

Index

Annexes

National Union of Mineworkers
Report of Mr. Gavin Lightman Q.C.
to the National Executive Committee

CHAPTER 1: INTRODUCTION

1.1:The Background to the Enquiry

1   Between 5th and 9th March 1990, the Daily Mirror and Central Television's "The Cook Report" published and broadcast a number of allegations relating to the conduct of the finances of the National Union of Mineworkers ("the NUM") by the National Officials of the NUM during the 1984-5 National Strike. In particular, it was alleged that the NUM, or the National Officials, had accepted money from Libya and the USSR in the course of the strike; and that Mr. Scargill and Mr. Heathfield had used part of the money given by Libya for hardship purposes in order to pay off sums owed to the NUM by Mr. Scargill, Mr. Heathfield and Mr. Roger Windsor, then the Chief Executive Office of the NUM.

2   On 9th March 1990, Mr.Scargill and Mr. Heathfield gave an explanation of the matters raised by the Daily Mirror and Central Television to the National Executive Committee; and the National Executive Committee resolved as follows:

"the National Executive Committee, at its meeting on 9th March 1990 unanimously accept the recommendations of the National Officials to appoint an Independent Enquiry into the allegations made by Central Television and the Mirror Group of Newspapers against the National Officials.

The National Executive Committee agree that the Enquiry should consist of an eminent Q.C. whose terms of reference shall be to investigate the allegations made by Central Television and Mirror Group of Newspapers in respect of the National Officials accepting money alleged to have come from Libya in December 1984 and Soviet finances alleged to have come into the funds of the NUM, and the allegation that in December 1984 the Officials used money alleged to have come from Libya to pay off their personal mortgages/loans.

The Committee agree that a 5-man Sub-Committee consisting of Messrs. J. Taylor, G. Rees, G. Butler, I. Morgan and H. Richardson should meet the Haldane Society of Lawyers and ask them to appoint a suitable Q.C. to conduct this Enquiry."

3   On 21.3.90, after consultation with the Haldane Society, the sub-committee approached me and asked me to carry out this Enquiry. My terms of reference were as follows:

1.   **Were any monies paid to or for the benefit of the NUM or its members from the beginning of the 1984-5 miners' strike to date by Libya or the USSR?**

2.   **If any monies were so received then how were these monies applied and where is the residue now?**

3.   **Were any monies, being either monies received from Libya or the USSR or any other monies of the NUM or monies received for or on behalf of the NUM or its members, used to repay home loans or improvement loans for the benefit of Mr. Scargill, Mr. Heathfield or Mr. Windsor?**

4   These terms of reference were proposed by me after reading the press reports and were agreed by the sub-committee. It was also made clear to me by the sub-committee that if, in the course of the Enquiry, it seemed to me that the terms of reference were too narrow, I should come back to the sub-committee in order to invite them to extend my terms of reference. By the 1st June 1990, it became apparent to me that the terms of reference were too narrow, and accordingly I requested the sub-committee to extend my terms of reference to include one further question and this they agreed to do on the 7th June 1990. This further question was as follows:-

"4.   **Has there been any misapplication of funds or assets of the NUM or any breach of duty by the National Officials in connection with or arising out of the financial arrangements made by the NUM or the National Officials during or in connection with the 1984-5 Miners Strike?"**

5   On my appointment I also considered, and informed the sub-committee of my views on, the form of the Enquiry. The decision to be made was whether the Enquiry, whole or in part, should be held in public or in private. The answer, it seemed to me, depended on which of these courses was the better calculated to achieve the truth or an approximation to the truth. I have, of course, no power to compel witnesses to give evidence or to compel those who are prepared to give evidence to do so on oath or to answer any question which they are unwilling to answer. It seemed to me that on balance witnesses would be more likely to be forthcoming if interviewed in private and my experience during this Enquiry has proved this view to be correct. A large part of the Enquiry necessarily consisted of investigating and analysing financial records and this certainly could not be done in public. I had to balance on the other side the intimations already given by certain potential witnesses reported in the press that they would decline to co-operate with a private Enquiry and the implication that they might co-operate if the evidence was given in public. I reached the conclusion that the better course was to carry out

3

the Enquiry entirely in private, and whilst the decision whether to publish my report is a matter for the National Executive Committee, the expectation must be that if the contents of the Report raise matters which the members of the NUM have an interest in knowing, and which in their interest ought to be disclosed, the National Executive Committee will publish my Report.

6 I was also given full authority by the sub-committee to engage whatever professional or other assistance I needed in order to carry out my Enquiry.

7 I immediately made two such appointments which I (correctly) perceived were essential to the prompt and effective execution of my task. First I appointed a practising barrister, Ms Elizabeth Jones, to act as my assistant. Secondly I appointed Messrs. Cork Gully to carry out the necessary accounting and financial investigations. The team from Cork Gully, working under the supervision of the Senior Partner Mr. Michael Jordan and Mr. David Graham Q.C., consisted of Mr. Richard Coleman, Mr. David Brookland and Mr. Kevin McDonald. I must share with them any credit due for this Report. I must especially express my appreciation for the untiring efforts and invaluable contributions of Ms Jones and Mr Brookland.

8 It is convenient to state here that where a conclusion reached by Cork Gully is expressed in this report, I accept that conclusion and treat it as my own.

1.2 Procedural steps

9 I invited co-operation, in the first instance, from the Daily Mirror and Central Television. They saw no advantage in doing so. I was disappointed, but not surprised, when both organisations declined to assist.

10 I also wrote to the three individuals whose services the Daily Mirror and Central Television obtained for the purposes of their publication and broadcast, namely Mr Roger Windsor, the former Chief Executive Officer of the NUM, Mr

James Parker, Mr Scargill's former chauffeur, and Mr Abbasi, the alleged conduit for the payment of monies from Libya to the NUM. In view of the attitude taken by the Daily Mirror and Central Television, it is no surprise, and perhaps no coincidence, that they either declined to assist or did not reply.

11 The National Executive Committee, at my request, instructed all NUM members, employees, officers and officials to co-operate with my Enquiry. From time to time, the sub-committee has also written, at my request, to various witnesses with whom the NUM has some connection, requesting them to offer me full co-operation.

12 In the first instance, I invited evidence from the principal witnesses or potential witnesses in writing. A list of witnesses from whom I have received written evidence is set out in Part I of Annexe A to this report. In the case of some witnesses, I received unsolicited evidence. I also received certain further evidence from witnesses who were only prepared to assist on an assurance of anonymity. I only accepted evidence on these terms when I was satisfied that good grounds existed for anonymity and that such anonymity could not result in any injustice to any other party.

13 A list of the witnesses from whom I have taken oral evidence (other than those to whom I have promised anonymity) is set out in Part II of Annexe A.

14 I also received all documentation from the NUM which I requested, through the sub-committee who appointed me. Two important documents which were supplied to me very early on in the Enquiry were the NUM's Press Release of 5th March 1990 and the National Officials' report to the National Executive Committee dated 9th March 1990, both of which are set out in Annexe B to this report.

15 I should also acknowledge here the invaluable help given both to Cork Gully

and to me by the former Finance Officer of the NUM, Mr Stephen Hudson, and by Mr Ian White, Finance Officer, and Mrs Hazel Riley, Assistant Finance Officer.

1.3 Limitations of this Report

16 There are limitations upon the scope and depth of this Report arising from a number of factors.

16.1   I have no power to require witnesses to attend or to produce documents and a number of witnesses have refused to assist. It is right, however, to point out that the NUM and its officials have given me full co-operation.

16.2   There is the constraint of costs. This is self imposed and not imposed by the National Executive Committee but it would be irresponsible for me to incur greater costs than can reasonably be justified by the likely return, having regard in particular to the financial state of the NUM.

16.3   There is the constraint of time in that this Report is intended to be of practical assistance to the NUM and accordingly should be made available to the NUM in order to enable any necessary action to be taken as soon as practical. It seemed to me highly desirable that the period of uncertainty, suspicion and rumour should be prolonged as little as possible and that the interests of the Union, its members and officials were one in ensuring that this Report (if it could be ready in time) should be available for consideration at the Annual Conference due to be held on the 9th July 1990.

16.4   In the event, there has been a limitation imposed by the reluctance and eventual downright refusal of the International Miners Organisation (through its General Secretary Mr Simon) to co-operate, the lack of any response from the miners union in the USSR, and the lack of meaningful co-operation from the CGT in France.

16.5   However, I am satisfied that I have been able to reach answers to all but one of the questions which I have been asked.

17 There are a number of areas of background information which are essential to an understanding of the scope and conclusions of this Report, and I have set these out in the next Chapter. Much or even most of this will be familiar to members of the National Executive Committee; but I bear in mind that many current members of the National Executive Committee were not members in 1984-5, and ask indulgence from those for whom the next Chapter adds nothing to their understanding.

18 In order to assist the reading of this very lengthy and complex Report, a list of the principal characters, and a list of abbreviations used in this Report are set out in Annexe X at the very end of the Report.

CHAPTER 2: BACKGROUND INFORMATION

2.1 Constitution of NUM and Duties of National Officials

19 For the sake of convenience, I set out here a brief description of the constitutional matters which are important for the understanding of this Report. A more detailed note on the Constitution of the NUM is contained in Annexe C to this report.

20 The National Union's members are divided into "Areas", some of which are themselves registered trade unions. An Area which is also a registered trade union is called a "Constituent Association".

21 The government of the Union is vested in the Conference of Delegates, which may function in Annual or Special Conference. Between Conferences, the business and affairs of the Union are administered by the National Executive Committee which also has the duty to perform all duties laid down for it by resolution of Conference. The National Executive Committee may not act contrary to, or in defiance of, any resolution of Conference. The National Executive Committee may delegate any of its powers to sub-committees comprising members of the National Executive Committee.

22 There are two full-time officials, the President and the Secretary. The Vice-President is not a full time post. The full duties of the President and Secretary are set out in Annexe C; but it should be noted that their authority and power derives only from the National Executive Committee. The President is under an express duty to ensure that the business of the Union is conducted according to the Rules. The Secretary is under an express obligation each year to prepare and submit to the National Executive Committee a balance sheet showing the financial position of the Union.

23 The property and funds of the Union are vested in the Trustees. The trustees are, however, obliged to act on the instructions of the National Executive Committee or Conference (but see paragraphs 7 and 9.1 of Annexe C). The trustees have no power under the rules to authorise expenditure.

24 The remuneration of the National Officials must be determined by Conference on the recommendation of the National Executive Committee.

2.2 Brief History of the 1984-5 National Strike

25 The strike began on 13.3.84 and continued until 4.3.85. On 10.10.84 the NUM was fined £200,000 for disregarding orders made in the action Taylor v. NUM (Yorkshire Area). On 25.10.84, the fine not having been paid, Sequestrators were appointed to sequestrate the property of the Union.

26 On November 8th 1984, 16 members of the NUM commenced proceedings (entitled Clarke v. Heathfield) against the trustees of the Union's assets and various officers of the Union, seeking orders for the removal of the trustees on the ground that the assets of the Union were in jeopardy whilst in their hands. On November 30, 1984 an opposed ex parte application came before Mervyn Davies J. for interim relief over until December 6, 1984. On that application he made an order for the removal of the trustees and the appointment of Mr. Brewer as Receiver of the income and assets of the Union (save in so far as the same might be in the possession or control of the Sequestrators). On Saturday December 1, 1984, the Court of Appeal dismissed an appeal from this Order.

27 The inter partes hearing of the application for interlocutory relief came before the judge on December 6, 1984. Before this date, objection having been taken to

the fitness of Mr. Brewer to act as Receiver, the Plaintiffs in his place sought to appoint a Mr. Arnold, a partner in Arthur Young & Co. The learned judge granted the application. He also held that jeopardy to the trust assets of the union required the appointment of the Receiver to be made. "...the trustees activities have placed the [union's] funds in jeopardy by subjecting the funds to obligations to pay a substantial fine and by leaving no conclusion but that their conduct, if now unchecked, may lead to further fines". In concluding his judgment, he said "Since I am removing the trustees, there will be an appointment of a Receiver to act for the time being until new trustees are appointed, or, on a change of heart, the removed trustees are restored". The hopes of an early discharge of the receivership order engendered by these words proved misplaced. Though the strike ended on the 4th March 1985 and the sequestration order was discharged on the 14th November 1985, the Receiver was only discharged on the 27th June 1986. (I have written a detailed account on the legal history of the receivership and sequestration in 1987 Current Legal Problems pages 25-54).

28 The efforts made by the NUM to place its assets beyond the reach of the Sequestrators and later the Receiver, and in particular the export of funds abroad, led to the institution of proceedings in the name of the Union against the National Officials (Mr Heathfield, Mr Scargill and Mr McGahey), the trustees of the Mineworkers Trust (Mr Burrows, Mr Homer and Mr Windsor) and a number of banks through whose accounts the monies passed in their travels. These were initiated by the Receiver in August 1984, were continued after the discharge of the Receiver by the Union trustees, and were finally settled on the 29 January 1988.

29 I should make it clear, as I did before and after my appointment, that I acted for the NUM, the National Officials and the NUM trustees during the legal proceedings described above. I should also make it clear that on one occasion I advised the trustees of the Mineworkers Trust in conference in respect of the breach of trust action mentioned above, when I advised that the action should be

settled on the basis that the assets settled by the NUM on the trustees of the Mineworkers Trust should be returned to the NUM.

2.3 The MTUI and the IMO

30 The Miners Trade Union International ("MTUI") and the International Miners Organisation ("IMO") play an important part in the events investigated in this Enquiry and accordingly something should be said at this stage about these organisations, before returning to the narrative of the events of 1984-5.

31 Until 1985, miners' unions were affiliated to organisations roughly following the political division between east and west. Most of the eastern bloc miners' unions were affiliated to the World Federation of Trade Unions ("WFTU"). The miners' division of the WFTU was the MTUI (founded in 1949). In 1985, and indeed since 1977, the Secretary General of the MTUI was Alain Simon ("Mr Simon"), an executive committee member of the French CGT.

32 The western bloc miners' unions were generally affiliated to the Miners International Federation, part of the International Confederation of Free Trade Unions ("ICFTU").

33 From about 1982 onwards, ongoing discussions took place between a number of different unions, including the NUM and the CGT, with a view to establishing an international miners union. In September 1985, the IMO was formed, to which the NUM became affiliated. The IMO is not affiliated either to the WFTU or to the ICFTU. Mr. Scargill was one of the prime movers in the creation of the IMO and on its creation became the President of the IMO. The general secretary is and has at all material times been Mr Simon. After the formation of the IMO, the MTUI dissolved itself and its undertaking was, it appears, taken over by the IMO.

Mr. Scargill and Mr. Simon were at all times the driving force behind the subsequent operations of the IMO and Mr. Heathfield has occupied a senior position. Mr. Scargill is the President, an unpaid position. Mr. Simon has been since the inception of the IMO its general secretary, a post vesting in him, in effect, the day to day management of the affairs of the IMO. Mr. Heathfield has been Chairman of what he describes as the Business and Policy Committee, but what Mr Scargill describes as the General Political Committee.

34 The IMO apparently now has over 6,000,000 members from 46 organisations around the world. The supreme organ of the IMO is a Congress which meets at least once every four years. Between meetings of Congress, the affairs of the IMO are managed by the Executive Committee. Between the Executive Committee meetings, the constitution of the IMO provides for management by the executive Bureau, but Mr Scargill has told me that in fact it is managed by the permanent secretariat. There is also a full time General Secretary. In effect, the IMO is controlled on a day to day basis by the General Secretary (Mr Simon) and the permanent secretariat.

35 The composition of the permanent secretariat, the executive bureau and the executive committee are set out in Annexe D to this Report.

36 The constitution of the IMO (also included in Annexe D) provides that the accounts of the IMO shall be audited and prepared by the Finance Committee. However, Mr. Scargill has told me that the Secretary of the Finance Committee merely gives a brief oral report to Congress, and no accounts are prepared, let alone audited.Mr. Scargill has also told me that the IMO does not keep minutes of its decisions.

37 The secrecy surrounding the finances of the IMO is practically impenetrable without the co-operation of Mr Simon. As I will detail hereafter, the finances of

on the one hand the MTUI until its absorption into the IMO and thereafter of the IMO, and on the other hand of the NUM, over the period of and since the strike have been so interwoven, and the records available are so limited, that no satisfactory picture can be obtained without the full cooperation of Mr Simon. Mr Simon has afforded much less than this cooperation.

38 I wrote two letters to Mr. Simon, one enclosing a long list of detailed questions relating to this Enquiry. Mr Simon wrote me two letters which gave some limited information in a very general form, and totally failed to answer the detailed questions. Mr. Simon also declined to be interviewed by me in connection with this Enquiry.

CHAPTER 3: FINANCIAL ARRANGEMENTS MADE IN CONSEQUENCE OF THE 1984-5 STRIKE, THE SEQUESTRATION AND RECEIVERSHIP

3.1 Protection of Assets

39 I return now to the events of 1984. The NUM perceived before the strike that in the course of the strike the Union was likely to come into conflict with the law, and that this conflict was likely to give rise to proceedings against the Union for contempt and the appointment of Sequestrators. The precedent of such an appointment in the case of the National Graphical Association in 1983 was ever present to their minds.

40 The successful prosecution of the strike required that union assets (or at least some union assets) remained available to enable the NUM to continue to function or (as it was generally put) to maintain the fabric of the Union, and accordingly steps were set in train at an early date so far as possible to place the NUM property and funds beyond the reach of the law (or at least of the Sequestrators). There was no anticipation of any appointment of a Receiver until about the time that such appointment was made.

41 On the 7th March 1984, a meeting was held "in camera" of the Finance and General Purposes Committee. At this meeting, the decision was taken that the Union funds should be invested abroad and that Areas should be advised at a further private meeting of the National Executive Committee of steps to be taken by them to do likewise, in order that their funds should be available at all times for use by the membership. The report of this decision was accepted by the National Executive Committee at a meeting on the 8th March 1984.

42 On the afternoon of the 8th March 1984, there was held a further "private" meeting of the National Executive Committee and Area Finance officers at the

Royal Victoria Hotel. At this meeting, following a report made by Mr Roger Windsor, unanimous agreement was reached that the National Officials implement the decisions taken at the earlier meeting of the Finance and General Purposes Committee.

43 The Minutes of the three meetings have to this day remained secret and have not been reported to Conference. Full copies of the Minutes appear in Annexe E to this Report.

44 Mr Scargill in his evidence before me first brought these minutes to my attention and he relied on the decisions taken at these meetings to explain actions taken by him. The message to the National Officials (he said) was clear: in the rules of the forthcoming engagement with the Government (which for the Union was a battle for survival), no holds (legal or otherwise) were barred. In the circumstances, I think that I must take them into account and refer to them in this Report. Further, members of the Union are entitled to know what was done, and in fairness to the National Officials any judgment of the actions taken by the National Officials during the strike should be made with these matters in mind.

45 The decisions taken at these meetings were implemented. Some funds were channelled to Switzerland, and this led to proceedings in Switzerland for their recovery by the Receiver and two subsequently publicised flights to Switzerland by Mr. Windsor by private jet at the cost of £12,000 in efforts to protect these funds. The funds in Switzerland were eventually remitted to the Receiver in England. The action of the National Officials in transmitting funds abroad led to the breach of trust action referred to in paragraph 28 above.

3.2 Arrangements for Financing the Strike

46 It must be appreciated that the financial arrangements made fall into 2 distinct

periods. The first period (March 1984-21 October 1984) is the period prior to the appointment of the Sequestrators, when steps were being taken to conceal the Union's assets, but the Union could continue to function and to receive money. The second period is the period after the appointment of the Sequestrators (21st October 1984) and the Receiver (30th November/6th December 1984), when the Union could no longer (at least lawfully or openly) use its own funds to pay its bills and other outgoings essential to its continued functioning. This second period lasted after the strike was over until the Receiver was discharged on 27.6.86.

The first period

47 The NUM required financial assistance to sustain the strike and also needed to conceal its assets in case Sequestrators were appointed. The National Officials assumed the responsibility of procuring this assistance and of concealing the Union's funds abroad pursuant to the "in camera" decision of the National Executive Committee.

48 The financial assistance sought and given was of two characters;

(1) there was financial assistance to the Union itself to maintain the fabric of the Union.

(2) there was financial assistance to alleviate the hardship occasioned by the strike to the families of striking miners.

49 A charitable trust was thus set up to alleviate the hardship to the families, namely the Miners Solidarity Fund (see paragraph 61) and contributions came in for this trust throughout the strike. Prior to the sequestration, I have been told that substantial sums were also coming in for the benefit of the Union itself from well-wishers in Britain and abroad. At this stage, however, receipt of the money posed

no problem and the money could be openly accepted by the NUM.

The second period

50 During this period, donations to the Miners Solidarity Fund could be and were made openly, for the funds could not lawfully be used for the benefit of the Union itself and, since the Union had no legal or equitable interest in the funds, the Sequestrators and Receiver had no right to seize the funds or interfere with the running of the trust.

51 Financial assistance for the Union itself during this period could take one of three forms.

(1) The provider of the money could pay creditors of the NUM direct.

(2) The provider of the money could give money to a third party for the specific purpose of paying **specific** creditors of the Union.

(3) The provider of the money could give money to a third party for the general purposes of the NUM, or, as it was put "to maintain the fabric of the Union".

52 It is unfortunately necessary at this stage to describe briefly the legal issues involved. The Receiver and the Sequestrators could have had in my view (though other may take different views) no objection to the first or second course. However, if money was given or lent to third parties, whether they were the National Officials or any other person, for the purpose of maintaining the fabric of the Union, the result was

(a)   that the money should not have been paid, as a matter of law, to anyone but the Sequestrators during the sequestration and thereafter during the

17

receivership to the Receiver. (It is no part of my role in this Enquiry to comment or pass judgment on this aspect.)

(b)   that the money <u>became the property of the NUM</u>. (This, which may or may not have been appreciated by the National Officials at the time, is fundamental to this Enquiry, and particularly to the change in my terms of reference); and

(c)   that if any of that money was made available by way of loan, and was made available to third parties with the intention of evading the obligation to account to the Receiver or the Sequestrators, the loans would not, after the discharge of the Receiver and of the Sequestrators, be repayable, as a matter of law, by the NUM. (This aspect also becomes important in Chapter 15 below).

53 It follows that the interests of the providers of assistance, the recipients and the NUM generally coincided in ensuring that these payments were made secretly and kept totally confidential. As I have just said, after the appointment of the Sequestrators and during the receivership, any such payment by way of loan or gift to the NUM bypassing the Sequestrators or Receiver was illegal and irrecoverable, and if detected the money could have been seized by the Sequestrators or the Receiver. Huge sums (often as much as £100,000 at a time and sometimes more) changed hands in cash. I have heard evidence of meetings by appointment in shops where carrier bags were exchanged, one filled with cash, the other presumably empty. Receipts from well-wishers and distributions to staff, members (e.g. for picket duty) and creditors took place in cash. Monies were received in cash from many foreign trade unions including miners unions in Bulgaria, Czechoslovakia and France.

54 The financial assistance to the NUM with which I am concerned in this Enquiry

took the third of the above forms, namely payment to persons (principally the National Officials) to be applied by them for the benefit of the NUM and in particular in sustaining the fabric of the Union.

55 Cash to support the strike, both money intended for hardship and money intended to maintain the fabric of the Union, had, as stated above, been coming in since the beginning of the strike. However, once the Sequestrators were appointed, and then the Receiver, the Union could no longer receive money intended to maintain the fabric of the Union directly. In addition, the Receiver swiftly moved to gain control of the NUM's official funds overseas, and was not paying essential bills such as rent or staff wages.

56 There was therefore an acute need for even greater funds than had previously been received, in order to pay those bills and keep the Union functioning. A series of meetings was therefore held with senior trades union officials in London in late 1984 at which it was agreed that funds would be loaned or donated for the purpose of maintaining the fabric of the Union. It appears that all of this money was received in cash. However, its source and application had to be disguised at the time in order to prevent the Receiver from laying claim to this money.

57 Of the loans made as a result of the meetings referred to in paragraph 56 above , some were received by the National Officials for the purpose of maintaining the National Union. Others were received by the various Area Officials where those Areas were subject to court orders. Many (both to National and Area Officials) were routed through the Scottish Area. Others went direct to the relevant National or Area Officials. Repayments began after the Receiver was discharged and have now been, at least in the case of the National Union, though not all the Areas, substantially completed. Although not referred to in my terms of reference, the mechanics of the making of these loans, the terms on which they were made, the use to which they were put and the way in which they were repaid have

become central to the issues in this Enquiry and are dealt with in more detail in Chapters 6 and 15 below.

58 It is sufficient to say at this stage that the National Officials (and in particular Mr. Scargill) assumed complete control over the raising, expenditure and repayment of these monies and at no time sought any authority for what they were doing or made any report to the National Executive Committee, the Auditors or Conference. Disclosure was first made to the National Executive Committee in any form in March 1990. It is these actions of the National Officials which have led to this Enquiry.

59 I should make it clear that throughout this Report where I refer to the National Officials, I am referring to Mr. Scargill and Mr. Heathfield. Mr. McGahey, who was then Vice-president, was not a full time Official and did not play any part in the financial arrangements made.

60 I shall now set out the specific arrangements made, some with the authority of the National Executive Committee, and some by the National Officials without the authority of the National Executive Committee, for financing the strike. This falls into 2 parts

(1)   establishment of trusts (Chapter 4)

(2)   establishment of bank accounts (Chapter 5)

CHAPTER 4: ESTABLISHMENT OF TRUSTS

4.1 Official NUM Trusts

(1) The Miners' Solidarity Fund

61 This charitable trust was set up on 18th March 1984 to receive and distribute money intended for the benefit of miners and their families who were suffering hardship because of the strike. The trustees were Mr. Richard Caborn M.P., Mr. W. Michie M.P. and Mr. David Blunkett (then the leader of Sheffield City Council, now M.P.). The audited financial statements of this trust record donations of £6,095,193.00 for the period 18 March 1984 - 31st December 1986, much of which it paid out for the purpose of alleviating hardship both during and after the strike. The Receiver allowed this Trust to continue to function during the receivership. The Miners Solidarity Fund continues to operate today, albeit on a much smaller scale.

(2) The Mineworkers Trust

62 This trust was also intended to be a charitable trust. The Charity Commission declined to register the trust as a charity but Mr. Francis Barlow of Counsel in an Opinion dated the 21st December 1988 advised the trustees that it was a valid charitable trust, and I accept the evidence of the two trustees who have given evidence, namely Mr Burrows and Mr Homer, that they at all times proceeded on this basis. In these circumstances, I think that I should proceed in this Report on the basis that the trust is indeed a valid charitable trust.

63 The Mineworkers Trust was set up with the intention of insulating the NUM properties transferred to it from any Sequestrators. At the official meeting of the Finance and General Purposes Sub-Committee held on the 7th March 1984 a

resolution was passed to establish this Trust so as to provide education and other benefits for members, officials and dependents and to settle assets to the value of £1 million upon the trust. This decision was indorsed by the official meeting of the National Executive Committee on the 8th March 1984. It was intended that there should be set up by the trust a museum of mining and labour history. Legal advice was obtained from solicitors and counsel as to the propriety of setting up this trust and the Trust Deed which was executed on 9th March 1984 was settled by solicitors and counsel. The Trust Deed expressly empowered the trustees to borrow money, and also to expend money on the erection and equipping of a building at what is now Cambridge House, Division Road, Sheffield. This was one of the properties transferred by the NUM to the trust. The trustees appointed were Mr. Ken Homer, a Yorkshire Official, Mr. John Burrows, a Derbyshire Official and Mr. Roger Windsor, the chief executive officer of the NUM. It is fair to say that it appears that the Mineworkers Trust was very much Mr Windsor's brainchild.

64 A number of properties belonging to the NUM were transferred to the trustees. However, the transfer of properties of the NUM to the trust for the purpose of defeating claims by the Sequestrators involved a breach of trust by the trustees of the NUM. Accordingly the Receiver challenged the transfer of the NUM properties to the trust and commenced proceedings for their return. This action was settled by an Agreement dated 29th January 1988 which was approved by the Court under which the properties were returned. It was in connection with a proposed settlement of this claim that I advised the trustees of the Mineworkers Trust in early 1986.

65 Two transactions in respect of this trust have been the subject of media allegations and require separate consideration. These are dealt with in Chapter 13 below.

4.2 Unofficial Trusts

(3) The Miners Action Committee Fund Trust ("MACF")

66 The Miners Action Committee Fund Trust was constituted by a Deed apparently dated 21st October 1984 drafted by Mr. Scargill without any legal advice shortly after the sequestration order, and backdated to before sequestration. The purpose of the Trust was to enable the Union to continue to function by receiving donations and loans and using these funds to pay debts and liabilities of the Union. The trustees of this trust were Mr. Scargill and Mr. Heathfield. It operated on a cash basis and did not maintain a bank account. The records of the MACF show receipts of £1,219,905.25 and payments totalling £1,219,331.29 leaving a cash balance of £573.96 which is still in the possession of Mr Scargill. It should be clearly recognised that there was no National Executive Committee authorisation for this "Trust" and it was set up and operated only by Mr Scargill and Mr Heathfield.

67 The deed of 21.10.84 is contained in Annexe F to this Report. It is apparent that the trusts set out in that Deed were intended to benefit the NUM exclusively. I have no doubt that this deed created a trust in favour of the NUM and that the NUM was at all times intended to be the sole beneficiary (although the emphasis in the deed on the means of securing the benefit of separateness from the other funds of the NUM may have appeared to the draftsman to furnish some disguise). The monies held in this trust were therefore in no way insulated from the obligation on the part of the trustees to pay over such monies to the Sequestrators or the Receiver: but more importantly for the purpose of this Enquiry, they were monies of the NUM.

68 I should make it clear that both Mr Scargill and Mr Heathfield have told me that they took the view that this trust was genuinely a separate fund, and that the

monies held in it were not NUM monies. If they did indeed hold this view (and I bear in mind that Mr Heathfield originally told me that he regarded the trust deed as a form of words to "justify that account if it came under pressure") they can only have done so as a result of their, in the case of Mr Scargill at least, deliberate decision not to seek legal advice on the terms or operation of this "trust". Mr Scargill still, on the last occasion on which I took evidence, refused to accept that the effect of the MACF trust deed was that its monies were NUM monies.

69 As stated above, no bank account was ever set up for the MACF and all transactions were carried out in cash. In effect, the MACF was the cash fund operated by Mr Scargill from October 1984 to October 1989. During the strike and receivership its existence was known as the "special account" to a number of people including the NUM Finance Department. Its operation and its interaction with other accounts and trusts are set out in Chapter 6 below.

(4) NUM-IMO Trust

70 The NUM wished to set up a trust or account in Ireland to receive funds which could be applied to facilitate its continued operation, and to which gifts and loans from supporters could be channelled but which would be free from risk of seizure by the Sequestrators and Receiver. On the recommendation of Mr Michael Seifert of Messrs. Seifert Sedley & Co., Mr Scargill and Mr Heathfield sent Ms Myers, (Mr Scargill's personal assistant and the NUM's Press Officer), to Dublin to consult Professor Kadar Asmal of the University of Dublin. Professor Asmal, himself a lawyer, gave some advice and recommended Ms Myers to an Irish solicitor, Mr Michael White. Ms Myers reported back to Mr Scargill, and with the benefit of Mr White's advice and assistance there was set up in Ireland in January 1985 the Miners Research Education Defence and Support Fund Trust (originally, and until 1987, the Miners Defence and Aid Fund) of which the trustees were at all times Mr. Simon, then an executive committee member of the CGT and General

24

Secretary of the MTUI, and Mr. Norman West MEP. (This trust is referred to throughout this report as the "MIREDS" trust or fund, notwithstanding that its name became "Miners International Research Education Defence and Support" Trust only in 1987.) The original Trust Deed (which was executed on 18.1.85) cannot be found. It was drafted by Mr White, but amended by someone, probably Mr Scargill. Mr Scargill has told me that it was destroyed in 1987 because it was not anticipated that it would be needed again. This seems to me to be a rather surprising attitude.

71 The trusts of the 1985 deed cannot therefore be now known. Mr Scargill told me that although it had initially been intended that a trust for the benefit of the NUM should be set up in Ireland, by the time he actually consulted Mr Seifert in December 1984 - early January 1985, the ideas had changed, and the trust which he then conceived of setting up, after discussion with Alain Simon, was a trust on behalf of the MTUI which could benefit miners internationally, and not a trust exclusively for the NUM. This is supported by Mr Seifert and by Mr White, and by Ms Myers who told us she regarded herself as acting for the MTUI, although her instructions came from Mr Scargill alone. There is a question which is fundamental to this Enquiry as to whose idea this change was, and who consented to it. I will return to this question in Chapter 8, which deals with the receipt of money from Libya and Russia.

72 The trust opened a bank account with the Irish Intercontinental Bank Limited in Dublin on the 29th January 1985 in the names of Mr West and Mr Simon, and standing instructions were given to the bank that all communications should be made to Mr. West alone and that there should be no communication to Mr. Simon in order to avoid any complications arising for Mr. Simon under French Exchange Control law. Mr. West has told me that as an NUM sponsored MP he was willing to assist the NUM in any way that he could and that when requested to become a trustee and signatory to the account he agreed without question; when requested

to execute the original trust deed and the 1987 trust deed, again he did so without question and without reading either in detail; and that as such signatory he has executed without question all and any documents, including authorities for transfer of money from the accounts, as instructed by Mr. Scargill; and that at no time did he receive any such request or instruction from Mr. Simon or anyone else. Mr West does not know what the trusts either of the 1985 deed or the 1987 deed referred to below are. In reality and in the eyes of the law, Mr Scargill has been a trustee, if not the sole trustee, of this Trust. It is apparent that Mr West was appointed a trustee in place of Mr Scargill to avoid the attention to this trust by the Receiver and others which any association with Mr Scargill would have necessarily attracted.

73 Mr Scargill has urged upon me that he had no involvement with this trust, other than the assistance he gave in setting it up, prior to September 1985. It is true that there was little activity on this account prior to that date, but the only instructions to the Bank were drafted by Mr Scargill. Mr Scargill says that this was done on the instructions of Mr Simon.

74 The MTUI's undertaking was subsequently taken over by the IMO and a new Trust Deed was then executed, on the 11th May 1987, to some degree altering the trusts, although it cannot now be determined what alteration was effected. This Trust Deed was drafted by Mr. Scargill, and no legal advice was sought in respect of it.

75 The IMO is expressed in the 1987 Deed to be the settlor. The trustees are required to act in consultation with the IMO and the IMO is given a right of veto over the appointment of new trustees and in the event of simultaneous incapacity of the existing trustees the IMO is itself given the power to appoint new trustees. The objects of the trust are expressed as follows:

(a) To alleviate hardship and suffering among miners and their families arising

26

from such occurrences as mining disasters, health problems, industrial disputes and anti-trade union legislation.

(b) To provide assistance by among other things maintaining a national office and officials and staff of a mineworkers' trade union anywhere in the world which is recognised and accepted by the Settlor.

(c) To authorise the issue and defence of any legal proceedings in any jurisdiction relating to the affairs and functions of a mineworkers' trade union referred to in (b) above, and to instruct and remunerate lawyers regarding such proceedings.

(d) Research into and public education concerning health and safety problems associated with mining and energy industries in general.

(e) Research into and public education concerning the history of trades unions in general and mining unions in particular.

(f) To give financial support to unions engaged in industrial disputes and the aftermath of such disputes.

(g) To provide finances and expenses of persons undertaking work in connection with the purposes referred to above.

The Trust Deed also provides for proper books of account to be kept and audited annually, but no such accounts have been kept,and no audit has ever taken place.

76 Under English law, this trust would be void as a non-charitable purpose trust. I have been told by Mr White that Irish law, which is the proper law of the trust, is more lenient and flexible and that the trust is valid under Irish law. It is also the

case that under English law the execution of the 1987 Trust could not alter the trusts affecting the money already in the account, which were the trusts of the 1985 Deed, unless the 1985 Deed contained a provision for those trusts to be altered. Again, Irish law may be more flexible, but it is possible that the money held in the accounts of this trust is still held on the terms of the January 1985 Deed.

77 The IMO, and (before its absorption into the IMO) the MTUI, treated the trust as a trust for their benefit and indeed the funds as their own monies, and the trustees, Mr Simon and Mr West's alter ego Mr Scargill, took the same view. Thus for example when Mr. Scargill requested a loan from the MTUI and Mr. Heathfield, later, from the IMO, and Mr. Simon on behalf of the MTUI and IMO respectively agreed to them being made, the payments were directed to be made out of this trust fund. (This is dealt with further in Chapter 11 below.) Mr. Scargill and Mr. Simon are insistent that the trust was at all times a trust for the MTUI and then the IMO, and indeed the moneys in this trust have been used to make all such payment as the IMO has required. If this is the case the 1985 and 1987 trust deeds and the trust therein contained are shams, never intended by the settlers or trustees to be given effect to, but a facade and convenient receptacle for funds which were in effect at the free disposal of Mr Scargill and Mr Simon. On this basis alone can there be any justification for the repayment of Mr Scargill's loan not to the trust, but to the IMO. The puppet role of Mr West and the total failure of the trustees to act as trustees, for example, to consider whether the loans to Mr Scargill and Mr Heathfield or other expenditure was proper and in furtherance of the objects of the trust, and the absence of any accounts or audit, are also explicable only on this basis. This scenario also helps to explain the nonchalance with which the 1987 Deed "replaced" the 1985 Deed and the 1985 Deed was destroyed. If it is correct that the MIREDS trust was a sham (and I think that it is so) this made the trust the ideal receptacle for NUM funds (and in particular the MACF funds) and the Soviet and other monies intended to be held for or given to the NUM. The facade of an international trust afforded by the

existence of the trust deeds and the identities of the trustees (persons separate and distinct from the NUM and its national officials) gave the trust and the monies held the desired immunity from the attentions of the Receiver, but the monies could still be retained and applied for the benefit of the NUM alone.

78 I am quite satisfied that a substantial sum of money was received into the account of this trust which originated from the miners' union in the USSR during the 1984-5 strike. It is probably also the case that large donations from other unions in Eastern Europe raised during that period were received into this account. These monies are dealt with in Chapter 8 below. In addition, there was paid (indirectly) into this account in January-April 1985 approximately £580,000 which was money held by Mr Scargill and Mr Heathfield for the MACF, and which, for the reasons set out in paragraph 67 above, was NUM money. This is dealt with in Part II of Chapter 6 below.

CHAPTER 5: Bank Accounts

A OFFICIAL BANK ACCOUNTS

79 As described above, the funds of the NUM were moved offshore in an attempt to avoid the effects of sequestration, pursuant to the decision "in camera" of the National Executive Committee, and the Miners' Solidarity Fund was set up to alleviate hardship. The allegations made by the Daily Mirror and the Cook Report do not appear to relate to the operation of the official bank accounts of the NUM, (including the offshore accounts) or to the Miners Solidarity Fund. Nevertheless, Cork Gully examined records of both the NUM's official accounts and the accounts of the MSF. The steps taken by Cork Gully and their conclusions are set out in Annexe G to this Report, and a list of the bank accounts of the NUM and the MSF as disclosed to Cork Gully are set out in Annexe H. Cork Gully have confirmed that the records presented to them do not disclose monies being received from Libya or the USSR, although they point out that without third party verification of all sources of income, it is not possible to conclude whether or not the records are correct. Cork Gully are satisfied that the official bank accounts of the NUM and the MSF are not implicated in any way in the other questions addressed by this Enquiry or the allegations made by the Daily Mirror or Central Television.

80 The operation of the Mineworkers Trust is dealt with separately in Chapter 13 below. It is quite clear that the Mineworkers' Trust did not receive money from the USSR or Libya.

B "UNOFFICIAL" BANK ACCOUNTS

81 At the meeting of the National Executive Committee on 10th March 1990, Mr Scargill and Mr Heathfield revealed to the National Executive Committee the

existence of 13 bank accounts and one cash account (i.e. the account of the MACF). At the beginning of this Enquiry Mr Scargill revealed a further 3 accounts material to this Enquiry, making a total of 17 accounts. Details of these accounts are set out in Annexe I to this Report. This section describes the establishment of those bank accounts by reference to the numbering in Annexe I. I should make it clear that there exist further IMO bank accounts for which neither Cork Gully nor I have received documentation. Cork Gully discovered these because money has been transferred from the accounts for which they have been provided with documents to those other accounts. Mr Scargill has told us that although he knows of the existence of those other accounts he has nothing to do with them and has no details relating to them.

82 The records provided by Mr Scargill to Cork Gully relating to all these accounts and the investigations undertaken by Cork Gully are set out in Part I of Annexe J to this Report.

83 It should also be made clear that Cork Gully's investigations into the receipt of money from the USSR or Libya extends to the end of the receivership in 1986. There are no allegations that any sum was received from those countries after that date, and neither Cork Gully nor I thought it right to incur further costs on investigating the period after the discharge of the Receiver.

84 This multiplicity of bank accounts referred to above was set up in order to conceal from any Receiver or Sequestrators assets of or available to the NUM which were necessary to enable the Union to continue to function, and later to conceal the movement and source of funds through and from various IMO accounts (included in the 17 accounts listed in Annexe I). These actions were therefore all taken after the appointment of the Sequestrators on 21st October 1984 and of the Receiver in early December 1984.

85 The first tranche of accounts was set up in October 1984 - January 1985, i.e. while the strike was continuing. These were as follows:

86 **The Miners' Action Committee Fund Account**
(Account 1)

This was the cash account operated by Mr Scargill, with the knowledge of Mr Heathfield, pursuant to the Deed dated 21.10.84. This account is fundamental to this Enquiry and is dealt with in Part 1 of Chapter 6 below.

87 **The Sheffield Womens Action Group Account**
(Account 2)

(This account is referred to in this Report by the perhaps unfortunate acronym "SWAG"). The Sheffield Womens Action Group was constituted by a deed dated 4.1.85 and an account was opened in January 1985 at the instance of Mr Scargill as a repository and conduit for money held for the benefit of the NUM under the control of Mr Scargill. The trustees and sole signatories were Doris Askham (now the Lord Mayor elect of Sheffield) and Jean McCrindle and the signatories at all times operated the accounts at the bidding of Mr Scargill. The trusts declared by the deed of 4.1.85 were -

(a)   To assist in the general, industrial and political campaign being conducted by the National Union of Mineworkers in defence of jobs, pits and mining communities.

(b)   To provide financial assistance to maintain the fabric of the National

Union of Mineworkers, St James House, Sheffield, by making available monies from the Fund for the purposes of paying bills etc. which cannot be met by the Union as a result of sequestration and or receivership.

(c)   To provide for alleviating hardship in mining communities.

(d)   To authorise the issue and defence of any legal proceedings in relation to the affairs and functions of the NUM and or of Sheffield Womens' Action Group.

This trust deed was also drafted by Mr Scargill, without the benefit of legal advice. A total of £1,124,887.97 was routed through this account. The Sheffield Womens Action Group account was used during the receivership to route money donated or lent by, inter alios, other unions, to pay wages and other bills of the NUM which were not paid by the Receiver. A payment was also made to the Miners Solidarity Fund. After the Receiver was discharged the account was used as a channel for repayment of loans which had been made to the National Officials during the strike and receivership; and was also used to channel monies from "IMO" accounts to various recipients on behalf of the IMO. In all cases the signatories acted as requested by Mr. Scargill, implicitly trusting him. I should make clear that the two signatories were motivated only by a desire to assist the NUM and placed implicit trust in Mr Scargill that all payments out of this account were made for the benefit of the Union. They had no knowledge of the detail of where the money was coming from or going to.

88 The Receiver was aware of the existence of this account, but not of the source of the funds or the terms of the trust deed.

89 The Apex Hallam Welfare Association Account
(Account 10)

This account was opened in May 1985 at Midland Bank, Sheffield. Its function was to receive money from other British trades unions and to pay staff wages, expenses and other creditors. The signatories were Mr M. Clapham and Ms. J. Ashton. It was operated in close connection with the NUM's Finance Department. Mr Scargill did not direct the operation of this account. This account received money direct from one particular trade union.

90 The SWAG account and the Apex account do not have any substantial significance to this Enquiry. A slightly more detailed account of their operation is set out in Annexe K to this Report.

91 The operation of the SWAG account and its relation to the MACF account is also further touched on briefly in part I of Chapter 6 below. However, it can here be stated that there is no evidence that any money from Russia or Libya was received directly into either the SWAG account or the Apex account.

92 Other accounts opened during the strike

Also opened during the strike at the request of Mr Scargill were the following accounts in the name of N. Hyett (the married name of Mr Scargill's personal assistant, Ms Nell Myers).

First National Bank of Chicago (Account 8)

Chase Bank (Account 9)

Ms Nell Myers has told me that she opened these accounts at the request of Mr

Scargill and operated them on his instructions alone. Mr Windsor also travelled to Dublin with Ms Myers to set up the First Chicago account. These accounts were operated as post box accounts, and do not need further comment save to say that the Chase Bank account received MACF (and hence NUM) money in January 1985. This is also dealt with in Chapter 15 below.

93   In addition, the account of the Miners' Defence and Aid (MIREDS) Fund was opened on 29th January 1985 as described in paragraph 72 above (Account 14(a)).

November 1985

94   In November 1985, that is still during the receivership but after the strike, another set of accounts were opened at the behest of Mr Scargill, as follows:

Jean McCrindle
Allied Irish Bank plc (Account 3)

Ms McCrindle has told me that she was asked to open this account by Mr Scargill, and was told that its purpose was to channel money back to repay loans made to the MACF. This account was used as a post box and needs no further comment.

T. Sibley
Bank of Ireland (Account 11)

The account in the name of Mr Sibley (who I am told was the WFTU representative in Britain) was inactive save for an initial deposit of £50 and the withdrawal of that sum.

IMO

Bank of Ireland (Account 16)

This IMO account is the account to which the NUR loan was paid by the
Mineworkers Trust, and from which it was repaid to the NUR. It is dealt with in
Chapter 15 below.

<u>1986-7</u>

95 Further accounts were opened in the course of 1986 and 1987 as follows (in
date order), again at the behest of Mr Scargill:

J. McCrindle
Allied Irish Bank plc, Leeds (Account 4)

IMO
Co-Operative Bank
Sheffield (Account 15)

Y. Schneider (the married name of Mr Scargill's secretary, Ms Y. Fenn)
Bank of Arbeit und Wirtschaft AG
Vienna (Account 7)

Y. Fenn
Co-Operative Bank
Sheffield (Account 6)

IMO
Bank fur Arbeit und
**   Wirtschaft AG**
Vienna (Account 12)

Jean McCrindle
Bank of Ireland
Dublin (Account 5)

96 Ms McCrindle and Ms Fenn have both told me that again these accounts were opened at the request of Mr Scargill and were operated entirely on his instructions. Both have told me that Mr Scargill told them that the purpose of these accounts was to route money from the IMO into Britain to repay loans made to the MACF during the strike, and that they opened and operated the accounts out of a desire to do anything they could to assist the NUM.

97 Mr Scargill described to me accounts 3, 4, 5, 6, 7, 12 and 15 above as being "opened at the request of the IMO". However, the letters from the IMO to Jean McCrindle in respect of accounts 3 and 4 postdate the dates on which the accounts were opened, and Ms McCrindle did not initially regard them as IMO accounts, although Ms Fenn did regard accounts 6 and 7 as IMO accounts. Secondly it is quite clear that all these accounts (with the possible exception of Account 12) have

been operated on the sole instructions and decisions of Mr Scargill throughout. Finally, because of the apparent lack of proper records kept by the IMO (see paragraph 36 above) and certainly because of the failure to produce any documents of the IMO to me, it is impossible to ascertain what knowledge the IMO (apart from Mr Scargill and Mr Simon) had of these accounts. In fact, Mr Scargill indicated to me that they were opened as "IMO" accounts in order to make it clear that they were not personal accounts containing money to which the signatories were entitled. In my view, these accounts were only nominally IMO accounts (again with the probable exception of account 12) and can be regarded as accounts controlled by Mr Scargill.

98 I should also mention that Mr Scargill told me that these accounts were set up on legal advice. However, Mr John Hendy Q.C. has told me that his only involvement was to draft a bank mandate, which he was asked to do informally. Mr Hendy does not recall being told any detail about the accounts or their purpose. To be fair to Mr Scargill, I do not think he was seeking to suggest that he had received legal advice on the purpose or operation of the accounts.

99 These 1986/7 accounts (i.e. Nos. 4, 5, 6, 7, 12 and 15) were all used as "post boxes" and do not need further comment.

1989

100 Finally, in 1989, and after Mr Windsor had left the NUM and Mr Scargill was aware that the Daily Mirror had in its possession bank statements of the IMO, two further accounts were opened, as follows:

A. Simon and N. West (2 accounts)
Bank fur Arbeit und Wirtschaft AG
Vienna (Accounts 14(b) and 17)

"Internationaler Hilfs und
Verteidigundfond" (i.e. IMO)
Bank fur Arbeit und Wirtschaft (Account 13)

101 Account 14(b) received £1m from account 14(a) in August 1989. Account 13 received the balance held in account 8 ($1, 000 = £684. 77) in February 1986.

CHAPTER 6 :THE OPERATION OF THE UNOFFICIAL ACCOUNTS AND TRUSTS

PART I: THE MINERS ACTION COMMITTEE FUND

102 The MACF was controlled and operated by Mr Scargill. Mr Scargill told me that the MACF was operated as a cash fund because it was not possible to operate a bank account without being subject to court action and possible seizure. Mr Scargill contends that even if it had been found to be legal to have operated a bank account, the legal process of determining its legality would have frozen the funds for a considerable period of time.

103 Mr Scargill told me that the MACF cash was held in the NUM's offices and applied for NUM purposes as required. For example, as the Finance Department required monies to pay creditors, Mr Scargill released funds to the Finance Department. These funds were recorded in both the Miners Action Committee records and the Finance Department's records provided to Cork Gully. Both sets of records confirm that £195,103.23 was transferred from this fund to the Finance Department in this manner.

104 As stated in paragraph 57 above, during the strike and the receivership period several British trade unions made funds available for the NUM, Scotland Area which were to be forwarded to the NUM National Union and other NUM areas. The funds were made available by the trade unions in the notional form of "interest free loans to the Scotland Area" so that the unions were not seen to have funded the NUM and its Area offices direct. These funds were then routed on to the National Officials or to the relevant Area Officials.

105 Loans totalling £170,103.23 were received by the MACF via the NUM (Scotland Area). A further £193,475.70 was received in the Sheffield Womens Action Group

account in the same manner. It must be remembered that in effect this was simply Mr Scargill receiving and transferring money through 2 different routes. These monies were ultimately repaid by both the MACF and the Sheffield Womens Action Group account direct to the original lenders, bypassing the NUM, Scotland Area.

106 The repayment of the loans by the MACF and SWAG, and the source of the money to do so, are dealt with in Chapter 15 below. The loans made, via Scotland, to Areas have been partly repaid, but some are still outstanding. I am not aware of any complaint from the lenders in respect of the outstanding loans.

107 I should make it clear that I do not propose in this Report to name any of the trade unions who lent money in this way. It has been made clear to me from a variety of sources that those trades unions do not wish to be named, and I can see no need or advantage in doing so. I am satisfied that I am aware of all loans which were made, and of all repayments which have been made by the National Officials. These come within my terms of reference because of the source of the money to make these repayments. It is no part of my brief to investigate loans to, or repayments by, Areas or their Officials. Details of the loans made to the National Officials, (whether notionally to the MACF, or the SWAG account or paid directly into the Apex account), and of the repayments of those loans are set out in Annexe L to this Report.

108 The records for the MACF to the end of the strike also show a number of sums coming in direct from British trade unions rather than via the Scottish Area. The details of the verification of this money are set out in part II of Annexe J.

109 Mr Scargill has told Cork Gully that there were a number of occasions when he had received cash from people supporting the miners strike or wishing to assist in the operation of the NUM. Mr Scargill passed these monies to the Finance

Department and he considered that it was the Finance Department's responsibility to record receipt of these monies. The Finance Departments records do contain evidence of such receipts. If Mr Scargill passed these monies to an Area representative, it was the Area's responsibility to record the receipt of these funds. Mr Scargill told me that he effectively passed these monies "straight on" and therefore did not record them in the MACF. An example of how this operated is set out in Part III of Annexe J to this Report. Further it seems possible that cash was received by Mr Scargill which was not recorded in the records of the unofficial accounts or by the Finance Department. Mr Scargill has also told me that he operated a "teeming and lading" system with cash in his possession. This means that, for example, if Mr Scargill had £10,000.00 he could pay away £5,000.00 and replace it at a later date with another £5,000.00 taken from new receipts; thus restoring the cash in his possession to £10,000.00. The records provided to us by Mr Scargill do not detail the workings of this "teeming and lading" exercise. As set out in part III of Annexe J there are discrepancies in the records relating to the MACF which suggests that there could be cash receipts unrecorded which were used to make some payments. Cork Gully has concluded that there is now no way of ascertaining what amount of cash may have passed through Mr Scargill's hands.

110 There are 3 further significant factors about the operation of MACF, as follows.

111 First, in January 1985 there was a very large amount of cash in the account of the MACF, i.e. in Mr Scargill's hands. A safety deposit box had been used for some time (in the name of Jean McCrindle), but Mr Scargill then decided the money should be placed offshore. With the assistance of another trade union, a total of £580,608 was transferred eventually to the account of the MIREDS Fund (account 14(a)) in Dublin, and £71,284.15 to the Chase Bank account in the name of N. Hyett (account 9). Details of the mechanics of these transfers are set out in Annexe M to this Report.

112 Mr Scargill has told me that this money was received in account 14(a) on the understanding that it was there for safe keeping and that the trustees of the MACF could call for it at any time. There was, however, no documentary evidence of this understanding, and if anything had happened to Mr Scargill, the NUM (whose money it was) would have had no idea that the asset existed. Mr Heathfield was not aware of the details of this alleged arrangement. Further, it was a serious breach of trust to mingle the NUM's money with the money of the MIREDS fund, unless, as indicated in Chapter 8 below the MIREDS Fund was indeed a trust intended exclusively for the benefit of the NUM.

113 The second significant factor about the MACF is that the records produced by Mr Scargill show that after May 1986, all receipts and payments passing through the MACF are on behalf of the IMO. This clearly was in no way justified by the deed constituting the trust of the MACF, and is another example of Mr Scargill's failure properly to distinguish between the IMO and the NUM.

114 The third significant factor relates to the source of the monies received from sources abroad by Mr Scargill on behalf of the MACF (as he tells me he believed) in October 1984 - January 1985. The records for the MACF to the end of the strike show the following sums received from abroad:

Date	Sum	Source
1. 25.10.84	100,000.00	CGT
2. 4.11.84	25,000.00	CGT
3. 4.12.84	50,000.00	Int.Coll. via CGT
4. 6.12.84	834.11	Finland (MJ)
5. 7.12.84	63,365.39(FF)	CGT (Nell and Jim)
6. 19.12.84	50,000.00	Int.Coll. via CGT
7. 7.1.85	65,000.00(FF)	CGT (Jim) via TGWU
9. 8.1.85	36,003.00(US$)	Bulgaria
10. 15.1.85	96,009.00(US$)	Czechoslovakia

115 Cork Gully wrote to the miners' unions in Bulgaria and Czechoslovakia, but have received no response. However, Mr Heathfield has described to me in

graphic detail the receipt of those funds, and I am satisfied that they were received from trade union sources in those countries. The sum from Finland is confirmed by a receipt for Finnish Marks. However, the sums shown as received from or via the CGT are crucial to the question whether monies were received from Libya, and are dealt with in more detail in Chapter 10 below.

116   For the sake of completeness, I must mention here that the summary receipts and payments schedule of the MACF shows sums totalling £191,955.41 received from various of the other accounts set out in Annexe I. Those receipts can, however, be dated from the bank statements, and were all received after May 1986. Apart from one small loan repayment to a British union, all these sums were used for IMO purposes, as indicated in paragraph 113 above, and none of them came from Libya.

PART II: THE MIREDS FUND

117   The only receipts into this fund's account in Dublin (account 14(a)) were as follows:

(1)   A total of £580,608 received indirectly from the MACF. (Received January-April 1985). (Annexe M)

(2)   A total of £1,404,616 received on the instructions of "Intern. Solidariteet Prag." between February and December 1985. I shall return to this in Chapter 8 below.

All other receipts into the account are attributable to bank interest.

118   For reasons which I set out in Chapter 8 below, I am satisfied that the sum

of £1,404,616 referred to above represents money deposited in the Narodny Bank Polsky account referred to below by the miners' unions including at least those of the USSR, the GDR and Hungary. Mr Simon has confirmed to me that this money represents money donated by the miners unions of the USSR and other Eastern European countries. However, he has declined to confirm that the money was deposited in the Narodny Bank Polsky, or to give us details of the route by which it reached Dublin. While I am satisfied that the money did go into the account at the Narodny Bank, I have been unable to ascertain how it was transferred from there to Dublin.

119 The first withdrawal from this account (which, it will be recalled, was operated by Mr West on Mr Scargill's instructions) was the sum of £100,000 which was borrowed by Mr Scargill for the purpose of purchasing his current house in August 1985. This is dealt with in Chapter 11 below.

120 On 3.8.89, £1m was transferred to account 14(b) where Mr Scargill has told Cork Gully it is earning interest. The balance as at 31.12.89 standing to the credit of MIREDS Fund in account 14(a) was £650,227. It can therefore be inferred that the total now standing to the account of the MIREDS fund is at least £1,650,227.

121 Sums totalling £1,050,000 were transferred from the MIREDS account 14(a) to others of accounts 4, and 12 and one of the IMO accounts for which I have not seen documentation and thence to account 2 during the period 1986 to 1989. Because of the constant movement of money between all the accounts controlled by Mr Scargill and/or the IMO, it is impossible to say exactly how that money has been spent or where it now is. I therefore set out in Chapter 15 below the payments which have been made out of the mixture of IMO and MIREDS fund money. I repeat again that the MIREDS fund comprises money belonging to the MACF (i.e. the NUM) and money received from miners' unions including those of the USSR, the GDR and Hungary.

CHAPTER 7: CONCERNS ARISING OVER THE UNOFFICIAL ACCOUNTS

122   I have been gravely concerned about these unofficial accounts and trusts and in particular (a) why they were never disclosed to the National Executive Committee or the NUM's auditors prior to January 1990 (b) why they were continued after the discharge of the Receiver (c) why there were not full records kept after discharge of the Receiver (d) the reason for their production for examination by KPMG Peat Marwick, Leeds, in January 1990 and (e) whether the statement by the National Officials to the National Executive Committee on 9th March 1990 that they had been examined by KPMG Peat Marwick, Leeds, was correct and true.

A   Reason for Non-Disclosure

123   It is apparent that during the period of sequestration and receivership there was perceived to be a need to conceal these accounts if the moneys were to be made available to preserve the fabric of the Union and avoid seizure by the Receiver (or during the period of sequestration by the Sequestrators). I understand from Mr. Scargill that he could not trust the National Executive Committee itself to keep these matters secret at the time and secrecy was vital. It leaked like a colander. During the receivership, Mr Scargill told me, publicity would have led to seizure of the funds and proceedings for committal for contempt of those involved: publicity thereafter would not have led to these consequences, but would have involved a breach of the obligation (albeit unenforceable) of confidence owed to the providers of funds, put at risk the scheme for repayment and generally damaged the standing of the Union. Mr. Scargill said that the National Executive Committee by its actions on the 8th March 1984 and by keeping these actions secret even to this day set a precedent and example to the National Officials of continuing secrecy of actions taken in or about the strike long after the occasion for

secrecy was over.

124   It may be thought not surprising that the National Officials followed suit. But in my opinion, these matters are in law no justification or excuse for a serious breach of duty, though the members of the Union may think that these matters go to blameworthiness and the need for action on their part. Mr. Heathfield has told me (although Mr Scargill does not agree) that one reason for non-disclosure of the asset of £580,000 held in the MIREDS account was the urgent need to rationalise the structure of the union, integrate and cut costs and expenses. Only financial stringencies would persuade the Union to agree to these measures, and disclosure of that asset would have destroyed this impression and this scheme. If (as I think it is) this statement is true, I am gravely concerned that the non-disclosure was utilised to achieve this objective, however desirable, quite improperly.

125   Both the National Officials have sought to persuade me that the NEC was well aware of the existence of the loans referred to above, and also aware that those loans were being repaid over the period since the end of the receivership. However, I have taken evidence from a number of NEC members who told me they were not aware of the loans to the MACF/SWAG set out in paragraph 103 above, or of the repayment of those loans, although most members seem to be aware of loans to Areas. And of course, no-one on the NEC knew of the existence of the substantial MACF assets which had been placed offshore. Mr Heathfield told me that he and Mr Scargill took a positive decision to keep those loans "close to their chests". I do not think that the National Officials can now say that the NEC knew all along what the National Officials were doing.

B   Need for continuance

126   Mr. Scargill says that it was necessary to continue the accounts until all debts and loans had been repaid and these included 5 year loans which only

47

became repayable in 1989. He considered that loans made in cash had to be repaid in cash. I find it difficult to believe that creditors and lenders would have refused earlier repayment. Mr. Heathfield has told me (but Mr. Scargill does not accept) that the loans were not 5 year loans, but that after the strike was over Mr Scargill and he requested up to 5 years to repay. I accept Mr. Heathfield's evidence on this question. This makes the delay in repayment the less justifiable on this score. Mr. Scargill also justified the delay in repayment on the ground that the repayment should await the result of the breach of trust proceedings, for the monies were available to pay the costs and any award against officers of the Union in those proceedings. I do not think that the monies were properly available for this purpose, and in any event I do not think that repayment proceeded promptly even after settlement of that action. I think that the deliberate decision was made to delay repayment as long as possible in order to retain hold of the funds in question and the interest thereon so long as possible. This accords with Mr Scargill's and Mr Heathfield's repeated statements that "it was thought advantageous" to retain a capital fund and to be able to use the interest to pay outstanding loans. (Advantageous to whom is another question.) This, in particular when accompanied by non-disclosure to the National Executive Committee and the membership, was, in my view, totally wrong.

C   Absence of complete records

127   The state of the records is dealt with in Annexe J referred to above.   It may be understandable that complete records of receipts and payments would not be kept during the receivership because of the risk of those documents falling into the hands of the Receiver, but there was no such risk after the Receiver was discharged. In addition, as also set out in Annexe J, the narrative accounts were written up by Mrs Riley in late December 1989. While there is no impropriety about writing up these accounts in this way, I have heard evidence from a number of sources of rumour that accounts were being "re-written" in secret at about this

period. While I have no way of knowing if these rumours refer to the writing up of the narrative accounts from the unofficial accounts, I suspect this may be so. Again, the secrecy in relation to the unofficial accounts has led to a very unhappy atmosphere of suspicion at the Head Office of the NUM. I should make it clear that absolutely no criticism at all is made or intended by me, or could be made by any person, of Mrs Riley or any employee in the Finance Department in respect of the writing up of these accounts.

D   Reason for disclosure

128   Mr. Scargill has told me that the reason for the disclosure of the accounts to KPMG Peat Marwick in 1989/90 was because all debts and loans had been repaid and had nothing to do with the imminent revelations by Mr. Windsor. Mr. Scargill says that on completing all repayments he wanted an audit to prevent any question arising thereafter. Mr. Steven Hudson has however told me that Mr. Scargill revealed the accounts to him and asked his advice specifically because he was concerned about imminent revelations by Mr. Windsor in the Press. Mr Hudson advised Mr Scargill to consult KPMG Peat Marwick, the Sheffield office of which audited the NUM's accounts, and Mr Hudson and Mr Scargill agreed that the Leeds office of KPMG Peat Marwick should be approached. That the imminent revelations by Mr Windsor were the immediate cause of the disclosure to KPMG Peat Marwick is confirmed by the evidence of the accountant consulted at KPMG Peat Marwick in Leeds, Mr Anthony Richmond who told me that Mr Scargill told him that this was the background. Mr Heathfield also told him that the officials had always intended to have these accounts audited, but accepted that the imminent revelations by Mr Windsor may have speeded up this process.I cannot accept Mr. Scargill's evidence on this question. I do not believe that there would have been any disclosure or any report by KPMG but for the falling out with Mr. Windsor.

E.   "Audit" by KPMG Peat Marwick Leeds

129   In their Report to the National Executive Committee dated 9 March 1990, the National Officials stated (on page 6):-

> "All the accounts for which we were signatories or trustees have been examined by Messrs Peat Marwick McLintock and they have confirmed, in relation to each and overall, that every receipt and every payment has been in accordance with the books and records of each individual trust fund"

As regards all accounts of which Jean McCrindle was sole or joint signatory, they said:-

> "... all the accounts had been fully examined by an independent firm of auditors".

130   The impression given by these statements, their language and choice of words, and by the accompanying commentary by Mr Scargill when he read out these statements, was that the accounts had all been audited and passed the audit with flying colours. I heard evidence from a number of members of the National Executive Committee who attended the Meeting that they so understood the statement. I have no doubt that this was the impression intended to be created.

131   This state of affairs was very far from the truth. In fact, all that KPMG Peat Marwick had been able to do (as set out in detail in Annexe J) was to check the narrative accounts which had been drawn up in 1989 against the documents from which those accounts had been drawn up, and to confirm that one matched the other. KPMG Peat Marwick were not able to do more that this very limited, and for practical purposes, meaningless exercise, because of the state of the records as referred to above and in Annexe J. I should make it clear that no criticism of KPMG Peat Marwick is intended. They made it clear to Mr Scargill what they were and were not able to do, and the letters which they wrote in respect of each account make it absolutely clear what was done.

CHAPTER 8:   MONIES FROM LIBYA AND USSR

132   I turn now to the heart of this Enquiry, namely the receipt of money from the USSR and Libya.   Again, it is first necessary to give some background information.

8.1   ACCOUNT AT NARODNY BANK POLSKY

133   In late 1984 and early 1985, the National Officials were making significant efforts to raise money overseas in addition to the money raised in Britain.   As indicated above, it appears that money was received by the National Officials in January 1985 from Bulgaria and Czechoslovakia.

134   Particular efforts were made to raise money from Eastern Europe. In this connection, a further bank account assumes great importance.

135   Mr Scargill disclosed to me in his submission the existence of a bank account held by the MTUI at the Narodny Bank Polsky in Warsaw. This account is No. 111-12-6973-151-6797.

136   This is the bank account number that Mr. Roger Windsor alleges, in the Daily Mirror of 6.3.90, he was told to give to Colonel Gaddafi. Mr. Scargill has told me that he was given details of the number of this account by Mr. Simon on behalf of the MTUI in about October 1984; and that Mr. Simon told Mr. Scargill that the account could be used to receive donations from organisations which wanted to assist the NUM in continuing to function during the strike. Mr. Scargill told me that he is not aware of any transactions which took place in connection with this account. However, he gave this account number to Mr John Platts-Mills Q.C. and to Professor Allen of Leeds University, both of whom travelled to a number of countries to try to raise money for the NUM, with the intent that they

should tell the people they talked to that donations could be made to this account. I have seen two letters from Mr. Scargill to Mr. Platts-Mills asking Mr. Platts-Mills to help in an international effort to raise money for the NUM. (In one of these letters, the account number ends in -6797; in the other, in -6796. Neither Mr Platts-Mills nor Mr Scargill could explain this). More importantly, those letters, dated 4th January and 25th February 1985, state that the account will only be operated on the instructions of Mr. Scargill. This would indicate to anyone receiving that letter that even if Mr. Scargill was not in fact a signatory, he did control the account. In addition, Mr. Platts-Mills has told me that he believes that he, Mr. Platts-Mills, gave this account number both to a Soviet official with responsibility for trade union matters, and to Colonel Gaddafi. Mr. Platts-Mills met Colonel Gaddafi on several occasions, and in particular met him on at least one of his two visits to Libya in August 1984 and March 1985. Professor Allen has also told me that he gave the number to various miners' leaders and officials in a number of countries in Eastern Europe. I will return to this below.

137   Mr Platts-Mills is emphatic that his interest was only in obtaining money for the Solidarity Fund as opposed to money for maintaining the fabric of the Union. But the same account number as was given to Colonel Gaddafi by Mr Platts-Mills for any donation was made generally available for receipt of donations to the NUM. It is highly doubtful that any Libyan would have distinguished between the two distinct objects rather than have a generalised intention "to help the miners". It is even more doubtful that any receipt into the account was or could be analysed to determine its intended destination; the natural assumption would surely have been that all receipts were for the benefit of the NUM, bearing in mind the arrangement between Mr Scargill and Mr Simon for this account to be available for receipt of funds for the NUM, and the possibility of making donations to the Solidarity Fund quite openly and with no disguise. Any full and complete investigation of actual or intended receipts for the NUM requires an examination of this account and its receipts and payments. Only Mr Simon as Secretary General of the IMO, the

successor to the account holder the MTUI, can obtain or authorise access. Mr
Simon has refused and failed to provide such access.

138   Mr Scargill has sought to persuade me that the agreement with Mr Simon
was that only funds donated into that account for the benefit of the NUM were to
be notified to him by Mr Simon or to be subject to Mr Scargill's direction.   Mr
Scargill told me that Mr Simon has assured him that no donation has been made
into that account for the NUM.   In my view, donors were unlikely to indicate who
the money was for,and any money received into that account at that time can be
regarded as having been intended for the benefit of the NUM.

8.2   THE USSR AND LIBYA AS SOURCES OF MONEY

A The USSR

139   Mr. Scargill has told me that repeated efforts were made to persuade Soviet
diplomats and trade unionists to support the NUM during the strike. Two forms of
assistance were sought, the first political, the second material. The political help
sought was the creation of pressure on the British Government in particular by
disrupting trade relations between the two countries. With regard to material help,
repeated requests were made for money. The miners' union in the USSR did
provide substantial assistance in the form of free holidays in the USSR for miners'
families and sent food and other gifts. As regards the provision of money there was
a serious problem in making available hard currency. Nonetheless it appears that
the decision was made to give approximately £1 million.

140   Professor Allen of Leeds University has told me that at the request of Mr
Scargill, he visited Moscow, the German Democratic Republic and Budapest to
raise funds urgently needed to maintain the fabric of the Union. On each occasion,
Professor Allen gave the number of the MTUI account in Warsaw supplied to him

by Mr Scargill for the receipt of money for the NUM. After discussions in Moscow with Soviet Trade Union officials, including Mr Srebny, then the President of the Coal Employees Union (CEU), he left with the impression that the CEU would pay one million roubles or (after exchange at the official rate) £1 million, to be channelled through the account in Warsaw to the NUM to maintain the fabric of the Union. In the GDR, the Head of the International Department of Free Trade Unions agreed to provide $500,000 through the same route, and in Budapest there was agreement to pay 80,000 shillings (approximately £20 - £30,000) through the same route. Professor Allen reported back the results of these trips to Mr Scargill.

141   Mr Scargill also had a number of meetings with high-ranking Soviet officials at the Soviet Embassy in London and at the CGT headquarters in Paris, as a result of which he believed that the Soviet miners would send a substantial sum.

142   That the Soviet miners raised a considerable amount of money for the NUM by way of a levy of at least one day's pay on each miner is supported by evidence from the following people, who reported that Soviet delegates had told them this money had been raised, namely, Mr G. Bolton, Mr E. Clarke and Mr M. McGahey. Mr G. Rees also told me that Soviet representatives had told him that a substantial amount had been raised. This was also reported in various newspapers in June 1990, as a result of the visit of two Soviet miners to the UDM Conference, who also said that there had been a levy to raise money. Although it is not clear what the credentials of these miners were, they would in my view be likely to know if there had been a levy, because it would have affected them personally.

143   I conclude therefore that it is highly likely that the Soviet miners, and miners in the GDR and Hungary, did contribute money to the Narodny Bank account which they must have believed was operated on Mr Scargill's instructions and was the appropriate channel to pay money for the benefit of the NUM.

144   An effort was apparently made to pay the Soviet money into the NUM's (official) bank account in Zurich. According to Mr. Scargill, however, the Bank would not "touch the money with a barge pole" and the money was returned. Whether this was before or after the money was paid to the Narodny Bank cannot now be discovered.

145   I received evidence from several people including Mr Scargill, Mr Hudson and Mr Simon, relating to the receipt of £1 million or $1 million by a bank in Switzerland, on behalf of the NUM. I was told that the bank returned the funds to the sender, although nobody was able to provide me with an explanation as to why or when the bank had taken this action. Cork Gully have reviewed various records relating to the NUM's overseas bank accounts and in particular accounts operated at EBC (Schweiz) AG in Zurich and can find no record of such a receipt. It seems strange that a bank should return funds received for the benefit of its client, without corresponding with the client. Cork Gully have written to EBC (Schweiz) AG who have been unable to provide further information.

146   If this money had been paid it would have been the free money of the Union. However, Mr. Scargill told me that the Soviet miners were not prepared to pay any money which would become the free money of the Union in case it might be seized by the Sequestrators or Receiver. (This change of mind must logically have occurred after the abortive attempt to pay into the NUM's bank account in Switzerland). Mr Scargill told me that after consultation between the Soviet trade union, the MTUI and the NUM it was agreed that the money should go to a special fund of the MTUI to assist miners anywhere in the world who were in a struggle with their employers. In fact, the sum of £1,404,616 was paid into the account of the MIREDS Fund in Dublin (Account 14(a)) between January and December 1985. Mr Scargill told me that he believes, although he does not know, that the money included the money from the miners union in the USSR, and probably also from the GDR and other countries. Mr Simon has confirmed that

the receipt into the MIREDS fund did include money from the miners' union in the USSR and other Eastern European countries.

147   As indicated above, that money was received by order of "Intern. Solidariteet. Prag." Cork Gully have written to the bank from which the funds are believed to have been remitted, namely Bank Fur Arbeit und Wirtschaft in Austria. On 25th June 1990, Cork Gully received a letter, which is contained in Annexe N to this Report, stating that the bank had been instructed by the account holder not to divulge any information to Cork Gully. I believe that this account holder must have been Mr Simon or the IMO.

148   Mr Scargill has been at pains to explain to me that the decision to pay this money to the MIREDS Fund was a decision of the Soviet miners, and that he had no choice but to agree. Mr Scargill told me that several ways of donating money for the benefit of the NUM were offered to the Soviet miners including using the accounts in Chase Bank or First Chicago Bank in Dublin in the name of N. Hyett, or via trades union in Finland or an account in Malta, but that Mr Simon and a Soviet official at the Soviet Embassy in London told him that the Soviet Miners' Union (the CEU) was not prepared to use any of those routes. According to Mr Scargill it was the Soviet miners who said that they would only give the money to an international trust fund which could benefit miners anywhere in the world. However, Mr Scargill did not speak to any Soviet representative or officials on the question of an international trust, and his only negotiations, in that respect, were with Mr Simon, who as General Secretary of the MTUI, had a vested interest in that money going to the MTUI rather than the NUM. Further, I cannot ignore the fact that at this time (as Mr Scargill has told me) the NUM, and/or plainly Mr Scargill himself, were committed to the formation of and affiliation of the IMO and, Mr Scargill must have had in mind his likely position in the IMO. In addition, Mr Scargill has told me that the decision to set up an international MTUI trust was taken before January 1985 (when the MIREDS fund was originally set up), and that

it was the idea of the Soviet miners who did not want their donation to go to the NUM, but offered no explanation for this change of heart in the middle of the strike. Mr Simon, however, wrote a letter to Mr Heathfield shortly after the revelations had been made in the press and on television in relation to this matter. That letter has been produced to me, and in it Mr Simon says that the Soviet miners had taken this decision <u>after the strike was over</u> (i.e. March 1985). This is a striking inconsistency. Neither has Mr Scargill explained to me if or how the miners' unions in the GDR and Hungary also suffered such a surprising change of heart at the same time.

149   Mr Scargill has produced to me a transcript of a speech made by him to the Soviet Miners' 15th Extraordinary Congress held in Moscow in March 1990. (The accuracy of the gist of the material part quoted below is confirmed by letters obtained and supplied for this purpose by Mr Scargill dated the 13 June 1990 and 12 June 1990 from Mr Marcel Golding, Assistant General Secretary of the NUM of South Africa and from Mr T. Wilks, General Secretary of the United Mineworkers Federation of Australia, both of whom attended the Congress). The relevant passages read as follows:

"When I spoke in January in Voroshilorgrad, the question was asked about the Soviet miners' assistance to Britain's miners during the 1984/85 miners' strike, and I believe that this Congress has a right to know from the British miners exactly what took place and what is still taking place.

The Soviet miners provided for our families hundreds of holidays during the course of the strike and in the years following the strike. Secondly, they sent a shipload of food and clothing to assist with the hardship of British miners and Margaret Thatcher's Government refused to allow food to be unloaded in Britain.

In consultation with our Soviet comrades we agreed rather than let our food go to waste on the dockside in England, we sent it jointly to the starving people of Ethiopia.

Thirdly, throughout the strike the Soviet miners tried to send financial assistance to the British miners, but because of sequestration and receivership by the Courts during the course of the strike the miners in the Soviet Union were not able to send it.

However, when the strike ended in 1985, our Union in consultation with the Miners' Trade Union International (the MTUI) and the Soviet miners decided that the money would go to the MTUI into a special fund to assist miners anywhere in the world who were involved in struggle.

The Soviet miners' contribution was sent to the international fund and from that international fund Britain's miners have received very substantial financial assistance from 1985 to date. And can I say to each and every one of you, from the bottom of my heart, my thanks for showing tremendous solidarity with our Union at a time when we needed help."

Mr Scargill tells me that it was on this basis that the money was paid to the MIREDS fund, but that the MTUI recognised that the NUM had a substantial claim on this trust because of what the NUM had suffered.

150   Mr Srebny, the former Secretary General of the Coal Employers Union (C.E.U.) in the USSR would have been a valuable source of information. I wrote to him, by registered post on 10th May 1990, but received no reply. He has, I

understand, retired or been retired following the reforms in the USSR and this may explain his reticence. However, I also bear in mind that until his recent retirement, Mr Srebny was one of what Mr Heathfield described as the "inner group" running the IMO. It may be that his reticence is also explicable on this ground. Mr Shestakov of the IMO, (a Russian, but now a member of the IMO Secretariat) has in a letter confirmed to me that the money went to the MTUI, but not the details of when or why. I have also written to the current President of the CEU, Mr Louniov, by fax on 14th June 1990, but have received no reply. I also asked Mr Scargill to make any efforts he could to procure that the CEU should co-operate. I understand that Mr Scargill asked Mr Simon and Mr Shestakov to pass on a request that the CEU should co-operate: I have also seen a copy of a fax sent to Mr Louniov by Mr Scargill asking for co-operation. However, in view of Mr Scargill's statement at the beginning of the speech quoted above that the Soviet miners had, earlier this year, asked <u>Mr Scargill</u> what had happened to the money, it may well be that the current leaders of the CEU have no knowledge which could assist this Enquiry.

151   In the absence of any direct response from the CEU, I am quite satisfied that this money was raised for the benefit of the NUM. I do not believe that the Soviet miners refused to pay this money to the NUM. I think that they wished only to defer payment until the Receiver was discharged and all risk of seizure by the Receiver was removed. In my view, the international trust was the idea of Mr Simon and Mr Scargill, and it was they who decided that the money from the Soviet Union should go to the MTUI trust in Dublin. The creation of such a trust had the advantage that if the monies were paid to that trust, they would not be, or not appear to be monies of the NUM and hence, even if paid during the receivership would be exempt from the attention of the Receiver.

152   This payment to the trustees of the MIREDS Trust could have been made on one or other of the following bases: (1) the money was in reality for the NUM;

but it was disguised as an international trust because this was the safest way of making the money available to the NUM without risking it being seized by the Receiver; or (2) that the money was to be genuinely held on the international trusts declared by the 1985/7 Deeds which could benefit miners anywhere, and would be used or not for the benefit of the NUM as Mr Scargill and Mr Simon decided.

153   The decision by the NUM that the monies go to the MTUI as an international fund (i.e. basis (2)) which is referred to in Mr. Scargill's speech must have been a decision by Mr Scargill alone. No one else on the part of the NUM knew of or agreed to this course. I can see no possible basis on which this diversion could be justified unless it was cosmetic only, and the fund in fact continued to be held for the NUM. Such diversion on any other basis must involve a breach of trust and a breach of duty to the donors and the NUM; and any purported participation in such decision by Mr Scargill was both unauthorised and in breach of his duty as President of the NUM.

154   I am far from satisfied that any agreement for diversion of the true entitlement to the money was reached. Such an agreement would have (as I have said) involved the most serious breach of duty by all concerned and in any case Mr Scargill had no authority to commit the NUM to any such agreement. I incline to the view that the money was indeed at all times intended to be held (albeit in a disguised form) for the benefit of the NUM (i.e. basis (1)). Only on this basis could the payment of this money into the same account as the £580,000 from the MACF fund be justified. The role of Mr West as trustee in name only and the complete control over this fund of Mr Scargill is again consistent with this scenario; and so is the sham character of the 1985 and 1987 Trust Deeds to which I have referred in paragraph 75 above.

155   I conclude, therefore, that the money (£1.4m) received by the MIREDS fund by order of Intern. Solidariteet. Prag. between January and December 1985 was or

included money donated by the miners in the Soviet Union for the benefit of the NUM and transferred to the MIREDS fund by the MTUI, by arrangement with Mr Scargill, to be held for the benefit of the NUM.

156   Mr Scargill has given three differing accounts of his participation in the decision to pay the money to the MTUI: (a) the NUM (i.e. Mr Scargill) made the decision (see the speech); (b) Mr Scargill had to agree because he knew that British miners would benefit from the International Trust (in his final written submissions); and (c) he had no part in the decision.   I have no doubt that Mr Scargill, if he did not make the decision, participated fully in it.   His failure ever to make a full report to the NEC on the developments in relation to the Soviet monies is a remarkable breach of duty and it there was indeed a diversion of the benefit from the NUM to the MTUI (and later the IMO) to which he was a party, as he now maintains, the failure to report this (as well as his participation in the decision to divert) is a breach of duty of the most serious character.

157   If I am wrong in my conclusion and there was an agreement to divert the gift of the money from the NUM to the MTUI, there must be a real doubt whether the intention of the donors could be defeated in this way.   If the question were governed by English law, the intention of the donors would prevail, but as the monies were raised in the Soviet Union and probably remained at the relevant time either in the Soviet Union or in Warsaw, this may turn on Soviet or Polish law.

158   It is quite clear that even if the money was given to the MTUI rather than the NUM, it was at all times intended that the NUM should at least indirectly receive part of the funds provided from the USSR.   However, as appears from Chapter 15 of this Report, when account is taken of the c.£580,000 payment of NUM money into the MIREDS account, and c.£71,000 paid into the Chase Bank

account, it is clear that either this £580,000 and £71,000 plus interest thereon remains payable to the NUM or, if treated as used in repayments, no benefits have been received by the NUM out of the money donated by the Soviet miners. However, donations of £135,000 have been made to the MSF out of a mixed fund which includes the money donated by the Soviet Miners.

B.   Libya

159   Mr. Scargill has made it clear that during the strike the NUM did seek support from Libya. However he contends that the support sought was political only and not financial. He says that he did make efforts to persuade the Libyan Government to stop supplying oil and thus bring political pressure on the Government. However he has said (in a Radio 4 interview on 6th March 1990) that undertakings were requested and given not to ask for financial support from Libya and not to accept such support. I fully appreciate that at a period shortly after the shooting of WPC Yvonne Fletcher, contacts with Libya might have had adverse public relations consequences for the NUM. Accordingly, whilst I could understand a decision to have no contacts and seek no support from Libya, I find it difficult to understand why political support should be acceptable but financial support not. This appears to be the view also of Mr. Heathfield, for he has told me that, whilst he would have stated the fact if he had known that any money had been received from Libya, he would have had no qualms in accepting it: to have refused to have accepted it would have been hypocritical. On the other hand, Mr Alan Meale MP told me that at this time he on behalf of the Campaign Group of MPs was seeking such political support for the NUM from a variety of countries but not (at least explicitly) financial support.

160   Mr Scargill's objection to receiving financial assistance from Libya did not appear to extend to objecting to assistance to the Solidary Fund. Mr John Platts-

Mills QC has told me (and, though Mr Scargill denies it, I accept the evidence of Mr Platts-Mills), that Mr Scargill authorised Mr Platts-Mills to seek such aid (if not aid for the NUM itself) on the occasion of his visit there. This is not surprising, since Mr. Richard Caborn, a trustee of the Miners Solidarity Fund, has also said that he would have accepted Libyan money as a contribution to the hardship fund.

161   In this context it is perhaps significant that in a broadcast interview on 29th October 1984 Mr. Scargill said "We would welcome financial assistance from Trade Unionists anywhere". Yet on the 6th March 1990 in another interview he said that if Libya had offered money he would have refused. It may be that there was a difference or there was perceived to be a difference (a) between payments by the Libyan Government and payments by Libyan trade unions and (b) between payments to the Union during the receivership which might be subject to seizure by the Receiver and payments in a form or to a recipient such that seizure could be avoided.

162   The evidence relating to requests for and the receipt of monies before me is very limited. It rests primarily on the statements reported in the media of Mr. Windsor that he received three instalments of £50,000. Mr Windsor has declined to assist me. It is clear that he was invited to visit Libya at no cost to the NUM and that Mr Scargill had agreed to him going (although Ms Jean McCrindle told me that at the time Mr Scargill told her that he had not sent Mr Windsor). He was in Libya between 24/26 October 1984. Mr Scargill has said that the purpose of his visit was to explain the Union's case. I cannot believe that at this critical stage of the strike Mr Windsor would have been sent merely to fulfil an academic exercise. It seems to me he must have been there to seek support and since at the time the NUM was in urgent need of funds and since it was combing the world for them it begs belief that the message did not and was not intended to get through. (I also bear in mind, that as stated in paragraph 136 above, Mr. Platts-Mills gave the number of the Narodny bank account in Warsaw to Colonel Gaddafi or his deputy.)

The question which remains, in my view, is whom Mr Windsor intended, and was intended by Mr Scargill, to ask for assistance when he visited Libya and in particular whether the trade unions or the government. (Mr Heathfield did not know that Mr Windsor would be visiting Libya until after the event).

163   Help on this Enquiry could have been provided by Mr Windsor and Mr Abbasi (who is alleged to have been involved in organising both the request for money and its receipt). Both have declined to assist. It is difficult therefore to assess their reported account of events. I have borne in mind the different stories told by each of these men in 1984 and now. In the case of Mr Abbasi I have listened to a tape recording made by a journalist, Mr Graham Hind, in October 1984, in which Mr. Abbasi denied having travelled to Libya with Mr Windsor. In the case of Mr Windsor, he was party to a report made to the National Executive Committee in late 1984 in which it was denied that Mr Windsor asked Colonel Gaddafi for money.

164   In weighing Mr Windsor's evidence, I have borne in mind a very significant piece of evidence provided to me by Mr P. McNestry, National Secretary of the National Association of Colliery Overman, Deputies and Shotfirers.

165   Mr McNestry told me that on an occasion some weeks or months after Mr Windsor's trip to Libya, Mr Windsor joined a train at London King's Cross bound for Doncaster, on which Mr McNestry was travelling. Mr Windsor joined Mr McNestry and at some point in the journey, Mr Windsor started to recount to Mr McNestry the story of his trip to Libya. Mr Windsor told Mr McNestry that he had gone to Libya to address a trade union meeting, and that he had duly spoken at that meeting which went on longer that he expected, with the result that towards the end of the meeting he was becoming concerned about missing his plane. He was assured that the organisers of the meeting would get him to the plane on time. When the meeting finished, Mr Windsor left the building with the organiser to see,

outside, the car which was to take him to the airport surrounded by military vehicles. Mr Windsor was told that Colonel Gaddafi wished to meet him. Understandably being considerably concerned, Mr Windsor attempted to remonstrate with the organisers of the meeting and those wishing to take him to see Colonel Gaddafi; but in the event he was told he must go. He was driven out into the desert through fortifications and rocket launchers, into a fort and eventually into the tent in which he met Colonel Gaddafi: Mr Windsor told Mr McNestry how worried he had been, and how he had not been aware that the interview was being filmed. He emphasised how totally unprepared he was for that interview and how unexpected the interview was. Mr Windsor did not tell Mr McNestry that he had asked Colonel Gaddafi for financial assistance, but said he had asked for "trade union support".

166 This is quite a different story from that told by Mr Windsor as reported in the Daily Mirror, which describes elaborate rehearsals with Mr Salim Ibrahim for a meeting with Colonel Gaddafi, and makes no mention of a trade union meeting. The story told to Mr McNestry has the ring of truth about it; further, I can think of no reason why Mr Windsor should have told Mr McNestry an elaborate lie (if his current story is true) some months after the affair when there was no media attention on it.

167 There is conflicting material relating to Mr Scargill's relations with Mr Abbasi. Mr Windsor, Mr Parker and Mr Abbasi are reported as saying that before Mr Windsor's trip to Libya, Mr Scargill met Mr Abbasi three times; once when he was introduced to Mr Abbasi at the TUC Conference in Blackpool in October 1984; once, in Mr Scargill's car shortly after the initial meeting, and once in the CGT headquarters on 8th October 1984. Mr Scargill has also told me that he met Mr Abbasi at the Conference in October 1984 and has also told me that he met Mr Abbasi and a Mr Ibrahim, whom he believed to be a trade unionist, at the CGT headquarters. Mr Scargill has also told me that he met Mr Abbasi in October

1985, when he saw Mr Abbasi in his car, on the question of whether the Libyan trade unions could be affiliated to the IMO.

168   Mr Scargill has represented his initial meeting with Mr Abbasi as being set up by Mr Windsor, and that he believed Mr Abbasi was involved in the trade union movement. Mr Windsor says that Mr Scargill asked him to contact Mr Abbasi after Mr Abbasi wrote to Mr Scargill.

169   Miss Marilyn Mitchell, an NUM employee at its Sheffield headquarters, has told me that she recalls putting phone calls through to Mr Scargill from Mr Abbasi in June, July and August 1984. The book that logged such incoming calls at the time has been lost or destroyed. I have also been told by an MP, whom I have agreed not to name, that Mr Abbasi approached him with an offer of money for the NUM, but that the MP declined to have anything to do with it.

170   I also attempted to obtain information from the Libyan Government. In the first week in June, I wrote to the Head of the Libyan Interests Section at the Royal Embassy of Saudi Arabia, Mr A. Ameish, enclosing a letter to Colonel Gaddafi's asking for information on a number of points. On about 18 June, after an intimation to me that Mr Ameish would be willing to see me, I wrote further to Mr Ameish himself.

171   Mr Ameish's response was to indicate (unfortunately, not until 29 June) that an approach for information through him would take several months to obtain a response, in part because of the lack of diplomatic facilities available to him, and because the matter would have to be raised with Colonel Gaddafi himself. He also indicated that he had no knowledge of the matters raised in my letter to Colonel Gaddafi, and that he did not know how my request for information would be reviewed in Libya. I think it is a fair inference that the Libyan authorities were not keen to provide information to this Enquiry.

172   I conclude that Mr Windsor probably went to Libya only to address a trade union meeting and probably did not expect to meet Colonel Gaddafi; but I also conclude that since Mr. Windsor did, in the event, meet Colonel Gaddafi, he probably did ask for financial assistance from the Libyan Government. I am also of the view that Mr Windsor had available the Narodny Bank account number, and is likely to have given it to Colonel Gaddafi, particularly as Mr Platts-Mills also did so. It cannot, therefore, be ruled out that Libya donated money to the MTUI account, number 111-12-6973-151-6797 at the Narodny Bank in Warsaw.

173   This does not, however, necessarily mean that the sums alleged by Mr Windsor to have been received in December 1984 and used to repay various sums to the NUM emanated from Libya. I also have to consider the account of Mr Windsor (again unfortunately through the newspaper reports only) and the evidence of Mr Scargill, Mr Heathfield and others concerning the repayment of money relating to the homes of Mr Scargill, Mr Heathfield and Mr Windsor, and the receipt of that money in the NUM head office. However, before dealing with this and evaluating that evidence (which is done in Chapter 10) I need first to deal with the history of Mr Scargill's, Mr Heathfield's and Mr Windsor's homes, and I turn to this next.

CHAPTER 9: MR. SCARGILL'S AND MR. HEATHFIELD'S HOMES AND MR. WINDSOR'S HOME LOAN

9.1   Mr. Scargill's and Mr. Heathfield's homes

174   In order to understand the actions taken in connection with Mr Scargills's and Mr Heathfield's homes, it is first necessary to describe the two National Officials' contracts of employment so far as they relate to accommodation.

175   Mr Scargill has provided me with a signed contract dated 17.11.82. (signed by Mr Daly on behalf of the Union) and an unsigned contract, making some changes to the 1982 contract, dated 25.7.83. Mr Heathfield has provided me with a signed contract dated 2.3.84 signed by Mr Scargill on behalf of the Union. All contracts contain the following clause:

"CLAUSE 12

ENDORSEMENT TO CONTRACT OF EMPLOYMENT REGARDING ACCOMMODATION

(1)   Accommodation will be provided at an Annual Rental (inclusive of rates) equal to 2% of the capital outlay of the Property.

(2)   Heating and lighting costs of this accommodation will be met by the Union.

(3)   Upon retirement you shall be given the option of:

    (i)   remaining in your present residence on the same terms and conditions as apply on retirement;

(ii)   living in another property of comparable value (purchased by the Union in an area of your own choice) at the same terms and conditions as apply to your present residence;

(iii)   purchasing your present residence from the Union at a cost price equal to a 5% depreciation per annum on a reducing balance method of the property during your period of office and on date of retirement.

NOTE: In the case of Option i) and ii), it is intended that whichever is chosen shall apply to your Widow (during her Widowhood)."

176   In addition, the Finance Officers have told me that the telephone bills of the National Officials are paid by the Union.

177   I am satisfied that the above contract term was properly authorised by the Union, having been agreed at a meeting of the F & GP Committee on 10.10.67 and approved by the National Executive Committee on 12.10.67. I am also satisfied that Mr Scargill was entitled to have his telephone bills paid, by reason of the decision of the F and GP Committee dated 8.4.82.

178   Copies of all minutes relevant to this Chapter of the Report are contained in Annexe O to this Report.

Mr. Scargill's home

179   Mr. and Mrs. Scargill bought their former home at 2b Yews Lane, Worsborough Dale, Barnsley on 24.11.67. On 23.5.73 Mr. Scargill became President of the Yorkshire Area of the NUM, and on 31.8.73, the trustees of the Yorkshire

Area agreed to offer Mr. Scargill a mortgage of £3,000 repayable over 24 years at an interest rate of $2^1/_2\%$.

180   During late 1981, Mr. Scargill, still the Area President, applied to increase his mortgage facility to £25,000 for the purpose of extending 2b Yews Lane. The request was considered by the trustees of the Yorkshire Area on 12.1.82, and they agreed to make a further advance. The additional finance was made available to Mr. Scargill on 6.4.82.

181   On 1.4.83, Mr. Scargill became President of the National Union, and so it became necessary for his mortgage to be repaid to the Yorkshire Area.

182   On 8.3.84, the National Executive Committee resolved, (further to a resolution of 7th March 1984 of the Finance and General Purposes Committee) to purchase property to provide accommodation for the National Officials i.e. Mr. Scargill and Mr. Heathfield in accordance with what I am satisfied was the usual practice of the Union and in accordance with the National Officials' terms of employment. This was, it appears, to be achieved in the case of Mr. Scargill by the National Union purchasing Mr. Scargill's house from him, and in the case of Mr. Heathfield, by the National Union purchasing (from the Derbyshire Union) the house which Mr Heathfield occupied as a tenant. In the case of Mr Scargill's home, this was to be achieved by the National Union repaying Mr Scargill's mortgage with the Yorkshire Area, and paying to Mr Scargill the balance of the value of the house. The house was valued at £50,250 on 7.3.84; and on 13.3.84 the sum of £22,255 (being the outstanding mortgage) was paid by the National Union to the Yorkshire Area in respect of Mr Scargill's mortgage.

183   By mid-March 1984, therefore, the position was that Mr. Scargill technically owed £22,255.45 to the National Union; but it was contemplated that the National Union would thereafter complete the purchase of Mr. Scargill's house by paying Mr

Scargill the balance and by Mr Scargill conveying the house to the National Union, and that it would then be rented to Mr. Scargill in accordance with his terms of employment. Whether because of this plan, or through oversight, the original 1973 legal charge to the Yorkshire Area was not discharged, and since the intention was for an outright sale to the NUM, neither was a new legal charge to the National Union executed. This was only discovered on the sale by Mr. Scargill of his property in August 1988.

Mr. Heathfield's house

184   In April 1966, Mr. Heathfield was elected an Area Official (becoming, in fact, Area Compensation Agent) of the Derbyshire Area of the NUM. In accordance with rule 44 (b) of the Derbyshire Area, Mr. Heathfield was provided with accommodation, free of charge, at 262 Newbold Road. 262 Newbold Road was purchased by the Derbyshire Area in 1969.

185   In January 1984, Mr. Heathfield was elected Secretary of the National Union. On 16.2.84, a valuation was carried out in respect of 262 Newbold Road on behalf of the Derbyshire Area, no doubt in anticipation of an imminent sale to the National Union. This valuation, by Messrs. J.M. Warwick & Co., contained the following statement:

> "It was, however, noted that the brick built garage had tilted to one side and will need considerable repair or rebuilding".

Mr. Heathfield has told me that the garage had become unstable because of the difficulty in opening and shutting the hinged doors, and was thought to be in danger of collapsing onto the neighbouring property.

186   On 7.3.84, as in the case of Mr. Scargill's house, the National Executive

71

Committee and the F & GP committee resolved to purchase accommodation for Mr. Heathfield.

187   Mr. Heathfield has told me that after the F & GP committee meeting on 7.3.84, he informally consulted the other two then trustees of the National Union who agreed that the work necessary to repair the garage should be carried out straight away. Mr Richardson, then one of the trustees of the NUM, has confirmed to me that he seems to recollect authorisation for urgent repairs being sought. However, Mr Richardson also told me that he would be most surprised if Mr Heathfield had asked the trustees for this authorisation, and that he would have expected it to be raised at an F & GP committee meeting.

188   In March 1984, therefore, the position in respect of Mr. Heathfield's house was that it was intended to be purchased by the National Union from the Derbyshire Area, and that Mr Heathfield appears to have had authorisation from someone for urgent repair work to go ahead.

9.2   The events of March 1984

189   By early March 1984, the national strike was imminent, and the National Officials and Mr. Windsor were giving thought to ways in which the Union's property could be protected in the event of the sequestration which was anticipated even then. On 8.3.84, Mr. Roger Windsor presented a paper to the special meeting of the National Executive Committee referred to in paragraph 42 above, setting out ways of protecting the union's real property, including the homes of National and Area Officials. Initial consideration was given to transferring the property to a private company, Oakedge, which would be owned by the Mineworkers' Trust. Mr. Richmond of KPMG Peat Marwick however, advised against this as creating tax problems but securing no advantages to the Union. He recommended that the Union's property, including the homes of the National Officials and former National

Officials, should be transferred direct to the Mineworkers' Trust. The National Executive Committee had resolved earlier that day to set up this charitable trust, and at a meeting later on 7.3.84, attended by the National Officials and Mr Windsor, it was decided not to use Oakedge at all.

190   At that same meeting, also attended by Messrs. Raley & Pratt, solicitors, steps were discussed how to set in motion this plan. Counsel's advice was taken as to the propriety and efficacy of the plan; and while expressing great concern as to the speed with which this scheme was being entered into, Counsel settled the draft deed and advised that it should be effective.

191   The trust deed was for the Mineworkers Trust was executed on 19.3.84, the trustees being Mr. K. Homer, a Yorkshire official, Mr. J. Burrows, a Derbyshire official, and Mr. Roger Windsor.

192   Messrs. Raley & Pratt then prepared the documentation for the transfer of the homes, inter alia, of Mr. Scargill and Mr. Heathfield to the Mineworkers' Trust; and in about mid-March (1) contracts between Mr. Scargill and the Derbyshire trustees on the one hand and the NUM trustees on the other hand; and (2) conveyances transferring 2b Yews Lane and 262 Newbold Road to the trustees of the Mineworkers' Trust as an endowment by the trustees of the NUM, were executed in escrow, (which means that they would be ineffective unless and until a certain condition was met) together with acknowledgments by the trustees of the Mineworkers' Trust of the tenancies of Mr. Scargill and Mr. Heathfield. However, in the event, those documents never came into force, and eventually the whole plan to transfer Mr. Scargill's and Mr. Heathfield's homes to the Mineworkers' Trust was abandoned. Mr. Scargill sold his home to a private purchaser in August 1988. In 1987 there were negotiations for the sale of Mr. Heathfield's home to Mr. and Mrs. Heathfield, but this sale did not proceed and on the 31st December 1988 the sale to the NUM by the Derbyshire Area was completed after some negotiation, for

£53,512. This sale was made at a price reflecting the value of the property including the improvements already paid for by the NUM as referred to below. It appears to me that the NUM accordingly paid twice for these improvements.

9.3   The repayment of Mr. Scargill's mortgage

193   As described above, Mr. Scargill's mortgage with the Yorkshire Area had been paid off by the National Union in March 1984, as part of the process of purchasing Mr Scargill's house and a contract (with the NUM trustees) and a conveyance in escrow (to the Mineworkers Trust trustees) had been executed. In August 1984, the transfer to the Mineworkers' Trust had not yet taken place, and Mr. Scargill had a mortgage loan of £22,455 from the National Union. Mr. Scargill therefore decided that he ought to repay that loan to the National Union. Mr Scargill has explained to me and I accept, that the repayment by the NUM of his mortgage loan to the Yorkshire Area had been part of the process of the purchase by the NUM of his house. However, the purchase had not proceeded, and there was no authority for the National Union to make a mortgage advance to him. In order to regularise the position, Mr Scargill therefore felt that he ought to repay to the National Union the sum paid by the National Union to the Yorkshire Area until such time as the purchase of the house should be completed.

194   On 8th August 1984 Mr. Scargill therefore repaid the National Union the sum of £22,255.45 being the sum then outstanding in respect of his mortgage loan. This repayment was made using two cheques. One cheque was drawn on Mr. Scargill's account with the Co-operative Bank in Barnsley in the amount of £5,255.45. The other cheque was drawn on a Bradford and Bingley Building Society account in the amount of £17,000.00. This cheque was made payable to Mr. Scargill and represented a withdrawal of funds from Mr. Scargill's building society account. Mr. Scargill has told me that he endorsed this cheque to the NUM. Both of these

cheques were deposited in an NUM bank account held with the Co-operative Bank in Sheffield on 14th August 1984. Cork Gully have reviewed financial records of the NUM and documentation held by both Mr. Scargill and KPMG Peat Marwick relating to Mr. Scargill's mortgage repayment and have confirmed to me that Mr. Scargill's mortgage was repaid in this manner.

195   Mr. Scargill has made available to me his bank statements for the accounts and periods referred to in Annexe P hereto. Cork Gully have confirmed to me that the two bank accounts used by Mr. Scargill to make his mortgage repayment of £22,255.45 contained monies built up over a number of years prior to the 1984-5 strike.

196   There is therefore no doubt that Mr. Scargill's £22,255.45 mortgage was paid by Mr. Scargill in August 1984 using two cheques drawn on accounts containing his own monies and not, as alleged by Mr. Windsor, in cash in December 1984. To this extent, therefore, the allegation of the Daily Mirror is quite incorrect.

9.4   Repairs and alterations to Mr. Scargill's and Mr. Heathfield's homes

Mr. Scargill

197   In December 1983, Mr. Scargill had obtained a quote from Wm. Goodyear & Sons for various alterations to his house, including the installation of various pieces of fitted furniture. This work was completed in about mid March 1984, and the invoice is dated 16.5.84. This bill was paid by the NUM on 30.6.84, in the sum of £6,118.00.

198   In addition, the following bills were paid by the NUM in respect of 2b Yews

Lane:

18.4.84	Yorkshire Water	£113.72
16.5.84	Barnsley MBC (rates)	£475.88
31.5.84	YEB	£ 83.61
4.9.84	YEB	£ 69.37

199   Mr. Scargill in his statement to me says that following the decision of 8th March taken by the National Executive Committee to purchase his home, the Union trustees Messrs. S. Thompson, T.H. Richardson and P. Heathfield agreed that as from the 8th March 1984 all bills for rates and electricity should be met by the NUM and that the NUM should pay for improvements. I do not think that the Union trustees had any authority to enter into any such agreement relating to improvements (although electricity bills would come within clause 12 of Mr Scargill's contract of employment.)   This was surely a matter for the National Executive Committee or Finance and General Purposes Committee or should at least have been reported to them. Mr. Thompson is dead. As regards this statement, Mr. Richardson recalls no such agreement and has told me that this is not an agreement the trustees would have felt competent to make, and that if they had done so, they would have reported the agreement to the F & G. P. Mr. Heathfield says that he recalls this matter being mentioned at about the same time he mentioned the works to his house. Later, in his oral evidence, Mr Scargill has told me that it was only the improvements which were raised with the trustees, and that the payment of rates and electricity would be automatic after the agreement to purchase his house. I do not believe that any of these matters were mentioned to anyone except perhaps Mr Heathfield.

200   Mr Scargill has produced to me the minutes of an F & GP Committee meeting of 13th March 1983 which (he says) give the National Officials authority to approve all expenditure relating to repairs, alterations and improvements to the property (included in Annexe O). I do not agree. The authority is to authorise

such expenditure as has been already projected by the F & GP Committee in their Annual Budget, or similar expenditure which may arise <u>when any delay would be detrimental to the interests of the Union.</u>

201   I also have doubt whether the works carried out constituted an enhancement of the value of the property in the sum expended as stated in the Press Release of 5th March 1990. (Annexe B).

Mr. Heathfield

202   The following bills were paid by the NUM in respect of Mr. Heathfield's home at 262 Newbold Road (which was still owned by the Derbyshire area, but in respect of which a conveyance to the Mineworkers' Trust had been executed in escrow):

13.6.84	Brayshaw Harrison Partnership (Architects)	£614.21
29.10.84	R.K. Morrell (building contractor)	£5,750.00
12.11.84	Andrew Reaney (Kitchen design)	£7,147.00

203   Mr Heathfield has told me that there was an urgency in carrying out the work, primarily to correct structural defects in property the NUM owned, and that he decided to contribute as the work would provide improved amenities, and accordingly he obtained a home improvement loan. Mr Heathfield told me that he

spent some £10,000 of his own money on the work on his house above and beyond the £13,511.21 expended by the NUM. Mr Heathfield has provided Cork Gully with information relating to payments totalling £5,010.71 made through his bank account during the period August to December 1984. These payments, so far as Mr Heathfield can recall, related directly to the rebuilding and refurbishment works. A number of other payments were, so Mr Heathfield says, made in cash, and cannot be traced to Mr Heathfield's bank account. Receipts for material purchases by Mr Heathfield were not retained, and a number of cash payments were also not recorded. There is therefore no documentary evidence available to substantiate this expenditure by Mr Heathfield. I am inclined to believe that Mr Heathfield did spend at least some thousands of pounds of his own money on the works, but I do not accept that it was as much as £10,000.

204   The National Officials in their Report to the National Executive Committee on the 9th March 1990 (Annexe B) stated that necessary building work was carried out to the coal house and adjoining garage attached to the house which was unsafe and leaning heavily on a neighbouring property; that Mr. Heathfield took out a personal loan and the NUM paid the balance as the NUM was responsible for repairs and accordingly paid £13,511.21. In the Press Release dated 5th March 1990 it was stated that the only benefit of this work to Mr. Heathfield was the removal of a dangerous structure and the provision of a safe one.

205   As indicated above Mr. Richardson has a recollection of his agreement that the Union should pay the cost of urgent repairs. Any authority given on behalf of the NUM was plainly obtained on the basis that the work to be done was urgently needed repair work. It is scarcely conceivable that in the middle of, or at the beginning of, the strike there could have been authority for expenditure beyond this.

206   It seems to me quite clear that the works went far beyond any repairs of

the type suggested in the report of the Officials or the Press Release, and beyond any authorisation on the part of the NUM. There was an extension to the kitchen/garage. I do not see how payment of this bill so far as it goes beyond repairs was authorised by the NUM. There was apparently no disclosure let alone a full disclosure to the National Executive Committee, and I am satisfied that proper authorisation was never sought. I incline to the view that the NUM has paid twice for these improvements, for the value of the house in 1984 before the improvements were carried out was £48,000 with vacant possession and £31,000 subject to the tenancy of Mr. and Mrs. Heathfield; and the price eventually paid by the National Union (subject to the tenancy of Mr Heathfield) was £53,512, based on an open market valuation of £59,000 which was of the property as improved. I am even more concerned that the description of the works and the explanation for the expenditure in the Report of the National Officials is clearly misleading and incomplete. I accept that this part of the Report was prepared by Mr Heathfield and that Mr Scargill relied on what was said by Mr Heathfield.

207   By 12.11.84, therefore, the NUM had expended £6,560.58 in respect of Mr. Scargill's house and bills, and £13,511.21 in respect of Mr. Heathfield's building works.   As stated above 262 Newbold Road was eventually transferred by the Derbyshire Area to the National Union in 1988.

9.5   Mr. Windsor's home loan

208   On 1st March 1983, Mr. Roger Windsor was employed by the NUM as Finance Officer. On 18th April 1983, the date the NUM opened its offices in Sheffield, he became Chief Executive Officer.

209   Mr. Windsor had previously worked in Stroud. At some stage in 1983-4, Mr Windsor told the National Officials that he had difficulty in selling his house in Stroud, and asked the National Officials if the Union could grant him a bridging

loan in order to help him purchase a house in Sheffield. The National Officials agreed to grant Mr. Windsor a £29,500 interest free loan repayable by the end of December 1984 and this was made on 27th June 1984. Mr Scargill told me that Mr Windsor was promised a bridging loan if he needed it when he joined in March 1983, and Mr Heathfield confirmed that Mr Scargill had told him the same, although it was of course before Mr Heathfield became General Secretary. Mr. Scargill says that the Finance and General Purposes Committee gave him or Mr. Heathfield and himself plenary power to negotiate terms of contract for relocation of employees on the occasion of the relocation of the Head Office from London to Sheffield, but nothing was minuted, and that it was in pursuance of this power that the loan to Mr. Windsor was agreed. Later, Mr Scargill produced minutes of various F & GP committee and National Executive Committee meetings which he relied on to show the authority given by the National Executive Committee to grant such a loan. Those minutes appear in Annexe O to this Report, and in my view they do not give the National Officials power to make such a loan.

CHAPTER 10: REPAYMENT OF THE SUMS PAID IN RESPECT OF MR. SCARGILL'S AND MR. HEATHFIELD'S HOMES AND OF MR. WINDSOR'S HOME LOAN

210   On a date which cannot now be precisely ascertained in late 1984, Stephen Hudson, the NUM's then finance officer, was given a large amount of cash to repay to the NUM 3 sums of money. These were

(1)   the sums which the NUM had expended on Mr. Scargill's house, namely of £6,860.58

(2)   the sums which the NUM had expended on Mr. Heathfield's house, namely £13,511.21

(3)   the loan owed by Mr. Windsor to the NUM, namely £29,000. (The sum owed was in fact £29,500, but when asked what sums were due, Mr Hudson did a swift calculation and gave an incorrect figure of £29,000. This was later corrected and the £500 later paid)

211   Mr. Hudson has told me that sums (1) to (3) above were paid to him on the same day. Mr. Heathfield and Mr. Scargill have told me the same. Mr. Hudson has also told me that he was given instructions by Mr Scargill and Mr Heathfield to date receipts for the 3 sums on 3 different dates. Mr Hudson was told that this was because the National Officials and Mr. Windsor feared that if, they were dated the same day, the Receiver or Sequestrators might seek to attack the repayments and hence make claims in respect of the homes of Messrs. Scargill, Heathfield and Windsor. The letters and receipts relating to all three sums, and to the sum of £12,000 referred to below, are set out in Annexe Q to this Report. I should mention that Mr Heathfield does not recall dating his receipt incorrectly.

81

212   However, in the National Officials' report to the National Executive Committee dated 9.3.90, the National Officials certainly imply that the sums set out in paragraph 210 above were paid on the date that the falsely dated receipts show, and hence _not_ all on the same date, as has been alleged by Mr. R. Windsor, and as is indeed the case. Mr Heathfield and Mr Scargill say that they did not intend to mislead the National Executive Committee. In the case of Mr Scargill, who prepared this part of the Report, I find this difficult to accept.

213   The date on which these payments were made is of some importance, since Mr Scargill has sought in his submission to me to disprove Mr Windsor's story by showing that the payments were made before the date on which Mr Windsor alleges he brought the money into the office of the NUM.

214   On some occasion, the sum of £12,000 was given by Mr Scargill and Mr Heathfield to Mr Hudson in respect of legal fees relating to members of the Nottinghamshire Area which could not be paid out of the Notts NUM funds. Mr Scargill and Mr Heathfield insist that this payment was not made at the same time as the three sums set out in para 210 above. Mr Hudson is "pretty convinced" that it was the same day. Mr Richardson, who was in the Head Office on the day when £12,000 was given and who gave a receipt for that money, is not said by any person to have been present when the other three sums were paid over, and so would not know if this was done on the same day. I am inclined to accept the evidence of Mr Hudson, who has struck me as an entirely honest and very careful witness who does not say he remembers things if he does not.

215   Mr Scargill has said that he is positive that the payments were made in about the first week of November 1984, and certainly not long after the appointment of the Sequestrators (i.e. 21.10.84). However, it is absolutely clear that the payments were made after 12 November, since this is the date on which the

last of the payments in respect of Mr Heathfield's house was made. Further the records of the MACF (see paragraph 114 above) do show £50,000 being brought in, possibly by Mr Windsor, on 4.12.84, the date on which Mr Windsor says he brought in £150,000. The total sum repaid to the NUM on that day was, of course, £49,871.79. Mr Windsor's story cannot, therefore, be disproved by reference to the date on which he says the payments were made or by reference to the written up accounts of the MACF.

216   However, it is quite clear that Mr Windsor's allegation that the cash he had brought in was used to repay Mr Scargill's mortgage of £25,000 is entirely untrue, since the mortgage has been repaid in August, and what was in fact repaid was the sum of £6,860 expended on repairs. Further, every figure given by Mr Windsor is incorrect. Even in respect of his own loan, the sum originally repaid was £29,000, not £29,500 (though this figure does appear on the receipt contained in Annexe Q, and the further £500 was repaid later as set out in paragraph 210). There are other inconsistencies in Mr Windsor's story as reported in the Daily Mirror and on the Cook Report. The sums received vary between £150,000 and £163,000. The money is implied, in the reports contained in the Daily Mirror, to have been brought in all at once on 4th December, but in the taped conversation with Mr Hudson reported in the Daily Mirror on 6th March, Mr Windsor refers to bringing in £50,000. Further, the story told in the Mirror on 6th March 1990 appears to suggest that Mr Windsor told his wife his debt was paid off with Libyan money 10 days before he claims the money was taken into the National Office.

217   I do not entirely discount Mr Windsor's story on account of those inconsistencies. I bear in mind first that all this took place over 5 years ago, and that anyone's memory is likely to confuse details over that length of time. Secondly, I am mindful that I have Mr Windsor's account of event only at second or third hand and in the medium of a sensationalist article in a newspaper and on television, so that details may very easily have been mixed up by the reporters

rather than Mr Windsor.

218   Two questions then arise:

    (1) Why were these sums repaid?

    (2) Where did the money to repay them come from?

Question 1

219   The explanation given for these payments in the report to the National
Executive Committee was that they were made to prevent any claim by the
Sequestrators that these were debts due to the Union. As regards the payment of
the loan owed by the Mr. Windsor, by common consent there was such a debt. As
regards the payments expended on Mr. Scargill's house, Mr Scargill has told me
that he believed the payments had been properly made at the time they were
made, but that Mr Windsor told him that since his house had not yet been
transferred to the NUM (or, as it was intended, the Mineworkers' Trust), the
Sequestrators could claim that NUM money had been expended on the house and
therefore attack Mr Scargill's house. As regards Mr. Heathfield I cannot see how
the payment can have been regarded as otherwise as a loan to him, and hence as
a debt due to the Union. However, Mr Heathfield has also told me that the
payment was made on the advice of Mr Windsor in the terms described above. In
my view, however, Mr Heathfield at all times knew that the money should not have
been paid by the NUM.

220   It should also be noted that on any basis the "repayment" was only a very
short time after the final payment was made by the NUM (on 12.11.84) in respect
of Mr Heathfield's improvements.

221   Both officials say that the whole transaction was Mr Windsor's idea. However, Mr. Hudson was certain that the National Officials had been expressing their concern for some time before the date on which the cash was paid to him. He indicated to me that part of this concern may have arisen out of fear of adverse publicity if it became known that the National Officials were having substantial home improvements carried out at the Union's expense in the middle of the strike. Further I do not understand why or how Mr Windsor would have known that those sums had been paid by the NUM in respect of Mr Scargill's and Mr Heathfield's homes, or indeed the circumstances in which those payments had been made. Indeed, if he had known the precise circumstances, I do not understand how he could possibly have made the mistake of saying that it was Mr Scargill's mortgage of £25,000 which had been paid off, instead of (as was in fact the case) payments for improvements and some bills, totalling less than £7,000.

222   Mr Windsor is reported in the Daily Mirror as saying that the National Officials wanted "to clean up" the books before the Receiver was appointed. Mr Hudson also thought he recollected that the transaction was triggered by the appointment of the Receiver, rather than, as suggested by Mr Scargill and Mr. Heathfield, of the Sequestrators. If the concern had been the appointment of the Sequestrators, I would expect the receipts to have been backdated to before 21st October 1984, as was the MACF deed. In fact, the three receipts are dated to the month preceding the appointment of the Receiver. In my view Mr Scargill, who knew that his house had not been conveyed and therefore that the union should be repaid their money, and Mr Heathfield, who knew, in my view, that the union should not have paid the money in the first place, were both likely to have been very worried by the appointment of the Receiver. Further, I find it hard to believe that the appointment of the Sequestrators was the problem, since two of the payments in respect of Mr Heathfield's house were made after the Sequestrators were appointed. Finally, Mr Hudson told me that Mr Scargill asked him how much

each of them owed, and that he initially got the sum in respect of Mr Hudson wrong, giving the figure as £29,000 not £29,500, so that the further £500 was repaid later. The receipt which the NUM has provided to me, and from which the union's cash book has been written up, is dated 30th November and is for £29,500. The receipt which the Daily Mirror alleges it has, but which I have not seen, allegedly refers to £29,500 on 4th December 1984, and £500 on the 10th December 1984. Mr Hudson has not been able to explain the apparent existence of two receipts, but tells me it does not surprise him.

223   All the above leads me to believe that the payment was indeed linked with the appointment of the Receiver. However, there is a receipt for £12,000 from Mr Richardson dated 18.11.84 which Mr Richardson says was dated the day it was given. This would indicate that the whole transaction was indeed mid-November. However, even if it was 18th November, the action in which the Receiver was appointed was commenced on 8th November and his appointment must have been contemplated even by 18th November. On balance, I am of the opinion that the payments were probably made because of the appointment of the Receiver, and were probably made in late November, but possibly early December, 1984. I am also of the opinion that the repayment was not wholly, though it may have been in part, the idea of Mr Windsor.

Question 2

224   I have been told by Mr. Scargill and Mr. Heathfield that this money came from the cash fund which they describe as the "Miners Action Committee Fund". I see no reason to doubt this. There is no entry on any other account which I have seen which could be those sums. Neither am I aware of any allegation that it came from any account other than those set out in Annexe I. Further, the "Miners Action Committee Fund", being in fact the cash which came into Mr. Scargill's hands from October 1984 onwards, is the logical place to look for this cash payment.

225   The "accounts" drawn up for the Miners Action Committee Fund were in fact drawn up in late 1989. The narrative account was compiled by an employee of the NUM in the Finance Office on the instructions of Mr. Scargill, from receipts and other documents provided by Mr. Scargill (see Annexe J). Among those receipts are the 4 receipts for the sums set out in paragraphs 210 and 214 above, and this is why the narrative account I have seen shows those false dates. However, this clearly casts doubt on the validity of the records for the whole account, and for this reason, the source of the money received by Mr. Scargill and used to pay these sums can only be verified by checking the entries with the parties who are said in the account to have paid the money.

226   Of course, as stated above, it is likely that there are other sums of cash which Mr Scargill received which are not recorded. However, there are clearly receipts of at least £150,000 which Mr Scargill and Mr Heathfield have told me were brought in by Mr Windsor at approximately the time alleged by Mr Windsor, and out of which Mr Heathfield and Mr Scargill agree the sums set out in paragraph 210 above were paid. It is fair, therefore, to assume that these are the sums Mr Windsor is reported as talking about in the Daily Mirror and on Central Television.

227   Of the six sums set out in paragraph 114 above, which are shown as emanating from the CGT, there is no contemporaneous record now available showing the source of those sums. In relation to the six receipts, the reconstructed records provided to Cork Gully by Mr Scargill show only what is recalled by Mr Scargill and Mr Heathfield, namely that the sums of £100,000 shown as received on 25.10.84 and the sum of £50,000 shown as received on 4.12.84 were brought in by Mr Windsor and that Mr Windsor told Mr Scargill and Mr Heathfield that the money came from the CGT. It was therefore necessary to go back to the CGT to ascertain whether the money shown above as emanating from the CGT was in fact

received by Mr. Scargill and Mr. Heathfield from the CGT; and also, to ascertain whether that money came from the CGT's own funds or from some other source.

228   On 25th June 1990, after two letters from me, and communications from the sub-committee and from Mr Scargill at my request asking for co-operation, Mr Bernard on behalf of the CGT replied saying that "if Mr Scargill says he received [the six sums referred to above], we have every confidence in him". This is less than helpful, and to my mind suggests that the CGT cannot confirm that they sent those six sums.

229   The following are the facts which I have to weigh in the balance in deciding whether the money from which the sums set out in paragraph 210 above emanated from Libya as alleged by Mr Windsor.

1. The records relating to the MACF are clearly (as freely admitted by Mr Scargill and Mr Heathfield) inadequate and misleading.

2. My conclusion set in paragraph 172 above that Mr Windsor did ask Colonel Gaddafi for money on his trip to Libya in October 1984.

3. Mr Scargill's and Mr Heathfield's evidence that Mr Windsor told them the money came from the CGT is corroborated by Ms Myers and Mr Richardson.

4. Mr Scargill and Mr Heathfield have told me that the CGT were also collecting money abroad. There must, therefore, have been the possibility that the money was simply routed from Libya through the CGT.

5. Other sums given by the CGT arrived in the NUM offices in French currency, not sterling.

6. The stories told by Mr Windsor on the one hand and Mr Scargill and Mr Heathfield on the other are inconclusive in respect of the dates on which the payments were made to the NUM.

7. There are a number of significant inconsistencies in Mr Windsor's evidence.

8. The failure of the CGT to assist the Enquiry in a meaningful way.

9. The absence of response from the Libyan authorities.

10. I regret that it has been my strong impression that Mr Scargill's story on a number of points has changed as it suits him throughout the conduct of this Enquiry.

230   However, I have reached the conclusion that on the material before me no clear or confident answer can be given as to the source of the money. There is a real possibility that the money came from Libya: but equally there is a real possibility that it came from elsewhere. The uncertain character of this conclusion is a reflection of the careless way the records of the unofficial accounts were kept and monies dealt with by the National Officials during this period.

231   A few days after whatever date it was that the payments set out in paragraph 210 above were made, Mr Scargill repaid the sum of £6,861.00 in cash into the brown paper parcel which was the MACF account. This was witnessed by Ms N. Myers, who signed a (again falsely dated) receipt. I am satisfied that this payment was indeed made, and that Mr Scargill had sufficient cash available to him

to do so. The only question which arises in my mind is why Mr Scargill did not use his own cash to repay the NUM in the first place, instead of using money of the MACF. As regards this, Mr Scargill has told me that he did not have the cash available at the time the payment was made out of the MACF fund. Mr Scargill tells me, however, that he intended, and told Mr Heathfield that he intended, to repay the MACF as soon as possible. Mr Heathfield confirms this.

CHAPTER 11: MR. SCARGILL'S AND MR. HEATHFIELD'S LATER HOUSE PURCHASES

232   In July 1985, Mr. Scargill wished to buy a house, Treelands Cottage, Hound Hill Lane, Worsbrough Bridge, Barnsley at the price of £125,000 which had just come on the market, and which he had wanted to buy for some time. The strike was over, but the Receiver was still in office, and Mr. Scargill was not being paid any salary and Mr. Scargill only began receiving his salary in November 1986. Mr. Scargill took the view that it would be impossible for him to obtain a loan from any bank, and so Mr. Scargill tells me he asked Mr Simon if the MTUI would make him a loan. Mr. Scargill needed both a long term mortgage and also a bridging loan to cover the period pending the sale of 2b Yews Lane. Mr. Simon evidently agreed and the money was paid and received in cash by Mr. Scargill on the 12th August 1985. The method of payment was a drawing of £100,000 (the first withdrawal) from the MIREDS account. The documentation was only drawn up later, consisting of two letters from Mr. Simon confirming the agreement to make the loans and purporting to enclose £100,000. Mr. Scargill acknowledged these letters and receipt on the 4th September 1985. By a letter dated 27th September 1985 Mr. Simon informed Mr. Scargill of the merger of MTUI and the IMO and that both loans were repayable to the IMO.

233   Mr. Simon on behalf of the MTUI agreed on 1.9.85 to loan Mr. Scargill £50,000 at 12% and £50,000 at 2½%. This was after Mr. Scargill had received the £100,000.

234   On 16.9.85, Mr. Scargill's son in law, Mr. D. Roberts, as nominee for Mr. Scargill, entered into a contract to purchase Treelands. Completion took place on 1.10.85. The purchase price was paid as to £91,000 out of the money loaned by the MTUI, and as to £34,000 out of Mr. Scargill's own savings. Mr. Scargill explains that he wished to conceal his identity as purchaser to avoid adverse publicity.

235   That £34,000 included £29,100 which had been held by Mr Scargill in accounts at the Jyske Bank in Denmark in the name of A. Pickering. Cork Gully have investigated that money and are satisfied that the sum is Mr Scargill's own personal money built up over a substantial period of time. Details of Cork Gully's investigations are set out in part I of Annexe R to this Report.

236   Mr Scargill has told me, and I accept, that he placed the money with the Jyske Bank because he was afraid the Sequestrators would seek to attack his own personal funds. Mr Scargill also told me, and Mr Hudson confirms, that this transaction was carried out with the knowledge of Mr Hudson, the Union's finance officer, who recommended the Jyske Bank.

237   In September 1985, the IMO was founded, and "took over" the two loans of £50,000 each made to Mr. Scargill. The mechanics of this "takeover" are not known to me in the absence of co-operation from Mr Simon.

238   On 14.10.86, Mr. Scargill paid to the IMO interest on the loan of £50,000 at 2½% in the sum of £4,100 by cheque on the Co-op Bank, Sheffield. (This payment was in fact more than 2½%, because Mr Scargill was making repayments in accordance with the scale of payments he had in respect of his earlier mortgage with the Yorkshire Area, and which included capital repayments.)

239   In November 1986, the Co-operative Bank offered Mr. Scargill a mortgage of £50,000. This loan was advanced on 1.5.87, and was sent to Mr. Scargill's solicitors, Raley & Pratt. Also on 1.5.87, Treelands was transferred by Mr. Roberts to Mr. Scargill, and the IMO were repaid £50,000 by a cheque on Raley & Pratt's client account. This loan repayment was deposited into the IMO account shown as no. 16 in Annexe I on 19 June 1987.

240   On 30.4.87, Mr. Scargill paid, so he told me, interest to the IMO on the loan at 2½% in the sum of £2,733 in cash.

241   On 28.8.87, Mr. Scargill paid, so he told me, £12,000 interest to the IMO in cash on the 12% loan (i.e. 2 years to 1.9.87).

242   On 4.9.87, Mr. Simon agreed to convert the 12% loan to a loan at 2½% for 20 years.

243   On 20.1.89, following the sale of 2b Yews Lane, Mr. Scargill repaid, so he told me, £51,657.92, being principal plus interest at 2½% for 17 months. An amount of £49,847.63 is recorded as having been received into the IMO account no. 13 in Annexe I on 25th January 1989, and is noted in the supporting schedule provided by Mr Scargill as being his loan repayment, given to Mr Simon in cash, and presumably paid, as to this sum, into account 13 by Mr Simon.

244   In the case of the sums of £2,733, £12,000 and £1,657.92 interest referred to above, the only documentary evidence substantiating those payments comprises receipts from Mr Simon and letters from Mr Scargill "enclosing" the money. Mr Scargill told me he handed that money to Mr Simon in cash and that Mr Simon retained it and applied it for "IMO purposes". Further, although Mr Scargill explained to Cork Gully how he came to have such large amounts of cash available, and has produced a schedule which is reproduced in part II of Annexe R, it would be impossible for Cork Gully to substantiate those payments. There must therefore be some doubt whether those interest payments were in fact made, although I am inclined to believe that they were. That this doubt should exist is part of the price Mr Scargill must pay for borrowing money in cash from a trust fund and generally conducting his affairs and the affairs of the NUM and the IMO in the unbusinesslike manner in which they have been conducted.

245   In July 1989, Mr. Heathfield also approached Mr. Simon for a loan from the IMO to buy a new house at 16 Main Street, North Anston, since he had moved out of 262 Newbold Road. The loan was apparently intended to be repayable out of the lump sum payable to Mr. Heathfield on his retirement. Mr. Heathfield received £60,000 on the 26th October 1989 in cash; and there is an exchange of letters between Mr. Heathfield and Mr. Simon dated 15.3.90 and 2.4.90 stating that the loan was repayable on 26.10.94 and carried interest at 10% per annum. This money also came, with Mr Heathfield's knowledge, from the MIREDS fund account in Dublin.

246   These loans disturb me considerably. First the loans were made out of an account which either totally or substantially belonged to the NUM, since it comprises only NUM money (from the MACF Fund) and the donations from the miners of at least the USSR, the GDR and Hungary. Secondly no notice was given to and no consent sought from the NUM in respect of these loans. Mr. Scargill's attitude is that they were nothing to do with the NUM. I do not agree. It is to be borne in mind that Mr. Scargill is full time President of the NUM as well as President of the IMO. It must be quite wrong that he or Mr. Heathfield should receive any benefit out of funds in which the NUM were interested without the consent of the NUM in any event. It seems to me that where the NUM allows its President to become an unpaid officer, and its secretary to become a chairman of an important committee, of another organisation, those employees should not accept benefits of this character from that other organisation without the prior consent of their full time employer, at any rate where there are financial dealings, as there are in this case, between the two organisations.

247   It is fair to say that both Mr Scargill and Mr Heathfield have told me that it was Mr Simon's decision that this money should come out of the MIREDS fund; and also that they did not believe that the funds they were receiving were NUM

monies.

248   I have borne in mind the fact which both Mr Scargill and Mr Heathfield have sought to impress upon me, namely that they forewent a considerable sum in salary after the end of the strike and up to the end of 1985. This does not alter the views I have reached in any part of this report, but the National Executive Committee and members of the NUM may feel it appropriate to take this into consideration in deciding what steps to take in relation to this Report.

249   While dealing with accommodation of the full time Officials, I should for the sake of completeness mention two other matters;

(1) Mr Heathfield has told me that negotiations are going on between lawyers acting for himself and his wife in connection with Mr Heathfield's departure from the matrimonial home, which is of course owned by the Union. Any agreement must, of course, be approved by the F & GP Committee.

(2)   Various newspapers have also made allegations about the ownership of the Barbican flat used by Mr Scargill. Mr Scargill has told me that he pays the rent for the flat, but that the rent is paid out of the expenses of £60 per night which he claims from the NUM when he stays in London. The NUM pay the phone and fax bills in respect of that flat.

CHAPTER 12: TRANSFER OF ROGER WINDSOR'S LOAN TO THE IMO

250   The money out of which Roger Windsor's loan was repaid came, so Mr. Scargill and Mr. Heathfield told me they believed, from the CGT. However, for the reasons given above, that money, in my view, was the property of the NUM. If this is the case, then the money has simply been moved from one NUM account to another, and should still be repayable to the NUM.

251   However, after the strike, Mr. Scargill and Mr. Heathfield were anxious that Mr. Windsor should repay the £29,500 to someone, but believed that it could not be repaid to the NUM which would in that case be repaid twice. It therefore appears to have been agreed between Mr. Windsor and the National Officials that the sum should be repaid to the IMO; and an agreement to that effect was entered into by Mr. Windsor on 22.7.86, and a legal charge executed charging that sum on his house on 1.9.87. Unfortunately, that charge was not registered, since Mr Windsor failed, despite a number of requests, to provide the solicitors with the necessary Land Registry details.   The documents evidencing these transactions, including the signed legal charge, are contained in Annexe S to this Report.

252   Mr. Scargill has told me that the money out of which Mr. Windsor was paid the sum to discharge his debt to the NUM had been given by the CGT to maintain the fabric of the NUM and that Mr. Windsor was only asked to repay the IMO for convenience. On this basis, and as I have indicated above the money must have at all times belonged to the NUM; and in particular, in view of the offices held by Mr. Scargill and Mr. Heathfield in the IMO as well as the NUM, either the agreement to pay the IMO instead of the NUM must be legally ineffective or the IMO must hold any rights and money as constructive trustee for the NUM. Indeed, (although he initially told me that the IMO intended to use the money "internationally") Mr Scargill has told me that the IMO has at all times intended (though it acknowledged no obligation) to repay this sum to the NUM when it was

recovered by the IMO.

253   I therefore invited Mr Scargill to procure that a letter to the NUM should be written by the IMO undertaking to pay any money recovered from Mr Windsor to the NUM or the Miners' Solidarity Fund as the National Executive Committee should direct.   That letter was produced to me by Mr Scargill and appears at Annexe T to this Report.

254   Mr Windsor has of course indicated in the Daily Mirror and the Cook Report that he is happy to pay the £29,500 to the Miners' Solidarity Fund. If all parties who on any basis may be entitled to that money, namely the NUM, the IMO, (to whom Mr Windsor has agreed, in writing, to pay the money) and the Miners' Solidarity Fund trustees, (to whom Mr Windsor says the money should have gone in the first place), were to agree that the money should be repaid to the Miners' Solidarity Fund and ask Mr Windsor to do so, Mr Windsor should be happy that the matter should be finalised in this way. This Solomonic solution would short circuit the current legal proceedings in France and provides an opportunity for Mr Windsor to prove his good faith at least in this area of contention.

CHAPTER 13: THE MINEWORKERS TRUST

13.1 NUR Loan

255 Two other transactions in respect of this trust have been the subject of newspaper comment and require separate consideration. The first relates to a loan of £300,000 to the NUM. There are two versions of the purpose of this loan. The first, supported by some of the documents and by the evidence of Mr Homer and Mr Burrows, is as follows.

256 By 1985 the NUM urgently required the finance to commence the development of land the site of Cambridge House which was the subject of a Deed of Gift to the NUM for the purpose of the construction of their headquarters. The Deed required building to commence within 5 years in default of which the land was subject to forfeiture. The 5 years expired in March 1986. This was to be financed in part by a grant of £300,000 from Sheffield City Council. However due to the breach of trust action, there was difficulty in obtaining this grant, and so on the request of Mr Scargill, the NUR acting by Mr. Knapp, its General Secretary, agreed to advance this sum to enable this development to proceed. The NUR could not, however, pay the money to the NUM and thus risk seizure by the Receiver. Accordingly, a loan of £300,000 was made to the trustees of the Mineworkers' Trust in November 1985. The loan, apparently a 5 year loan, appears to have been secured by a promissory note (although I have not seen this document and Mr Burrows and Mr Homer could not remember signing or seeing it). For the purposes of form it was agreed that interest would be charged on the loan at 10% per annum, but it was agreed by Mr Knapp that the NUR would make a grant of £30,000 per annum to the Mineworkers Trust to cancel out this liability to pay interest. The NUR has now told me that the loan was made at interest.

257 The second version, given by Mr Scargill, is as follows. The £300,000 was

intended to be used for the general purpose of sustaining the Union during the receivership, and the documents suggesting that its purpose was to develop the headquarters were merely a blind. In addition, the agreement between Mr Scargill and Mr Knapp was that interest would be paid by the trustees of the Mineworkers' Trust to the NUR, and that the NUR would donate the interest to the NUM, not to the Mineworkers' Trust. This version of the story is supported by a letter from Mr Scargill to Mr Knapp dated 12th August 1985 which accompanies a letter referring to the building project, which it describes as being drafted in "a very neutral fashion," and also by a letter from Mr Knapp's secretary Mr Milton Rampersaud, which refers to a loan to "the NUM". Mr Heathfield's view of events falls somewhere between these two stories.

258   It is my view that the trustees were told and believed that the loan was given for the purpose of the Mineworkers' Trust and particularly for the building works referred to above. This is, as I say, supported by contemporaneous documents seen by Mr Homer and Mr Burrows. It must be remembered that Mr Burrows and Mr Homer at all times believed that they were the trustees of a charitable trust, and should act accordingly. It may be that Mr Scargill intended the money to be used for other purposes, but that was solely his own intention and not shared by the trustees, or at least by Mr Homer and Mr Burrows. I have not, of course, had the benefit of Mr Windsor's evidence.

259   This difference in the view of the loan underlines the different views of those concerned in the Mineworkers Trust as to the nature of the trust itself. Mr Scargill regarded it at all times as a facade and convenient receptacle for NUM properties and monies to be returned to the NUM on demand; and this explains his view of the loan and his later actions. His view is expressly set out in a letter of 24th October 1988 to the Trust's solicitors where he states that all the assets of the Mineworkers' Trust were always regarded as assets of the NUM. The trustees (or at least Mr Homer and Mr Burrows) regarded it as a bona fide trust (while of

course wishing to act in the best interests of the NUM so far as was consistent with their duties as trustees). This explains the tensions between the trustees and Mr Scargill set out below.

260   On 19 March 1986, the sum of £310,411.70 was paid by the trustees of the Mineworkers' Trust to the IMO. This sum represented the NUR loan of £300,000 together with the accrued interest thereon. Again, there are two versions of how this transfer came about.

261   Mr Scargill told me that the National Officials and the trustees became concerned that the Receiver might succeed in recovering the £300,000 in the breach of trust action, and so the trustees decided, on legal advice, to "donate" the £300,000 plus interest to the IMO, which would hold it until required.

262   Mr Homer and Mr Burrows have told me that they recall Mr Scargill asking them to transfer this money to the IMO, and that they did so for reasons which both of them described as "blind loyalty" on the understanding, but (so far as they knew) without any written undertaking to that effect, that it would be repaid to the trustees of the Mineworkers' Trust at some point. Mr Burrows told me that he thinks he believed it was handed over to enable the IMO to continue the building works. Mr Homer and Mr Burrows also told me that it was certainly not a donation, although they did not specifically put their minds to the question of interest. Mr Homer told me that he assumed it would be repaid with interest because of the interest formally due to the NUR.

263   There is great difficulty about ascertaining whether this sum was intended as a loan, and if so at what rate of interest. The minute of the relevant meeting refers to a donation. Mr Homer and Mr Burrows also told me that they were deeply concerned at all times after the payment was made about the repayment of that money, and their personal liability to the NUR. Mr Burrows told me that

there were frequent verbal assurances from Mr Scargill given to Mr Windsor and reported to Mr Burrows by Mr Windsor that everything would be all right. The sum was certainly treated as a loan at interest at a later date by all concerned, particularly at a conference with Counsel in late 1989 attended by Mr Scargill on behalf of the IMO.

264   Further Counsel who was asked to advise on passing the money to the IMO was told that it would be by way of loan at an appropriate rate of interest, and that it was in order to enable the IMO to commence building work which would protect the Mineworkers' Trust's asset, namely the Cambridge House site.

265   Both Mr Homer and Mr Burrows told me that there had been no documentation relating to the payment to the IMO. Neither did the solicitor to the trust appear to recall any such documentation. However, on 28th June, Mr Scargill produced to me a document dated 17.3.86 from the IMO to the trustees of the Mineworkers' Trust in which the IMO undertakes to repay £300,000 and any interest due if they become repayable to the NUR. It is not clear to me who, outside the IMO, ever saw that letter.

266   Eventually, on 6.3.89 and in circumstances that I will describe below, the IMO repaid the NUR the sum of £300,000 by cheque signed by Mr Scargill alone. No interest was repaid to the NUR, but Mr Knapp signed a letter dated 13.3.89 confirming that the liability of the trustees of the Mineworkers' Trust was fully discharged. The interest was expended by the IMO in the ways set out in Chapter 15 below which deals with the mingling of the monies of the NUM and the IMO.

267   I should say that Mr Scargill has repeatedly stated that all transactions in respect of the Mineworkers' Trust were carried out on the basis of legal advice. However, it is clear to me that the lawyers involved whom I have seen were by no means fully informed. As I have said above, there was a conflict of views as to

whether the Mineworkers Trust was a bona fide trust or a mere vehicle for the NUM. Mr Scargill's view appears to have been that the trust was a vehicle for the NUM (although, to my surprise, in his final written submission to me, and notwithstanding the letter of 24.10.88 in which he states the absolute contrary, Mr Scargill stated that he had always regarded the Mineworkers' Trust as a bona fide trust whose assets did not belong to the NUM). The trustees, or at least Mr Homer and Mr Burrows, acted on the former basis. Legal advice obtained in these circumstances cannot be relied on to defend Mr Scargill's actions.

B. Gifts to the IMO

268   The second transaction relates to the donation of the residue of the funds of the trust to the IMO and the "sale" to the IMO of a piece of land belonging to the Mineworkers Trust, namely 12 Carver Lane, Sheffield. In 1988, following the National Executive Committee decision to wind up the Mineworkers' Trust, the trustees were advised by Counsel that they should sell their assets, and apply the money for charitable purposes within the objects of the Trust. The trustees wished to sell the land (which adjoins other land owned by the NUM), to the NUM, and then to apply the cash for educational purposes connected with the NUM, for example, provision of books in the public library intended to be set up at NUM headquarters, or the making of educational grants. However, Mr. Scargill has told me that when the Mineworkers Trust was wound up he decided that the balance of its assets (other than the land) should be given to the IMO on the basis that the IMO should purchase this land, that the IMO would permit the NUM to use the land and that the purpose behind this purchase was to keep away any predator who wished to build on the land.

269   A different picture is given in a letter dated 24th October 1988 to the Trust's solicitors which has been referred to above, in which Mr Scargill states that all the assets of the Mineworkers' Trust were always regarded as assets of the

NUM, and expresses his concern that if 12 Carver Lane were sold, NUPE would demand repayment of £25,000 which they had donated to the Mineworkers' Trust and out of which 12 Carver Lane had been purchased. This letter also indicates that if the trustees did not act as Mr Scargill wished, the IMO would not "pay any monies" to the Mineworkers' Trust. That letter apparently expressed his wish that the trustees should give all the assets of the Trust to the NUM. Later, when it became apparent that the trustees in accordance with their duties as trustees of a charity intended, on Counsel's advice, to apply the money in the Mineworkers' Trust for charitable purposes, Mr Scargill, apparently on the basis that he regarded those assets as NUM assets, decided he would procure that those assets should go to the IMO. Mr Scargill in his evidence to me expressed his horror that the assets should be given away for charitable purposes to third parties, and he told me that he intended that these assets should, at some point in time, come back to the NUM.

270   The trustees' minutes of the 6th March 1989 confirm the evidence of the trustees, and Mr Scargill in his evidence to me accepted, that Mr. Scargill threatened, by implication if not in so many words, that the IMO would not repay the NUR (thus leaving the trustees open to a claim by the NUR) unless these transactions in favour of the IMO (i.e. the sale of the land to the IMO and the donation of the purchase price of the land and all other remaining assets of the Mineworkers' Trust to the IMO) were approved by the trustees. Mr Scargill described this to me as a "tactical move". Under this pressure, the trustees conceded. The decision took the form of a grant of £32,000 to the IMO for educational purposes. (They had already been advised by Counsel that the monies could be applied by the trustees for educational purposes). Mr Simon on behalf of the IMO thereupon by a letter dated 18 November 1988 requested a financial contribution to education programmes being undertaken by the IMO. The trustees then decided to donate £32,000 to the IMO towards the costs of this programme. Counsel was certainly not aware of Mr Scargill's implicit threat, or aware that the

trustees were acting under that pressure.

271   12 Carver Lane was therefore "sold" to the IMO for £25,000 and a "grant" of £32,000 was made to the IMO for educational purposes. The balance of the funds of the Mineworkers Trust, being the sum of £1,733.53 was paid over to the IMO on about 4th October 1989. It does not appear that the £32,000 was used for the purpose set out in Mr Simon's letter.

272   On this basis, the IMO repaid the £300,000 to the NUR as described above. However, the question remains what happened to the interest. It appears that the NUR formally waived the interest on 6th January 1989. It is not clear whether the trustees of the Mineworkers' Trust were aware that the interest was formally waived, since I was not told this until 27th June by Mr Scargill, and so I have not had an opportunity to ask Mr Homer or Mr Burrows. Mr Homer and Mr Burrows have told me that they did not give specific thought to the interest, and certainly did not either waive or agree to make a donation to the IMO in that sum. Counsel who advised on the transaction in late 1988 advised on the basis that the IMO would repay principal plus interest which would all go to the NUR. In addition, Counsel advised that the additional £10,411.90 which had been paid over to the IMO in 1986 must be recovered and paid for the purpose of the Mineworkers' Trust.

273   In fact, the £10,411.70 and the rest of the interest on the £300,000 plus the £32,000 plus the £1,700 have been used by the IMO for a number of different purposes. Because it has been mingled with other money of the IMO, it is impossible to tell exactly how the Mineworkers' Trust money has been spent by the IMO, but the total receipts into and payments out of the account into which the Mineworkers' Trust money was paid are set out in Annexe U to this Report.

274 I can see no justification in law for the making of any such gifts as set out

104

above to the IMO, or for the use by Mr. Scargill of his authority as President of the NUM to benefit the IMO of which he was also President. He had no right to interfere at all unless the trust is to be regarded as a mere vehicle of the NUM, in which case all his efforts should have been directed to ensuring that the NUM rather than the IMO was exclusively benefited.

275   In my view, the IMO was unjustly enriched, but it is difficult to tell at whose expense. I return to this in Chapter 15 below. As regards the land at 12 Carver Lane, Mr Scargill told me that he and Mr Simon as trustees of the IMO have at all times regarded themselves as holding the land as trustees for the NUM and would transfer the land to the NUM at its request. I required execution of an acknowledgement by the IMO of the existence of such a trust, and Mr Scargill subsequently produced to me such an acknowledgement, dated 8th June 1990, which forms part of Annexe T hereto.

276   I should re-iterate that I am quite satisfied, having heard evidence from Mr Homer and Mr Burrows, that they at all times regarded themselves as trustees of a bona fide charitable trust and tried at all times to act in accordance with their duties as trustees. I have also gained the strong impression, both from Mr Homer and Mr Burrows and also from Mr Barlow of Counsel, that Mr Windsor also intended to act at all times in accordance with his duty as a charity trustee. The trustees were put in an impossible position by the uncertainty as to the nature of the transaction in 1986 when the £310,411.70 was paid over to the IMO. This led directly to the unhappy situation in 1989. I am quite satisfied that the trustees, though impelled to act as they did by the pressure placed on them by Mr Scargill, believed that they were entitled to make the grant of £32,000 for educational purposes and to sell the land to the IMO, and believed that they were acting properly and in accordance with legal advice in so doing.

CHAPTER 14: OAKEDGE AND OTHER ALLEGATIONS

A THE SPLIT BETWEEN STRIKING AND NON-STRIKING MINERS, AND THE ROLE OF OAKEDGE

277   The strike led in certain areas to a split in the ranks of the NUM between those supporting and those opposing the strike. The non-striking miners later formed the Union of Democratic Miners ("UDM"). The non-striking miners were a majority in two areas, namely the Nottingham Area and South Derbyshire Areas, and in these areas the NUM premises were taken over by the non-strikers.

278   The need on the part of the NUM to find replacement premises in these areas led to matters which have come within the scope of this inquiry.

1.   South Derbyshire

279   New premises for the South Derbyshire area were found at 62, Alexander Road, Swadlingcote, Burton on Trent. The IMO, (according to Mr Scargill in order to assist the NUM) brought these premises in the names of Mr. Scargill and Mr. Heathfield as trustees of the IMO for some £16,000 and the NUM South Derby Area occupied these premises rent free. The £16,000 came from the account into which the £300,000 representing the NUR loan was paid by the trustees of the Mineworkers' Trust (as set out in Annexe U.) With mine closures in the area, the premises have now proved redundant and are being offered for sale by the IMO. Its current value is about £70,000. No document existed recording any interest on the part of the NUM in this property or its proceeds of sale, and a question immediately arose whether the purchase by the IMO was intended as a gift or an investment. I have been anxious to resolve this question. Mr Scargill told me that the IMO intended at all times, though it acknowledged no obligation, to give the property or its proceeds of sale to the NUM. At my request however Mr. Scargill

assured me that the IMO would execute an acknowledgement that these premises were held as trustees for the NUM and that the entire net proceeds of sale will be paid to the NUM. Mr Scargill subsequently provided me with this signed document dated 8 June 1990. The document is the same document as acknowledges the bare trusteeship of 12 Carver Lane and is set out in Annexe T hereto.

2. Nottingham

280 In about February 1985 the Nottingham Area of the NUM found new leasehold premises at 42 St. John Street, Mansfield. A lease was signed in or about April 1985 and possession was taken on the 1st May 1985. The Nottingham Area required a loan of £10,000 to refurbish and equip the premises. The Derbyshire Area of the NUM was willing to make this loan at 12 1/2 per cent interest. But under the constitution of the Derbyshire Area such a loan could not be made to another Union. Accordingly the scheme was devised, apparently by Mr. Windsor, of a loan by the Derbyshire Area to a third party who would re-lend on the same terms to the Nottinghamshire Area. The loan was made on 27th January 1986.

281 The company chosen to occupy the role of intermediary was Oakedge Limited ("Oakedge").

282 Oakedge was incorporated on 22nd November 1983 as a private limited company and purchased as an off the shelf ready made company by Raley & Pratt, Solicitors for the NUM. It was acquired by the NUM as a wholly owned subsidiary. The three shareholders were all employees of the NUM and held their shares as nominees of the Union. They were Mr. Windsor, the former Chief Executive Officer, Mr. Clapham, the Industrial Relations Officer and Mr. Feickert the then Assistant Research Officer. Throughout its life, the company was financed out of funds of the NUM.

283   The original idea was that the company should acquire and hold property and assets of the NUM in conjunction with the Mineworkers Trust as a means of placing them beyond the reach of any sequestration order. But on advice being received from their auditors Messrs. Peat Marwick Mitchell that this was not a viable scheme, and not merely would fail to achieve this object, but would also lead to taxation disadvantages, this proposal was dropped in favour of the transfer of such property and assets direct to the Mineworkers Trust (see paragraph 189 above).

284   The company was thereafter left dormant, no change in shareholders or directors being made from the original nominees, until the proposal was made that the company be used as the medium for the loan to the Nottinghamshire Area. Mr. Scargill agreed to this scheme. He has told me that he saw this as merely a use of the Company's name as a device to enable the scheme to proceed: he did not intend or appreciate that the company would do anything or be activated. But of course, if the scheme was to be implemented, such activation was essential. There could be no advance and re-advance unless Oakedge was active, at least to this extent.

285   Mr. Windsor thereupon activated Oakedge. On the 25th October 1985, (1) he changed its registered office to 14 Carver Lane, Sheffield, the headquarters of the Mineworkers Trust; (2) he procured the transfer of shares and appointments of directors and (3) he also opened an account in the name of the company at the Midland Bank with Mr. Feickert and himself as signatories. The advance made by the Derbyshire Area to Oakedge was paid into this account and on-paid by Oakedge out of this account to the Nottingham Area. Subsequently the loan (together with interest) was duly repaid by the Nottingham Area to Oakedge, and by Oakedge to the Derbyshire Area. One peculiarity relating to this repayment is that after the initial repayment on the 22nd December 1986 of £6,667 of the capital (and £1,164.38 representing interest at 12 1/2%), Mr. Windsor caused a further

payment of £6,000 to be made via Oakedge to the Nottinghamshire Area. The reason for this payment was then unexplained and remains unexplained, but this sum and the balance of the loan were repaid by way of a deduction from an imprest payment due from the NUM to the Nottingham area.

286   Mr. Windsor also caused Oakedge to enter into certain other transactions, including the purchase of two computers for about £500 each. The decision to use Oakedge for these purposes was taken by Mr. Windsor on his own initiative and without reference to the National Officials. This was one of the matters which, when discovered by the National Officials, on or about the 30th September 1988, led, among other things, to a complaint by Mr. Scargill against Mr. Windsor to the Police in October 1989. Meanwhile, Mr. Windsor had left the NUM to live in France on the 15th August 1989.

287   The company itself was struck off the register as a defunct company under Section 652 of the Companies Act 1985 on the 19th April 1988 and dissolved on the 10th May 1988 by notice in the London Gazette. At the date of dissolution the company held £1,039.22 at an account with the Midland Bank branch at 17 Church Street, Sheffield and the two computers. Unless the company is restored to the register, the money is payable to and the title to the computers is vested in the Crown as bona vacantia. The computers are in the possession of the Union and in use. Their value today must be minimal. Whether the cost of an application to the Court to restore the name is justified in view of the small sums involved must be dubious. The fate of the company and the loss of the money in the bank account must be put down to the default of Mr. Windsor as Chief Executive Officer of the Union and a director and secretary of Oakedge, in ensuring that the company either was properly wound up or avoided being struck off. I can see no justification however for any complaint to the police against Mr Windsor in respect of Oakedge.

B   THE BURGLARY OF MR SCARGILL'S OFFICE

288   A burglary took place at Mr Scargill's office in about July 1987 when confidential files and papers were stolen. They included the typed list of receipts and payments in respect of the MACF account. The burglary was only reported to the police on 6th October 1989. Mr Scargill has explained to me that his immediate reaction on learning of the burglary was to consult solicitors Messrs. Seifert Sedley and institute proceedings for recovery of the documents taken in the hands of newspapers when possession of these was disclosed to them. Only after these proceedings were frustrated by destruction of the documents by the newspapers was he advised by his solicitors to notify the police, which he duly did.

289   Although Ms. S. Burton, the solicitor acting at the time, is quite sure that she was not told that a burglary was suspected until the date in October when she advised Mr Scargill to call the police, I do not think that this inconsistency (which may just be a difference in recollection) is important, or takes this Enquiry any further.

CHAPTER 15: MONIES HELD BY THE IMO FOR THE BENEFIT OF THE NUM OR OTHERS

There are a number of elements of mingling of monies with the monies of the IMO which now need to be disentangled, and which are dealt with in this chapter.

Part I: The payments by the Mineworkers' Trust to the IMO

290   The IMO bank account into which the Mineworkers' Trust monies were deposited in March 1986 and March and October 1989 was also used to receive other monies payable to the IMO, including the NUM's IMO affiliation fees. The same account made a number of payments, some of which appear to have been for the NUM's benefit and some of which appear to have been for the IMO's benefit. (As indicated above, a summary of the receipts and payments in this bank account are included in Annexe U to this report.)   Cork Gully have also prepared a calculation of the monies of the Mineworkers' Trust held by the IMO, including interest. This calculation is included as Annexe V to this report. The total sum is £159,550.42 to 31.3.90.

291   Mr Scargill initially told me that the interest on the NUR loan was to be used for the benefit of the objects of the IMO, i.e. to assist miners in various parts of the world. Subsequently, Mr Scargill told me that the interest was applied in payment of NUM creditors.

292   However, it is not clear to whom the monies received by the IMO from the Mineworkers' Trust really belong, although in my view it is unlikely to be the IMO. In respect of the interest on the NUR loan, the money may belong to the NUR, the NUM or the Mineworkers' Trust depending on the true nature of the payment over of £310,411.70 in March 1986, the true relationship between the NUM and the Mineworkers' Trust and the intention of the NUR when it waived interest on

the loan in 1989. In respect of the other monies, these may belong to the Mineworkers' Trust trustees or the NUM, again depending on the nature of their relationship. If the funds belong to the Mineworkers' Trust trustees, this will be on the basis that Trust was a valid charitable trust, and the monies will be impressed with those charitable trusts.

293   Insofar as money from the IMO account, some of which must have been money from the Mineworkers' Trust, has been expended for the benefit of the NUM, (for example, the property in Swadlingcote) I have included those sums in the general balancing account between the IMO and the NUM set out in the next part of this chapter. If, however, the money received by the IMO from the Mineworkers' Trust belongs in fact to the Mineworkers' Trust or, in part, to the NUR, the IMO cannot, of course claim the benefit of monies it has expended on behalf of the NUM.

294   This is not a matter which I am able to resolve in the context of this Enquiry. I have ascertained what has happened to the money; the legal consequences of that will have to be resolved by agreement or if necessary by legal action between the IMO, the NUR, the Mineworkers' Trust trustees, the NUM and possibly, (if the Mineworkers' Trust was indeed a valid charitable trust,) the Attorney General.

295   It is, of course, entirely a matter for the above parties how they choose to resolve this matter. However, in view of the possible charity involvement, one way in which it might be resolved is by a donation of £159,550.42 by the IMO to a charity or charities within the charitable objects of the Mineworkers' Trust, to be agreed by the relevant parties.

Part II: NUM funds which have come into the hands of the IMO

296   The deposit of £580,608.83 of MACF (i.e. NUM) money into account 14(a) and of £71,284.15 into account 9 has been described in paragraph 111 above.

297   Mr Scargill has claimed during this Enquiry that the IMO has contributed considerable sums of money to repay NUM creditors and make other payments for the benefit of the NUM. This is an important claim, and needs to be closely analysed.

298   Cork Gully have examined the total NUM funds located overseas including attributable notional interest earned by these monies, and also payments made out of overseas funds controlled by Mr Scargill /the IMO, in order to determine whether the NUM has received full benefit of the monies deposited overseas. A summary of their calculations is included as Annexe W to this report.

299   As indicated in paragraph 121 above, the sum of £1,050,000 has been transferred out of the accounts of the MIREDS fund into other accounts controlled by the IMO/Mr Scargill. Further, £105,998.82 has been transferred out of account 16 (which received the Mineworkers' Trust money) into the other accounts controlled by Mr Scargill/the IMO. The money in those accounts controlled by Mr Scargill/the IMO has been so thoroughly confused that it is not possible to say which money has been used to make what repayment. I have therefore looked at the general position of

    (1) What money the accounts controlled by the IMO/Mr Scargill (including the MIREDS fund) received, and

    (2) What money has been expended out of those accounts.

300   The first part of Annexe W sets out Cork Gully's calculation of interest on the money transferred to the accounts controlled by the IMO or Mr Scargill, giving

credit for money expended for the benefit of the NUM. The identifiable sums which belong to the NUM which were placed in accounts controlled by Mr Scargill and/or the IMO are as follows:

£580,608.83   transferred from the MACF to the MIREDS fund (see paragraph 111 above)

£71,284.15   transferred to the Chase Bank account (see paragraph 111 above)

£800.00   the initial deposit in the First Chicago Bank

£10,000.00   transferred from the SWAG account to the account at Co-op Bank Sheffield (Account 15)

301   Payments identified by Cork Gully and accepted by me for this exercise as being for the benefit of the NUM are set out in Part II of Annexe W and include amounts applied in repayment of NUM/MACF loans (a separate analysis of which appears at Annexe L) and in payment of NUM creditors. It appears that the NUM has not in fact received the full benefit of the monies and attributable interest earned on the funds deposited in the bank accounts controlled by the IMO/Mr Scargill. The shortfall is £61,373.81

302   It seems to me that the NUM is the owner of the funds deposited into these bank accounts (which I shall refer to in this chapter as "the overseas account"). These deposits were not disclosed by the National Officials to the National Executive Committee or its auditors and it seems to me that the NUM are entitled after giving credit for the sums set out in Part II of Annexe W to repayment of at least £61,373.81. I should, however, make one matter clear to the National

114

Executive Committee. Loans made to the National Officials for the benefit of the NUM during the receivership in order to allow the NUM to continue to function would not, in my view, be recoverable as a matter of law from the NUM. Strictly speaking, therefore, repayments of such loans are not sums paid for the benefit of the NUM. However, since the original loans were, on the whole, expended to pay genuine NUM creditors, or held to repay loans which were so expended, and since I am satisfied that the National Executive Committee knew that the Union continued to function notwithstanding the receivership, and that at least some members of the National Executive Committee knew of the existence of these loans, I have allowed these repayments as a benefit the NUM has received. It may, however, be open to the NUM not to give credit for such repayments and to claim repayment of this sum also. If the National Executive Committee or Conference does wish to take this course, it should take detailed legal advice before making such a claim.

303   Mr Scargill has also claimed that some of the payments made from the overseas accounts which I have treated as IMO expenses were made for the benefit of the NUM since they were payments which the NUM would otherwise have made. I consider that it is for the National Executive Committee to determine, on the basis of a full explanation by Mr Scargill, whether or not the NUM would have incurred any of the items of such expenditure, and for this reason these expenses have been treated as paid for the benefit of the IMO. These expenses identified by Mr Scargill as having been paid for the NUM's benefit are set out in part III of Annexe W. It will be seen that £135,000 of this is money donated to the MSF. I do not doubt that the National Executive Committee will be pleased that such donations have been made, but Mr Scargill and the IMO cannot claim that these are payments for the benefit of the NUM since the MSF is an entirely separate charitable trust. Given the state of its finances, the NUM may well not have decided to be so charitable.

304   If I am correct that the expenses set out in Part III of Annexe W are IMO expenses and not payments for the benefit of the NUM, then the result is that the NUM has not received any benefit at all from the Soviet etc money deposited in the MIREDS Fund; although on this basis the £135,000 donations to the MSF have been made out of money including the Soviet etc money deposited in the MIREDS fund.

305   If, however, the National Executive Committee do regard the expenses set out in part III of Annexe W above as payment made for the benefit of the NUM; (including the donation to the MSF) then the NUM may have received the benefit of the monies deposited overseas plus interest thereon, and the total benefit which may have been received (depending on how many of those expenses are ratified by the National Executive Committee) out of the Soviet etc. money is a maximum of £191,940.57 if all the expenses are accepted as NUM expenses. Because of the intermingling of the Soviet etc. funds with other funds of the IMO, it is impossible to say whether those payments set out in part III of Annexe W were made wholly or partly or not at all with Soviet funds.

306   Part IV of Annexe W sets out the remaining expenditure of the IMO out of the mixed pot of IMO money and money from the MIREDS fund. I have thought it right to include this in my Report because roughly 70% of the money in the MIREDS fund was originally constituted by money received from the USSR and other Eastern European countries (the other money being NUM money from the MACF). My terms of reference asked me to determine what has happened to the money received from the USSR. Because of the mingling of this money with other money of the IMO, (see paragraph 121 above) it is impossible to say that the expenditure in Part IV of Annexe W was made out of the Soviet money; but it is likely that the money used for that expenditure included some of the money which originated from the Coal Employees Union of the USSR.

307   In fact, a very, very substantial part of the money now controlled by the IMO and/or Mr Scargill is money which originated from the CEU and other Eastern European unions during or shortly after the 1984-5 strike.

308   Finally, I should say that it is quite clear that the payments for the benefit of the NUM have been made by Mr Scargill without giving any thought to the amount of money held by the IMO or its agents as constructive trustees for the NUM. That the discrepancy between amount held and amount received is not much greater is purely a matter of luck.

Part III: Alternative and additional claims

309   The whole of Part II of this Chapter has been dealt with on the basis that the repayments of loans and other payments set out in Annexe W part II (and possibly in Annexe III if the NEC accept those expenses or any of them as being NUM expenses) were made out of the MACF and other money which had been transferred to the MIREDS fund or other accounts controlled by Mr Scargill or the IMO (i.e. the money set out in paragraph 300 above); and also on the basis that the money transferred to the MIREDS fund from the miners' unions in the USSR and Eastern Europe was, contrary to my view, not in fact money to which the NUM was entitled. However, there are 2 alternative claims to the claims set out in Part II of this Chapter which in my view the NUM could make.

(1) If I am correct and the whole of the money transferred in the MIREDS fund was money to which the NUM was entitled then the NUM may be able to claim the whole of the sum transferred plus the interest which should have been earned on it.

(2) If I am wrong about this, nevertheless, Mr Scargill made it clear to me that the MTUI intended that the NUM should be treated as having a

substantial claim on the money received from the miners' unions of the USSR and Eastern Europe, and in his speech to the Soviet miners quoted in paragraph 149 above, Mr Scargill implies that the NUM has indeed done so. In this case, the payment listed in Annexe W Part II and III may have been made, or should be treated as having been made, out of the funds received by the MIREDS fund from the Soviet and other miners' unions. On this basis, the whole of the money set out in paragraph 300, plus interest which should have been earned on those sums, would remain payable to the NUM. Cork Gully has calculated this sum to be approximately £1,020,429.10.

310   Finally, I should mention one other sum of money received by the IMO which appears to be NUM money. The details of this are set out in Part III of Annexe J, and it appears that part, although what particular part cannot be accurately ascertained, of a sum of £37,116.04 deposited into account 13 on 15th April 1987 belongs to the NUM and should be refunded by the IMO.

Part IV: Assumptions and Calculations

311   I should make it absolutely clear that the calculations of figures due to the NUM set out in this chapter have been done on a very rough and ready basis, making a number of assumptions. This has been done to indicate to the National Executive Committee the sort of figures that the NUM may be able to claim. The reason why the calculations have had to be made on this basis is the total confusion of money belonging to various parties in various bank accounts, the inadequacy of records, and Mr Scargill's failure to appreciate or act in accordance with the fundamental principle that assets belonging to different bodies should be kept distinct.

312   I should also make it clear that Mr Scargill does not accept the views set

out in this chapter as to the ownership of money. This is primarily caused by his refusal to accept that the MACF money is money belonging to the NUM. Mr Scargill told me that if anyone could prove to him that any money now held by the IMO belonged in fact to the NUM, that money would be repaid by the IMO without question. However, I must question, having regard to the exchanges between us at our last interview, whether Mr. Scargill will accept any proof without, (and perhaps not even after) a judgment.

CHAPTER 16: THE IMO

313   As I said in paragraph 37 of this Report, the finances of the IMO are practically impenetrable. The only person who undoubtedly knows all the facts is Mr Simon. Mr Simon wrote to me saying that he had no intention of disclosing to me the accounts on which he is a signatory or the source of the funds of the IMO. Later, Mr Simon wrote to me saying that all the funds in the MIREDS fund were nothing at all to do with the NUM. Mr Scargill, who is President of the IMO, has told me that in that capacity he cannot procure any further information, in particular in relation to the Narodny Bank account in Warsaw which I believe was at least a conduit for the majority of the money now controlled by the IMO. It has now become clear that there are no financial records, nor minutes of decisions kept. Mr Simon and Mr Scargill, (either directly or through his alter egos, particularly Mr West) have unrestricted and unaudited access to funds currently in excess of £2 million, in accounts, which can, for the most part, be operated by one signatory. Mr Scargill and Mr Simon apparently think it is satisfactory to make personal loans to themselves or other IMO committee members out of those funds, and for payments to the IMO to be handed to Mr Simon in cash for him to deal with as he see fit. (I do not suggest that Mr Simon has made a personal loan to himself, but he has indicated that he thought it perfectly proper to make the loans to Mr Scargill and Mr Heathfield). Mr Scargill has told me that Mr Simon has authority to do anything he wishes in regard to IMO finances.

314   In addition Mr Simon has declined to co-operate fully with this Enquiry; and I believe it can be assumed that the refusal of the Bank for Arbeit und Wirtschaft to co-operate (see paragraph 147 above) must also be on the instructions of Mr Simon or the IMO.

315   It is for these reasons, I recommend that the National Executive Committee give very serious thought to the question whether the NUM should continue its

association with, and continue to pay substantial affiliation fees to, an organisation which conducts its financial affairs in such a way.

316   Mr Scargill has strenuously defended the IMO, telling me that the IMO's operations have to be clothed in secrecy because of the difficulties, including physical danger to the recipient, of giving financial assistance to trade unionists in certain countries. I entirely appreciate that trade unionists under some regimes operate under enormous difficulty, and that it may be necessary for the IMO to have a specific fund, operated in secrecy but under appropriate financial controls, which would have to donate money in cash and through unconventional channels. What I cannot accept is that the state of affairs disclosed in this Report is essential or inevitable, that any financial controls or audit are impracticable or that the making and repayment of loans to Mr Scargill and Mr Heathfield and the payment of a variety of other large sums needed to proceed in the extraordinary fashion described in this Report.

CHAPTER 17: CONCLUSIONS

1.   FINDINGS

My answer to the four questions raised by my terms of reference are as follows:

1.   **"Were any monies paid to or for the benefit of the NUM or its members from the beginning of the 1984-5 miners strike to date by Libya or the U.S.S.R.?**

(a)   As regards Libya, I am satisfied that not merely did the NUM by Mr Scargill seek political help (in the form in particular of cutting off oil supplies) but also financial help.   He certainly sought financial aid in the form of contributions to the Miners Solidarity Fund.   I incline to the view that the financial aid sought was not limited to aid to this fund, but included aid to sustain the NUM and the strike itself. The material before me suggests that a payment of £150,000 stated in the records to have been received from the CGT may have been received from Libya. The CGT have declined to assist as to the sources of these monies, and the two potential witnesses who apparently claim that the money did come from Libya have declined to assist. I can accordingly reach no concluded view on this question.

(b)   As regards the USSR it is clear that at least £1 million or possibly U.S. $1 million was raised by a levy on miners by their Union to support the NUM and that this money was paid (I infer through the bank account in Poland in the name of the MTUI) to the account of the MIREDS fund and has in effect been utilised as an accretion to the assets of the IMO. On the basis that recourse is treated as having been made to the NUM's £580,000 and other sums in making the repayment of loans to other trade unions and other expenses in Annexe W parts II and/or III, and those sums are no longer owing and due, the NUM received little or no benefit from this fund, and most certainly not the benefit intended. The payment to the account of the MIREDS Fund was in my view a payment exclusively for the benefit of the NUM, and on this basis, this sum and interest is not payable to the NUM. Any expenditure for the benefit of the IMO or for any purpose other than the benefit of the NUM constituted a misapplication of these funds. On the other hand if (contrary to my view) the payment to the MIREDS fund was a payment for the benefit of the MTUI (or later the IMO) or on the genuine trusts of the 1985 or 1987 Deeds, such payment constituted in my view a misapplication of funds of the NUM to which Mr Scargill was a party but to which he had no authority or right to agree.

2.   **"If any monies were so received then how were the monies applied and where is the residue now?"**

(a)   If the £150,000 does represent Libyan money, part was applied in the carrying out of three (paper) refinancing transactions relating to Mr Windsor's loan, Mr Heathfield's repairs and improvements and Mr Scargill's improvements, and the balance formed part of the Miners Action Committee Fund maintained by the National Officials. Mr Scargill did, I think, repay his £6,861.00 shortly afterwards to the Fund. Mr Windsor's further loan was assigned to the IMO, and the IMO is currently suing Mr Windsor for repayment. The IMO has acknowledged a duty to account for this sum to the NUM. The balance of the £150,000 has been expended in the maintenance of the fabric of the Union.

(b)   Part of the money from the Soviet Union has been paid to accounts of the IMO, out of which accounts (but not necessarily out of Soviet money) have been made the payments set out in parts II, III and IV of Annexe W. Part of the money remains in the accounts of the MIREDS fund, in effect for the benefit of the IMO.

3.   **"Were any monies, being either monies received from Libya or the U.S.S.R. or any other monies of the N.U.M. or monies received for or on behalf of the NUM or its members used to pay home loans or improvement loans for the benefit of Mr Scargill, Mr Heathfield or Mr Windsor?"**

No such monies were used to repay any home loan of Mr Scargill or Mr Heathfield. Mr Heathfield never had a home loan until much later, and Mr Scargill had some time before repaid his home loan out of his own monies.

Monies of the Union were used to pay £6,560.58 in respect of improvements to Mr Scargill's home at 2b, Yews Lane, Worsborough Dale, Barnsley. There was a degree of irregularity regarding authorisation for this payment, but since I believe that Mr Scargill repaid this money to the MACF, I think that no complaint can now be made.

Monies of the Union were used to pay £13,511.21 in respect of works to Mr Heathfield's home on the basis that such works constituted urgent repairs: they in fact constituted to a major extent substantial improvements. The National Executive Committee or Conference may wish to take into account in this regard the c.£15,000 in lost income during the period after the end of the strike for which Mr Heathfield did not receive any salary from the Union, but this is a matter for them.

Loans of £100,000 and £60,000 have been made by the IMO through the medium of the MIREDS trust to Mr Scargill and Mr Heathfield. The MIREDS trust held substantial funds on trust for the NUM. At the least these advances constituted payment to National Officers of substantial sums from a mixed fund of NUM and other monies, including monies donated by the Soviet miners. Mr

Scargill's loan and the interest thereon have been repaid, but to the IMO's general funds, not to the MIREDS trust.

4. "Has there been any misapplication of funds or assets of the NUM or any breach of duty by the National Officials in connection with or arising out of the financial arrangements made by the NUM or the National Officials during or in connection with the 1984-5 Miners Strike?"

In my view, as a matter of law, there have been a number of misapplications of funds and breaches of duty.

I   UNAUTHORISED AND UNDISCLOSED FINANCIAL DEALINGS.

Since the beginning of the sequestration the Union had in effect operated two separate sets of accounts, the official accounts properly administered and audited, and the unofficial accounts operated by the National Officials (in effect Mr Scargill) with no supervision or control. The very existence of these separate funds, their collection and distribution, their retention and investment, and most of all their non-disclosure, involved breaches of duty by the National Officials. Their seriousness may be viewed differently in two different periods in time in which this state of affairs continued.

(a)   Receivership period

As a matter of law, the fund raising and application of secret funds raised by the National Officials on behalf of the NUM during the sequestration and receivership were unlawful and accordingly in breach of duty by the National Officials. This action is justified or excused by them as of necessity to secure the survival of the Union. It is said that the National Executive Committee itself on the 8th March 1984 countenanced equivalent illegal actions in the war against the Coal Board and Government, and that there has been wholesale acquiescence during this period by the membership. This matter cannot in law constitute excuse, but the membership may accept this as such.

(b) Post Receivership

But whatever view is held as to the period of emergency, there was clearly a duty to make a clean breast of this matter and make a proper account to the National Executive Committee and the Union Auditors after the receivership ended. The (non legal) excuses are proffered that there was a continuing obligation of confidence to the (trade union) leaders and donors, and any disclosures would have resulted in damaging press publicity and may have led to the frustration of all efforts to make repayments; and further that many National Executive Committee members knew that off-balance transactions were continuing, and the National Officials were being left to do the dirty work of clearing up after the strike on their own. The continued suppression by the National Executive Committee of the meetings and resolutions of the 8th March 1984 was undoubtedly a comfort, if not a support for their actions. Again, these matters can constitute no excuse in law, and the National Executive Committee may find this default less excusable if excusable at all. The National Executive Committee and members were entitled to know the full facts and the true financial conditions of the Union, and to decide whether the loans (in law irrecoverable) should be repaid and if so when. A substantial price has been paid in loss of staff (and no doubt membership) morale, disturbed by the persistent evidence and rumours of secret accounts. I have heard a considerable body of evidence to this effect.

II   DELAY IN WINDING UP, DISCLOSURE, AND COMPILING RECORDS

There appears to me to have been quite unnecessary and excusable delay in winding up the accounts. Receivership ended on the 27 June 1986. The accounts continued to be operated until December 1989. I cannot see why the continuance of the breach of trust proceedings justified or excused any such delay: the use of the funds for the benefit of national officers sued by the Union could not be proper nor could delay in disclosure or distribution until the proceedings were concluded. Contrary to the evidence of Mr Scargill, I find that the existence of the accounts was prompted only by fear of revelations by Mr Windsor and, but for the fall-out with him, the accounts would never have been disclosed or audited. The deliberate suppression of the existence of Union assets (the £580,000 in the MIREDS account and the other sums set out in paragraph 300 above) cannot be justified as a means of achieving a rationalisation of the Union, however advantageous. The failure (at least after the discharge of the Receiver) to reconcile and maintain complete records is likewise inexcusable. Mr Scargill has told the National Executive Committee that the multiplicity of funds was "in all honesty to confuse and for secrecy". In my view, whatever view the National Executive Committee may take of the receivership period, there can be no excuse for the multiplicity of accounts once the Receiver had been discharged, and the confusion deliberately caused by Mr Scargill in his efforts to maintain confidentiality, and (I hope) unwittingly caused by Mr Scargill's intermingling of NUM and IMO assets has led inevitably to the Union being put to the expense of this Enquiry. The great problem is that Mr Scargill has acted throughout without the benefit of properly informed legal or accountancy advice. I regret that I am of the view that was in part because Mr Scargill was unwilling to accept the constraints which such advice would have placed upon him. Indeed when I put this view to Mr Scargill, he accepted that this was the case.

III   MISREPRESENTATION

(a)   Mr Heathfield's repairs

I regretfully find that Mr Heathfield has misled the Union as to the character of the works to be carried out to his house and in fact carried out. He secured the expenditure of £13,511.21 in the middle of the strike on the grounds that this was needed for urgent repairs and in the National Official's Report of 9th March 1990 the works done were so described. In fact they were very substantial improvements. It may be because the works were so misdescribed that the NUM in fact paid for them twice. The Union paid £13,511.21 as part of the costs of the works, and later paid the improved value of the property on the purchase of the property from the Derbyshire Area. Mr Heathfield is of the view that, taking into account his loss of salary and the terms on which the NUM brought his house, the NUM has no legitimate financial claim against him.

(b)   Disclosures to National Executive Committee of accounts

I have already recorded my views that the existence of the unofficial accounts was only disclosed by Mr Scargill and Mr Heathfield because of impending revelations by Mr Windsor.

The disclosure in the Report of the National Officials to the National Executive Committee on 9th March 1990, the amplification of that report given by Mr. Scargill during that meeting, and also the terms of the Press Release of 5th March 1990, were in my view misleading. The language chosen for this disclosure gave the impression (if it did not say specifically) that all the accounts had been checked and in effect passed an audit with flying colours. A number of members gave evidence that they were convinced that there had been an audit, and I think that this was the impression intended to be created. In fact all that could be and was done was for the accountants to check the figures against the very limited (and inadequate) documentation produced. This exercise was practically meaningless as any kind of verification or check upon the accounts.

IV   LOANS TO MR SCARGILL AND MR HEATHFIELD

In my view, it was a breach of duty and wrong for Mr Scargill and Mr Heathfield to obtains loans from the MTUI or the IMO, and still more so for these loans to be paid out of the MIREDS Fund without the prior consent of the National Executive Committee, or at least the F &GP Committee, and in any event such loans should have been reported.   Both may have believed that they were acting properly. However, I find it a matter for concern that in particular in the case of Mr Scargill, he did not recognise the impropriety of what seemed to me to have been so obviously wrong.

V   MISAPPLICATION OF SOVIET MONEY

I think that the MIREDS Trust has at all times held the Soviet and other monies as trustee for the NUM and that Mr. Scargill has wrongfully allowed such monies to be treated as, and has wrongfully maintained that such monies are, in effect IMO monies. If, contrary to my view, the Soviet money has not at all times beneficially belonged to the NUM, then I think that Mr Scargill acted wrongly in assenting to the passing of money raised for the NUM to the MTUI or the MIREDS Trust. The matter is made the more serious because he did not report, and continues to deny, his participation in the agreement for diversion, and has made no full or proper report to the National Executive Committee in respect of these funds, and because he has at all times been in substance (though not in form) the trustee in complete control of the MIREDS Fund, as well as President of the IMO.

VI   CONFUSION OF ASSETS OF AND DUTIES TO NUM AND IMO

In my view, Mr Scargill has failed to recognise or implement his overriding duties to the NUM, and has allowed his role in and duties to the IMO to result in substantial advantages being obtained by the IMO at the expense of the NUM.

This report records that the IMO has obtained benefit through the MIREDS Fund from the £580,000 transferred by the MACF and that the MIREDS Fund has been run as a trust for the IMO. The Mineworkers Trust trustees were quite wrongly forced by Mr Scargill to transfer its assets on winding up to the IMO. Mr Windsor's debt should not have been assigned to the NUM.

I have sought in this inquiry to right the balance where I can. I have obtained acknowledgement of the trusteeship of the IMO in respect of 12 Carver Lane and 62 Alexander Road, and the Windsor debt. The state of account between the two organisations is obscure and totally unsatisfactory - a situation aggravated by the lack of any audit of the IMO accounts and Mr Simon's limited cooperation.

B   RECOMMENDATIONS

1.   ACCOUNT

In my opinion a proper account is urgently required of the monies and property of the Union, as follows:

(a)   Soviet money

In my view, careful consideration should be given to proceedings for the recovery of these monies from the MIREDS trustees and the IMO. This would first involve taking detailed legal advice.

(b)   The £580,000 of the MACF and other monies received by the IMO

These monies were always held on trust for the NUM, and any balance of this sum and interest not proved to be expended in payment of NUM creditors should be recoverable. In my view the IMO and/or the MIREDS trustees should be asked to pay immediately to the NUM either the sum of £61,373.81, or such lesser sum as remains if the National Executive Committee are prepared to give credit for any of the sums set out in Part III of Annexe W. Alternatively, as indicated in paragraphs 309 - 310 above, if the sums set out in part II of Annexe W are treated as being made out of the Soviet and other monies in the MIREDS Fund, the whole of the £580,000 and the £71,000 and the other sums set out in paragraph 300 plus the interest thereon may be recoverable from the IMO or the MIREDS trustees. This alternative claim would also first involve taking detailed legal advice.

(c)   Account at Polish Bank

I am of the view that the IMO should be required to disclose to the NUM the statement of account at this bank and account for any receipts intended for the benefit of the NUM.

(d)   **Mineworkers Trust Distribution**

I have indicated in paragraphs 290 - 295 above the difficulties of ascertaining to whom the Mineworkers' Trust money belongs, and the course which the NUM needs to take.

(e)   **The loan to Mr Windsor**

The IMO acknowledges the obligation to account for any recovery to the NUM. Mr Windsor has expressed willingness to pay the full sum to the Solidarity Fund. As indicated in paragraph 254 consideration may be given to shortcircuiting the proceedings (and testing the good faith of Mr Windsor) by assigning all rights to the Miners Solidarity Fund or making an offer to Mr Windsor authorising the discharge of the debt by payment to the Miners Solidarity Fund.

2.   **THE IMO.**

Careful consideration should be given to the continuation of the present very close association with the IMO if a proper accounting is refused.   Careful consideration should in any event be given to the payment of substantial subscriptions (£105, 200 from 1985 to date) to an association which has declined to co-operate meaningfully with this Enquiry and appears to have no or no normal financial control or audits. (I have in particular in mind the loans to its President and the Chairman of an important committee). The question should be considered whether the holding of the office of President of both the IMO and the NUM by one man for a protracted period must not inevitably involve the problem of a conflict of interest between the two organisations and the risk of a sacrifice of the interests of the NUM (as has occurred) to the interests of the IMO.

3.   PUBLICATION

I cannot recommend too strongly that this Report be published whatever its shortcomings (and I am sure there are many). It must be right that the members of the Union be afforded such insight into the Union's affairs over the past 6 years as I have been able to gather and put together in this Report and which to date have been either concealed or the subject of ill informed or partial rumour or public statement. In his address to the 1990 Congress of Soviet Miners Mr Scargill said that the Soviet Miners had a right to know what happened to their money. So much greater is the right to know of the English miners. The membership should be able to make an informed decision what (if any) action should be taken. The public also has a real interest in knowing the facts, a matter recognised by the National Officials in making previous (at best incomplete) press statements. In my view, publication should be achieved

(1) by making a copy of this Report available to each delegate attending the Annual Conference, as early as possible and certainly some days before the Conference starts;

(2) by making copies available to Areas through such channels as the National Executive Committee thinks appropriate;

(3) by making copies available to such newspapers as the National Executive Committee thinks appropriate at the end of the meeting of the National Executive Committee to which this report is given.

GAVIN LIGHTMAN

THE NATIONAL UNION OF MINEWORKERS

REPORT OF GAVIN LIGHTMAN Q.C.

TO THE

NATIONAL EXECUTIVE COMMITTEE

ANNEXES

3rd July 1990

Part I:

Witnesses from whom written evidence obtained

<u>Name of Witness</u>

Mr A Scargill	President, National Union of Nineworkers
Mr P Heathfield	General Secretary, National Union of Mineworkers
Mr S Hudson	Former Finance Officer
Ms Jean McCrindle	Signatory on accounts
Ms Doris Askham	Signatory on SWAG account
Mr A Simon	Official of CGT, IMO and MTUI
Mr N West MEP	Signatory on MIREDS Fund
Ms Nell Myers	NUM Press Officer and signatory on accounts
Mr D Blunkett	Trustee of Solidarity Fund
Mr R Caborn M.P.	Trustee of Soliarity Fund
Mr John Platts Mills, Q.C.	
Mr P McNestry	National Secretary, National Association of Colliery Overmen, Deputies and Shotfirers

Mr A G Markham	Raley & Pratt, Solicitors
Mr M Seifert	Seifert, Sedley Williams, Solicitors
Mr K Barron M.P.	
Ms S Burton	
Mr M White	Solicitor, Dublin
Mr G Hind	Freelance journalist
National Union of Mineworkers	
National Union of Mineworkers (Derbyshire Area)	
National Union of Mineworkers (Yorkshire Area)	
National Union of Railwaymen	
South Yorkshire Police	
B.B.C.	(Provided manuscripts of relevant news items)
Mr N Clapham	
Mr D Feickert	
Mr G Bolton	

Mr M McGahey

Mr A Richmond   KPMG Peat Marwick, Leeds

Mr J R Ottey

Mrs A Booth

Mr W Chambers

Mr K Toon

Mr E Clarke

Sheridans   Solicitors for the NUM Trustees

Mr D Murphy

Mr H Hanlon

Mr O Briscoe

Mr T McKay

Mr R Chadburn

Mr J Weaver

Mr K Hollingsworth

Mr Guy

Mr S Vincent

Mr C Bell

Mr I Morgan

Mr T H Richardson

Mr D Hopper

Mr W Etherington

Mr J Colgan

Mr J Stones

Mr F Cave

Mr L Kelly

Mr J Ellis

Mr A Moffat

Note: It should be made clear that some of the witnesses listed above were replying to letters sent asking them if they had any relevant information, and indicated only that they had no relevant information.

ANNEXE A:

LIST OF WITNESSES

Part II:

List of witnesses by whom oral evidence given

Mr A Scargill

Mr P Heathfield

Mr S Hudson

Mr I White

Ms H Riley

Ms N Myers

Mr N West MEP

Ms J McCrindle

Ms D Askham

Ms Y Fenn

Mr L Daly

Mr G Rees

Mr D Blunkett M.P.

Ms M Mitchell

Mr R Brown M.P.

Mr A Meale M.P.

Mr K Homer

Mr J Burrows

Mr M Seifert

Mr A G Markham

Mr T H Richardson

Professor V L Allen

Ms S Burton

Mr I Morgan

Mr J Taylor

Mr G Barlow

Mr F Butler

Mr A Ameish

Mr J Stones

Note: Some witnesses gave evidence by telephone where it did not seem necessary or it was not possible for them to come to see me

142

PRESS STATEMENT OF 5th MARCH 1990 REPORT OF NATIONAL OFFICIALS TO THE NEC DATED 9th MARCH 1990

Publisher's Note

In the report submitted by Mr Lightman to the National Executive Committee the following documents were photocopies of original material. Because the quality of the photocopies made them unsuitable for photographic reproduction, they have been retyped. The retyped documents are faithful and accurate copies of the originals.

SCARGILL AND THE LIBYAN MONEY - THE LIES

Allegations in today's Daily Mirror that the NUM's two full-time National Officials used money from Libya to pay personal debts are nothing but vicious lies.

1.   There was no money received by the NUM either during or after the strike in 1984/5 which came from Libya or Libyan sources as far as the two full-time National Officials are aware.

THE FACTS

During the course of the miners' strike all monies brought into the National Office either by organisations, individuals, members of the public or members of staff were recorded. All members of staff who received money from outside or inside the office were required to indicate the source of the donations or loans and these were recorded. If any money emanating from Libya was brought in or received from any organisations or individuals including members of staff, the National Officials were not aware of it at the time nor have they been so informed since by Mr. Windsor or anyone else. The National Officials reiterate that to their knowledge no monies were received from Libya during or since the strike. If it is true that the former Chief Executive Officer, Roger Windsor, did obtain monies from Libyan sources, then he lied about it at the time to the National Officials. If it is not true, then he is lying about it now to the Daily Mirror.

2.   No Union money or money donated for Union members or hardship purposes was used for the personal needs of the National Officials.

THE FACTS

Neither the National President nor the General Secretary had a mortgage or loan, so no question of repayment could have been perceived. By the rules and longstanding practice of the Union houses occupied by the National Officials are owned by the National Union. These include former Officials like Lord Gormley and Lawrence Daly. Prior to the dispute, the NUM were in the process of purchasing the properties occupied by the President and General Secretary from, respectively, the President and the Derbyshire Area of the National Union of Mineworkers in accordance with the procedure of the Union. The Union had also, perfectly properly, spent some money on the properties thereby enhancing their value to the Union prior to completion of the purchases. The strike intervened delaying these transactions. There was a Sequestration Order subsequently made and concern was expressed that the Sequestrators might try to make out a case for seizure of those properties and other houses owned by the Union. A decision was therefore made to repay the NUM the sums it had spent. The money to do so came from a Trust Fund and in the President's case, was repaid to that Trust Fund within four days from his own personal savings. The house occupied by the General Secretary was eventually transferred to the Union some four years after the dispute finished and remains the Union's property.

The payments and transactions referred to above were completed weeks before the date identified by the Daily Mirror as that on which Mr. Windsor allegedly brought cash into the NUM office from Libyan sources.

An accurate record was kept of all monies paid into the Trust Fund along with the course of such monies and also details of all expenditure from the Trust Fund. These accounts have been fully examined and confirmed as accurate by one of the world's leading independent firms of auditors.

It is true that monies were paid perfectly properly to the Nottinghamshire Area of the NUM in respect of Area legal actions.

3.   Roger Windsor's role.

THE FACTS

Roger Windsor was an unelected member of staff in charge of the Union's administration. At his request, the NUM granted him a 12 month bridging loan to enable him to purchase his house in Sheffield to be near his work. That money was repaid from the Trust Fund into the NUM general fund in order to protect Mr. Windsor's property from the Sequestrators. Some two years after the dispute ended, Mr. Windsor signed a legal agreement confirming that he had received a personal loan and gave an undertaking to repay this loan plus interest to the International Miners' Organisation to whom the debt had been transferred.   To date, Mr. Windsor has not repaid this loan and he is the subject of legal proceedings which are currently under way in France by the IMO against him for the recovery of this debt.

He is also, as is widely known, the subject of a current investigation by British police who have confirmed that they still seek to interview him. That investigation was called as a result of information given to the police by the President of the NUM shortly after Mr. Windsor resigned as Chief Executive Officer when certain matters came to light.

4.   Meetings with Libyan representatives.

THE FACTS

During the strike National Officials met representatives from over 50 countries around the world. The only contacts which the National Officials had with any representative claiming to be from Libya were (a) when Mr. Windsor introduced a man named Abbasi to the President of the Union at the 1984 Labour Party Conference, and (b) at a meeting in the CGT Paris Headquarters on the 8th October, 1984. These facts were duly reported to the Union's NEC in November, 1984. Roger Windsor genuinely volunteered to go to Libya. The only contact since the dispute occurred was when the President briefly met a Libyan representative at the 1985 Labour Party Conference in Bournemouth and when the National Secretary, whilst attending a meeting in France, met a Libyan representative. This was also duly reported to the NEC. Financial assistance was not requested or given during or as a consequence of these meetings.

The Daily Mirror was requested to put any questions on these matters to the NUM. Had it done so, all of the facts to which we have replied would have been made available and this smear story would have been destroyed before publication. One can only conclude that the Mirror's primary purpose was to mount a malicious character assassination on the NUM's National Officials.

In view of the scurrilous attacks, the lies and distortions contained in the Daily Mirror article, the Union's Officials will make a report to a Special National Executive Committee.

NUM PRESS OFFICE
MONDAY 5th MARCH, 1990

A copy of the written statement provided by the National Officials to the NEC at its meeting on Friday, 9th March 1990, concerning the allegations raised by the Daily Mirror story and Central Television's "The Cook Report" programme.

Please note:

(a)   On page 2, paragraph 3, the figure to be inserted is £4,500 repayable over three years. This was obtained by Mr. Heathfield from his bank the National Westminster.

(b)   Item 14 "Miners' International Research, Education, Defence and Support Fund". The amount put down opposite withdrawals of £150,000 was a typing error and should, in fact, read £900,000.

REPORT OF THE PRESIDENT AND SECRETARY

TO THE NATIONAL EXECUTIVE COMMITTEE

This report is prepared for the information of the National Executive Committee in light of the unprecedented attacks by the Mirror newspaper and Central television on the Union's President and Secretary over the past week.

The Secretary reported to the NEC at its last meeting about the situation as it then was. His report, and all of the information he gave to the NEC at that meeting, was absolutely accurate. On the 5th March, shortly after the first Mirror article appeared, the NUM issued a Press Release condemning the lies and distortions published in the Mirror. The Press Release sets out the facts, all of which are true.

The most serious and hurtful allegation made in the Mirror is that the National Officials misused funds, provided during the 1984/85 miners strike for alleviation hardship amongst the striking miners, to pay off personal debts. This is utterly untrue. We set out below the full facts concerning the Secretary and President's homes, and that of Mr. Roger Windsor, the former Chief Executive Officer.

THE SECRETARY'S HOUSE

The Secretary was, in 1984, a tenant of the NUM Derbyshire Area and his house was being sold by them to the National Union in accordance with NUM practice and the Secretary's Contract of Employment. During that year, necessary building work was carried out to the coal-house and adjoining garage attached to the house which was unsafe and which was leaning heavily towards a neighbouring property (as was confirmed by the Derbyshire Area's valuer's report). Notwithstanding that he was a mere tenant, the Secretary took out a personal loan from his bank to pay a proportion of the costs of the building works (£   ). The NUM paid the balance of those costs, namely £13,511.21. As the NUM were to be the owners of the property it was the NUM's responsibility to pay for the full costs of repair in due course, but the Secretary waived his right to repayment of the monies he had spent, and to the interest he had paid in borrowing that money, in view of the Union's financial difficulties.

In the autumn of 1984 the Union's funds were put in the hands of Sequestrators by the Court. To prevent any claim by the Sequestrators that the sum of £13,511.21 was a debt due to the Union, that sum was repaid into the Union's General Account from monies held in a Trust Fund, the "Miners' Action Committee" Fund. This was an account set up immediately on Sequestration to enable the NUM to function without recourse to its own funds. Funds were paid in from various bodies, including national and international Trade Unions. No moneies were received, to our knowledge, from Libyan sources, Soviet Sources or members of the public. No monies raised or donated for hardship purposes were paid into the Trust Fund and it had no connection with the Miners' Solidarity Fund. Four years later, the house was transferred from the ownership of the Derbyshire Area to the National Union. The NUM has not repaid the sum of £13,511.21 to the Trust Fund and repayment is not required.

Far from making any gain on the transaction, the Secretary is out of pocket. His only benefit was, as a tenant, the removal of a dangerous structure from the grounds of the house he occupied and the provision of a safe one. His financial contribution and that of the Trust Fund to the rebuilding work has enhanced the value of a Union owned asset at no cost to the Union.

THE PRESIDENT'S HOME

The President owned his own home and, for the same reasons, the NEC agreed on the 8th March, 1984 that it should be conveyed to the National Union. In 1984 the President had an outstanding mortgage of £22,250.45 at 2½% interest which had been provided to him whilst an Official of the Yorkshire Area in line with its normal practice and was in common with other Yorkshire Area Officials. This mortgage had to be redeemed on or before the transfer of the property. In any event, the Yorkshire Area were quite properly requiring redemption of the mortgage following the President's election as a National Official. In fact, the only reason for any delay was due to the move of the NUM headquarters from London to Sheffield. The mortgage with the Yorkshire NUM was finally redeemed by the NUM on the 9th March, 1984 so that the President then had his mortgage with the NUM. On the 8th August that year, to remove any potential problems (as outlined above), the President redeemed his mortgage with the NUM in full from savings accumulated in his personal bank and building Society accounts over many years.

In addition to the payment to the Yorkshire NUM of the mortgage the National Union had also paid out a total of £6,860.58 in respect of improvements, rates and other related expenses. (In line again with the NEC decision in March, 1984).

By October, 1984 it was becoming clear that completion of the conveyancing to the NUM which had been set in hand by Messrs. Raley & Pratt, would be indefinitely delayed by the events of the dispute and the consequent legal actions against the Union.

On the 27th October, 1984, following Sequestration of the Union's assets, the President on the 27th October, 1984, arranged for a repayment to the NUM General Fund of £6,860.58 by using cash from the Miners' Action Committee referred to above. This was again done to prevent any claim by the Sequestrators that this sum was a debt due to the Union. The President received a receipt dated 29th October, 1984 from Steve Hudson, Finance Officer, and an undertaking to repay this amount to the President when the transfer of the property to the Union was completed.

On the 1st November, the President reimbursed the Miners' Action Committee Fund from his personal savings for the full amount. His house was never, in fact, transferred to the Union; He owed no money to the Union; he had no mortgage with the Union and had no outstanding loans on the house at all in December 1984 (the date which features in the allegations of Roger Windsor).

It should be remembered that neither the President nor the General Secretary – in common with other full-time Officials – drew any salary at all during the year of the dispute and in the case of the two National officials, for a period of 5 months after it ended.

ROGER WINDSOR'S HOME

On 27th June, 1984 Roger Windsor was, at his request, granted a bridging loan of £29,500.00 by the NUM to assist him in purchasing a home in Sheffield before his Gloucester home could be sold. Again, in order to protect him from claims by the Sequestrators, that loan was repaid to the NUM's General Account from monies in the Trust Fund already referred to. Mr. Windsor acknowledged that his debt remained due and owing to the CGT (who had, the National Officials understood, provided the funds to the Miners' Action Committee Fund) and on lst September, 1987 the debt was legally assigned to the International Miners' Organisation. Mr. Windsor signed an undertaking dated 22nd July, 1986 and a legal agreement on lst September, 1987, to repay the IMO the full amount of the loan plus interest. He has never done so. Proceedings against him in the French Courts by the IMO for the recovery of this money are continuing.

To remind the NEC, Roger Windsor's allegations are that, on the 4th December, 1984, he brought £150,000.00 into the NUM offices in a suitcase and the following distribution was made:

£10,000.00 to Notts Area for legal fees .

In fact £12,000.00 was (perfectly properly) paid to the Notts Area for legal fees on the 18th November, 1984. This was paid from cash held in the Trust Fund which it was understood had been donated by the CGT.

£29,500.00 to pay off Roger Windsor's bridging loan.

In fact, a receipt was given by the NUM's Finance Officer, Steve Hudson, to Roger Windsor on the 30th November, 1984 showing that the loan was repaid (from the Trust Fund, monies donated by the CGT) on that date. A copy of a note from Steve Hudson dated the 9th August, 1989 and his own draft of a letter to Roger Windsor following a telephone conversation is attached and confirms these details.

£17,500.00 to pay off a loan on Peter Heathfield's house.

In fact, there was no loan to the Secretary whether in that amount or at all.

£25,000.00 to pay off Arthur Scargill's mortgage to the NUM.

In fact, the President's mortgage of £22,255.45 was redeemed by the NUM and repaid by the President personally weeks earlier. The second sum which had been paid by the NUM, of £6,860.58 was similarly repaid to the NUM from The Mineworkers Action Committee Fund and the Mineworkers Action Committee Fund was reimbursed in full by the President. All receipts referred to were examined by the Receiver, Michael Arnold, during the period 19841986 and there is no doubt as to the dates when payments were made. All of the transactions involving the Mineworkers Action Committee Fund referred to above were made prior to the 4th December, 1984. There is no record of £150,000.00 or any similar lump sum being brought in on the 4th December. The records of the Mineworkers Action Committee for the 25th October, 1984 when it was established, to the 4th December, 1984 show:

Date	Deposit £	Source	Withdrawal £	Recipient	Balance £
25.10.84	100,000.00	CGT			100,000.00
27.10.84			6,860.58	Finance Department (AS 2b Yews Lane)	93,139.42
01.11.84	6,861.00	AS repayment			100,000.42
04.11.84	25,000.00	CGT			125,000.42
16.11.84			13,511.21	Finance Department (PEH 262 Newbold Rd)	111,489.21
18.11.84			12,000.00	Notts NUM (legal costs)	99,489.21
28.11.84	100,000.00	NUR	20,000.00	North Derbyshire	179,489.21
28.11.84			60,000.00	Finance Department	119,489.21
29.11.84			29,500.00	Finance Department (RW P. Loan)	89,989.21
04.12.84	50,000.00	Int. Coll. via CGT			139,989.21

As is apparent from the above, no money whatsoever came in, to our knowledge, from Libyan sources. If Roger Windsor took delivery of money from such sources, he either lied about it when he brought the money into the NUM or he never brought the money in at all.

It has been alleged by Abbasi (a self-confessed convicted terrorist) that Libya gave the NUM or made available to the NUM $9 million. This is a complete lie. There is nothing more that we can say about such fabrication.

It was alleged that the President met a man called Abbasi. The President has already told the National Executive that he met Abbasi in the Planet Room of the Winter Gardens, Blackpool in October, 1984 on the occasion of the Labour Party Conference (for a few minutes); in Paris on 8th October, 1984 along with another man from Libya; and in Bournemouth in 1985. This meeting was arranged at Abbasi's request in a car driven by Jim Parker. Abbasi wanted to discuss affiliation with the IMO. It lasted no more than a few minutes.The Secretary also met a Libyan whilst he was attending a meeting in France in 1986. The only other time the President ever saw this man Abbasi was when the President, with his wife, returning from a miners function in Nottinghamshire, called at Roger Windsor's house (the only time he had done so) to give Windsor some documents and found Abbasi was present in the house. There was no meeting on this occasion. Abbasi's presence was never explained to the President. Although at some of the earlier meetings the plight of the striking miners and the NUM was described, no funds were sought, nor offered nor received.

Jim Parker has alleged that he drove the President around Lytham-St-Ann's in 1984, during which time the President met with Libyan Officials in the car and requested funding. This is completely untrue. The President met Abbasi in 1985 in Bournemouth (at the latter's request) in the circumstances described above.

It was alleged that the National Union of Railwaymen was improperly repaid by the IMO. An NUR loan was advanced (not for hardship purposes but to help maintain the fabric of the Union) to the Mineworkers Trust in Sheffield. When it appeared likely the Receiver would seize the money from the Mineworkers Trust, the NUR loan was "donated" to the IMO's account in Dublin by the Trustees of the Mineworkers Trust acting on legal advice. The money was repaid in full to the NUR by the IMO. The interest which had accumulated in the IMO's account in Dublin and in the Mineworkers Trust itself, was forwarded through the international system and used in accordance with the purposes of the IMO to help repay loans to other trade unions.

It was alleged that $1 million dollars was donated by the Soviet Miners' Union to the British miners for the relief of hardship. This is not true. The Soviet Miners did wish to support the NUM financially but refused to place money in various accounts established for fear that it would be sequested. Eventually, after the end of the strike $1 million was sent by the Soviet Miners' Union solely for "international purposes". This money was sent to the MTUI in Warsaw and thence to the Miners' International Research, Education, Defence and Support Fund where it has been used in accordance with the wishes of the donor. At no time was any Soviet money intended for the relief of hardship. Nor was the money donated permitted to be used to sustain the fabric of the Union.

It was alleged that the IMO's bank account was established prior to formation of the IMO. This is purely and simply a lie.

152

References have been made to a bank account established by Jean McCrindle in Dublin. Jean McCrindle, in line with legal advice, opened three bank accounts. Two were in Ireland and one in Leeds. She was also a Trustee, along with a Sheffield City Councillor in a fourth bank account which was used by the NUM Scottish Area to provide monies to pay creditors of the Union whilst in Sequestration/Receivership. All these accounts inter-connected as indeed so did other Trust Accounts. The NUM's creditors and loans which had been advanced by other unions and required payment were paid through this system. Once the loans were repaid the NUM Scottish Area who had given a receipt for the loans, were able to clear their books. At all times monies held in these accounts were held in trust and all these accounts had been fully examined by an independent firm of auditors.

Indeed, there were a number of bank accounts established in the United Kingdom and elsewhere during the period when the NUM were unable to run its own affairs in the normal way due to Sequestration and Receivership. In addition, the Mineworkers Trust, established prior to the strike, held its own bank account. A self-explanatory schedule of the account is annexed. These are all wholly separate from the Miners' Solidarity Fund which was established to alleviate hardship and which has raised over £6.4 million todate.

All of the accounts for which we were signatories or Trustees have been examined by Messrs Peat Marwick McLintock and they have confirmed, in relation to each and overall, that every receipt and every payment has been in accordance with the books and records of each individual Trust Fund

We deplore the personal smears and attacks upon our integrity and we would welcome any investigation/inquiry which we know will vindicate everything which was done by the NUM and ourselves during the course of the 1984/5 miners' strike. We wish to conclude this report by saying we are proud of the role we played in doing everything possible to sustain the fabric of the National Union of Mineworkers.

A. Scargill   **P. Heathfield**
President   **Secretary**   **9th March, 1990**

153

Telephone call from R Windsor, Tuesday 8 August 1989 to S Hudson
at CISWO Office, Barnsley

File Note 9/8/89

Mr Windsor rang and commenced by saying did I know he had left
the NUM. I replied that I had heard through Vernon. He then
said he was ringing up about the loan(house). He said that do
you remember I repaid the money back to the NUM and that you gave
me a receipt. I was taken aback because this was going back to
1984 and instant memory recall is difficult. I said that yes the
money had been paid back, but I said that <u>I knew it wasn't his
money</u>. He told me he had received a letter from AS asking him
to repay the money to the IMO and did I know anything about it
(ie repaying the IMO). He asked me whether Peter, Arthur or
Henry (Notts) had repaid any money. I confirmed that as far as
the NUM was concerned <u>all</u> debts had been discharged. He said had
the individuals repaid the money - I indicated that I did not
know whether money had been paid back to third parties. I agreed
with him that the IMO wasn't in existence at the time. Roger
then said you know the money came from Mr "Akbusi" (Libyan
mediator) - I said I had no knowledge of that fact and that I
had never heard of the man and don't want to know about him.
(Though I subsequently recollected that the funds had been
provided through the CGT so that it would have been natural for
them to have assigend the debt). He asked me what I knew about
the IMO. I said nothing, I had nothing to do with the IMO apart
from the payment of our (NUM's) affiliation fees. He said that
certain information and questions on the IMO had been raised
I said I knew that George (Rees) had asked questions about IMO
accounts etc. I said I had never seen IMO Accounts, presumably
the Organisation would be subject to audit at wherever registered, UK
-France or whatever and that Accounts by law must exist. I again
confirmed I had no involvement with the IMO. Roger indicated he
thought the Orgaisation was AS's own bank or fund (I had
forgotton at the time that the IMO covers both the Eastern and
Western bloc mining unions so that may be why it is registered in
several countries.

He mentioned money coming into the IMO including Russia - I again insisted that I knew nothing of the IMO's internal affairs. I said I knew (as Roger knew becuase he had been involved at the time) that £1m touched the NUM's bank account with EBC as an in and out contra - the money being returned to the bank from which it came. I said the Receiver knew all about this and it was public record because it appeared on the NUM's EBC bank statement but couldn't do anything about it because the money was returned (or rejected by Kahrmann). Roger intimated that the money must have come back by another means such as IMO. I said that I knew nothing of this.

Roger seemed to think that I knew a great deal about the IMO when in fact I know very little (which I kept on telling him).

He obviously knew he owed £30,000 and was trying to get out of paying it (in my opinion he has been trying to get out of paying it ever since he received the money!) - At no time did he intimate that he would repay.

After the call I immediately telephoned AS to tell him what had transpired. I was concerned that he might 'edit' the tape (because I was convinced by a click at the end that I had been taped) especially the sentance 'but I know it wasn't your money, Roger'.

I later remembered discussing Roger's house position with Peter when Roger sold his first house (Moncrief Road). Roger should have repaid the loan then but never did. I remembered that Roger agreed a legal charge on his new property to ensure the same situation never happened again.

I do believe Roger has acted dishonourably with his house loan. The NUM bent over backwards to help him in 1984 (in retrospect it would have been better for the NUM to have kept the loan for the Receiver would certainly have got the money back from Roger or put it on a proper commercial footing). He has had £30,000 (and the interest on the money - or even greater the saving in back mortgage interest) and has known all along that its repayable).

I did draft a letter to send to Roger clarifying his 'phone call and my understanding of the loan but was advised not to send it to him at this moment in time.

S C Hudson
9/8/89

Dear Ray,

After your telephone call to me yesterday about your house loan I tried to ring you back with no success, so I thought I would drop you a line.

I remember the repayment of cash into the NUM funds, around November '84 to discharge your house loan, I think the amount involved was £30,000. Unfortunately I can't remember the exact details of which Organisation lent you the money to repay the NUM though I'm sure the North debt was repaid by CFT so this was probably the origin of the loan to you. The IMO wasn't in existence at the time so presumably if AS is saying that the debt is owed to the IMO then it will have been assigned so the CFT would be a logical source.

I have never had any access to IMO records so it was never part of my remit. As far as I was concerned the Union was no longer involved as the debt had been discharged in cash. Obviously, however, a loan remained between you and whichever party lent you the £30,000 to pay the Union back.

I remember when you changed house of being aware that no money had yet been repaid which caused a bit of consternation as presumably the loan should have been repaid from the sale proceeds.

PTO

156

From what you tell me yesterday, the loan must still be outstanding. Presumably, you simply want to verify who you owe the money to before you sell your present house and move to France. If AS is asking that you repay the MO I would have thought there should be either an MO document assigning the debt to them or a straight written acceptance by you of a house loan from the MO.

I'm afraid I can't help with any written evidence as it was a loan between you and a third party and nothing to do with the Union. If you want me to ask Ian if he has anything let me know.

Best Wishes

Steve Hudson.

THE BANK ACCOUNTS

The NUM and its members face two financial problems arising out of the 1984/5 strike. The first was the need to sustain the striking miners and their families, the second was to sustain the Union organisation.

The sustenance of the members was met principally by a National fund, the Miners' Solidarity Fund (as well as other including Area funds). There was no legal threat to these funds. These funds collected donations ear-marked for the relief of hardship and we assert that to the best of our knowledge and belief, not a penny intended for the relief of hardship of our members and their families was ever used for another purpose.

The maintenance of the Union organisation was a more difficult problem in view of the sequestration (a foreseen possibility) and receivership (an unforeseen possibility). The Union lost subscription income and its assets were seized or threatened with seizure. The seizure and protracted Breach of Trust litigation lasted long after the end of the strike. Recognising this plight National, overseas and International Unions (and many other individuals and bodies) donated funds to maintain our Union organisation but these funds had to be kept from seizure or from being frozen whereby they might be the subject of extended litigation as to whether, since they were not for the relief of hardship, they were Union assets or not.

The need to maintain the availability of funds, therefore, necessitated:

1)   A multiplicity of accounts,

2)   Secrecy, and

3)   The use of overseas accounts.

In fact 14 accounts were utilised and members of the NEC will recognise the use of various of them by their Areas during and after the dispute. As is made clear in the report, a number of the accounts were made available by the IMO.

The accounts are as follows:

1.   **TRUST FUND – MINERS ACTION COMMITTEE**

          Opened 21st October, 1984

          Trustees: A. Scargill and P. Heathfield

Total Deposits   £1,219,905.25

Withdrawals   £1,219,331.29

Balance   £573.96

2. **TRUST FUND – SHEFFIELD WOMENS ACTION GROUP**

    Opened 4th January, 1985

    Trustees: Ms. J. McCrindle and Councillor Doris Askham.

Total Deposits	£1,124,887.97
Withdrawals	£1,124,737.08
Balance £150,89	

3. **TRUST FUND – ALLIED IRISH, DUBLIN – JEAN McCRINDLE (National Treasurer of Women Against Pit Closures 1984/5)**

    Opened 22nd November, 1985

    Signatory: Jean McCrindle.

Total Deposits	£200,236.57
Withdrawals	£200,236.57
Balance	Nil – account closed 7th April, 1987

4. **TRUST FUND – ALLIED IRISH, LEEDS – JEAN McCRINDLE (National Treasurer of Women Against Pit Closures 1984/5).**

    Opened 31st January, 1986

    Signatory: Jean McCrindle

Total Deposits	£351,239.09
Withdrawals	£351,239.09
Balance	Nil – Account closed 16th July, 1987

5. **TRUST FUND – BANK OF IRELAND – JEAN McCRINDLE (National Treasurer of Women Against Pit Closures 1984/5)**

    Opened 8th April, 1987

    Signatory: Jean McCrindle

Total Deposits	£41,146.77
Withdrawals	£41,146.77
Balance	Nil – Account closed 24th July, 1989

6. TRUST FUND – CO–OPERATIVE BANK, SHEFFIELD – Y. Fenn (Secretary to A. Scargill).

Opened 22nd November, 1986

Signatory: Y. Fenn

Total Deposits	£236,664.37
Withdrawals	£236,664.37
Balance	Nil – Account closed 24th October, 1989

7. TRUST FUND – AUSTRIAN BANK – Y. SCHNEIDER (Maiden name of Y. Fenn)

Opened 22nd November, 1986

Signatory: Y. Schneider

Total Deposits Inc. interest	£615,805.01
Withdrawals	£615,805.01
Balance	Nill – Account closed 12th October, 1989

8. TRUST FUND – FIRST CHICAGO – N. Hyett (Nell Myer's former married name).

Opened 12th November, 1984

Signatory: N. Hyett (NUM Press Officer)

Total Deposits	$1,000
Withdrawals	$1,000
Balance	Nil – Account closed 11th February, 1986

9. TRUST FUND – CHASE BANK, DUBLIN – N. Hyett (Nell Myer's former married name).

Opened 10th January, 1985

Signatory: N. Hyett

Total Deposits Inc. interest   £223,682.91

Withdrawals   £223,682.91

Balance   Nil – Account closed 18th November, 1986

10. TRUST FUND – APEX HEAD OFFICE BANK ACCOUNT

Opened May, 1985

Signatories: M. Clapham, Ms. J. Ashton

Total Deposits   £157,544.37

Withdrawals   £157,544.37

Balance   Nil – Account closed December, 1985

11. TRUST FUND – T. SIBLEY

Opened November, 1985

Signatory: T. Sibley

Total Deposits   £50.00

Withdrawals   Nill

Balance   £50.00 – Account not used.

12. TRUST FUND – IMO AUSTRIA

Opened 7th November, 1986

Trustees: A. Scargill and A. Simon.

Total Deposits Inc. interest   £912,184.70

Withdrawals   £911,820.67

Balance   £364.03

13. TRUST FUND INTER-HILFS-U-VERTEIDIGUNGSFOND

Opened 19th February, 1986

Trustees: A. Scargill and A. Simon.

Total Deposits Exc. interest	£137,221.90
Withdrawals	£50,000.00
Balance	£111,588.64

14. MINERS INTERNATIONAL RESEARCH, EDUCATION, DEFENCE AND SUPPORT FUND

Opened 30th January, 1985

Trustees: A. Simon, N. West MEP.

Total Deposits Exc. interest	£1,985.227.00
Withdrawals Exc. interest	£1,150.000.00
Balance	£1,800.000.00

CONCLUSION

All the 14 Funds referred to were opened and operated at a time when the NUM was involved in strike action, sequestration, receivership or facing a breach of trust action. Out of the 14 Funds which were established only 5 are still open. The bank account of T. Sibley never operated. Out of the 5 Funds which are still active, 3 are under the auspices of the IMO. One is the Sheffield Womens Action Group, with a balance of £150.89 and the Miners Action Committee with a balance of £573.96. It can be seen from these records that all monies donated into these Funds were used for the benefit of the NUM or in accordance with the wishes of the donors. The Funds have at all times been operated with propriety. The Funds were established to maintain the NUM in one of the most difficult periods in history and we are proud of the fact that we were able to play a role which ensured that our Union could continue to function inspite of sequestration, receivership and all the various problems that it confronted.

ANNEXE C

CONSTITUTION OF THE NUM

Rules in force in 1984

1.	The authority and government of the Union is vested in the Conference of Delegates, which may function in Annual or Special Conference (see rules 8 and 23).

2.	Between Conference the business and affairs of the Union are administered by the National Executive Committee which shall perform all duties laid down for it by resolution of Confence, and shall not at any time act contrary to, or in defiancing of, any resolution of Conference (rule 8). The may may delegate any of its powers to sub-committees comprising members (rule 28).

3.	The Union has 3 National Officials, namely President, Vice President and Secretary. The President and Secretary are full time officials (rule 14).

4.	The duties of the President are defined as follows:

"15.	In addition to performing whatever other duties may from time to time be entrusted to him or her as a ful time official by the National Executive Committee, the President shall preside at all meetings of the NEC, Annual Conference and Special Conference, and see that the business of the Union is conducted in a proper manner and according to the Rules, and that in the conduct of affairs of the Union the Rules are duly and properly carried out".

5.	The duties of the Secretary are as follows:

(1)	to act as Treasurer

(2)   to conduct the correspondence for and on behalf of the Union and the National Executive Committee

(3)   to attend all meetings of Conference and the NEC and keep records of their proceedings

(4)   to prepare and submit to the NEC and the Auditors a balance sheet showing the financial position of the Union for each year

(5)   to recieve all monies payable to the Union, and to pay all monies not immediately require for the purpose of the Union to a bank to be invested by the Trustees (rule 17).

6.   The remuneration of full-time National Officials is to be determined by Conference upon recommendation of the NEC. A National Official is also entitleed to be paid reasonable and proper expenses, as determined by the NEC, for doing work on behalf of the Union (rule 16(b)).

7.   The Funds and property of the Union are vested in three Trustees (rule 21); and the Trustees are obliged to observe and carry out in all respects the lawful orders and directions of the National Executive Committee in connection with the property and funds of the Union, subject, nevertheless, to the authority of Conference (rule 22). The manner in which the funds of the Union may be invested is set out in Rule 22.

8.   Rule 45 provides that the books of the Union shall be available for inspection on reasonable notice to a member or to any person having an interest in the funds of the Union.

9.   The following significant changes have been made to the provisions set out above in the 1989 Rules which now govern the affairs of the Union.

9.1   The Trustees are obliged, by rule 24.D, to carry out <u>all</u> orders and directions of the NEC and of Conference, in place of the earlier obligation to carry out all <u>lawful</u> orders and directions of the NEC, subject to the authority of Conference.

9.2   The following indemnities are governed by the Rules:

"16.   **Indemnity of National Officials**

Each National Official shall be indemnified by the Union in respect of every act done as such a National Officer so long as such act was not contrary to the policy of Conference or of the NEC. If such act be not in accordancfe with the Rules then the National Official shall be entitled to be indemnified if the said act was done with the prior or subsequent consent of Confererence or of the NEC. For the purposes of this Rule the word "Act" shall include the not doing or the failing to do something as well as the doing of anything. For the avoidance of doubt this Rule shall apply whenever the Act as defined occurred whether the same occurred before the passing of this Rule or later.

19.C   Every Area Official/Agent shall be entitled to be indemnified by the Union in respect of every act done as such as Official/Agent whether in accordance with the Rules or otherwise so long as such act was done with the prior or subsequent consent of the Area Council and/or National Officials (or any of them), the NEC of Conference; but the Area shall indemnify the Union if the Area Officials/Agent act was subject only to the consent of the Area Council but not any other of the persons or bodies set out above. For the purposes of this Rule the word "act" shall include the not doing or the failing to do something as well as the doing of anything. For the avoidance of doubt this Rule shall apply whenever the act as defined occured whether the same occurred before the passing of this Rule or later.

24.C   Every Trustee shall be entitled to be indemnified by the Union in respect of any act as done as such a Trustee whether in accordance with these Rules or otherwise so long as such act was done with the prior or subsequent consent of Conference or of the NEC. For the purposes of this Rule the word "act" shall include the not doing or failing to do something as well as the doing of anything. For the avoidance of doubt this Rule shall apply whenever the act defined occurred whether same occurred before the passing of this Rule or later."

166

ANNEXE D
INTERNATIONAL MINERS' ORGANISATION
MANAGERIAL STRUCTURES

Permanent Secretariat

President	Arthur Scargill	Great Britain
Vice-President	Mikhail Srebny	USSR
Vice-President	John Maitland	Australia
General Secretary	Alain Simon	France
Secretary	Valery Chestakov	USSR
Secretary	Radko Stantchev	Bulgaria

Executive Bureau

Great Britain	Arthur Scargill	
USSR	Mikhail Srebny	
Australia	John Maitland	Permanent
France	Alain Simon	Secretary
USSR	Valery Chestakov	
USSR	Radko Stantchev	
Czechoslovakia	Vladimir Polednik	
GDR	Gunther Wolf	
Great Britain	Peter Heathfield	Committees'
France	Augustin Dufresne	Presidents
Chile	Juan Antinao	
Hungary	Lazslo Kovacs	

ANNEXE D

INTERNATIONAL MINERS' ORGANISATION
EXECUTIVE COMMITTEE

Great Britain	Arthur Scargill	
USSR	Mikhail Srebny	
Australia	John Maitland	Permanent
France	Alain Simon	Secretary
USSR	Valery Chestakov	
USSR	Radko Stantchev	
Czechoslovakia	Vladimir Polednik	
GDR	Gunther Wolf	
Great Britain	Peter Heathfield	Committee
France	Augustin Dufresne	Chairmen
Chile	Juan Antinao	
Hungary	Lazslo Kovacs	
Poland	Rajmund Moric	
India	Sunil Sen	
Congo	Henri Gankama	Regional
Zambia	T M Walamba	Representatives
Cuba	Ramon Cardona-Nuevo	
Iraq	....	

Note: Mr Srebny and Mr Dufresne have now retired and have not been replaced.

CONSTITUTION

ARTICLE I - Name, Objective and Location

1. The International Miners' Organisation is a democratic federation of trade union organisations of employees associated with mines, quarries and energy enterprises. The IMO will defend the economic, social and moral interests of employees associated with mines, quarries and energy enterprises, promote their international solidarity and campaign for peace and disarmament.

2. The IMO shall have its headquarters in Paris, France or such other place as may be determined by Congress.

ARTICLE II - Principles

1. The IMO will be independent and not differentiate between race, nationality and religion.

2. The IMO is open to all mining and energy trade unions of the world, who demonstrate a willingness to defend the economic and social interests of their members.

3. The IMO will prepare its programme, its orientations and actions on the basis of consultation with all member organisations and discuss specific experiences of each organisation between them and search for the definition of common interests relating to mine and energy workers of the world and will inspire the international solidarity of workers.

4. The IMO recognises the principle of sovereignty of the member organisations.

ARTICLE III - Objectives and Means

To achieve what is proposed, as in Article II the IMO will resort to the following:

1. Development of relations between unions nationally and internationally by the organisation of congress or international conferences, information, etc.

2. Preparation of a programme of minimum demands.

3. Development of solidarity among member organisations with a view to mutual assistance during disputes and support initiatives of member organisations.

4. Development of international initiatives, conforming to the programme clearly defined in point 2.

5.	Defence of the interests of members from affiliated organisations who reside and work abroad, e.g. migrant workers.

6.	Propogate the common ideas in those countries where there does not yet exist a union and help the trade union movement there where it is still weak.

7.	Representation of workers of member organisations in all institutes and international bodies where the economic and social interests of workers are liable to be debated.

ARTICLE IV - Membership

1.	Affiliation of an organisation to the IMO is admitted by the Executive Committee if the organisation declares in writing the recognition of the statutes and rules of the IMO and respects the obligations therein.

2.	The organisations will have their requests for affiliation accepted after examination and majority vote of the Executive Committee.

3.	Affiliated organisations cannot belong to any other international association of employees in mines, quarries and associated energy undertakings, subject to point 4 below.

4.	Affiliated organisations who have members in both mining and associated energy undertakings may affiliate their mining members to the IMO and their energy members to any other international organisation.

5.	An organisation may appeal to the Congress if its application for membership is rejected by the Executive Committee. In such cases, a two-thirds majority for acceptance is required.

6.	An affiliated organisation may leave the IMO when it notifies the Executive Committee in writing.

7.	An organisation affiliated to the IMO can be excluded by the Executive Committee or Congress if it deliberately contravenes the common interests.

8.	Any organisation which has been excluded from continued membership of the IMO may appeal to the Congress. An organisation whose appeal against exclusion is examined by Congress shall have the right of voice but not of vote.

ARTICLE V - Contributions

1.	The annual affiliation fee to the IMO shall be determined either by Congress or the Executive Committee and all member organisations are obliged to make the appropriate contributions.

2.   The Executive Committee can give special dispensation, if determined necessary, to those organisations who are unable to pay their full rate of contribution because of special financial circumstances.

3.   The Executive Committee or Congress can introduce a special levy for specific purposes.

4.   Any member organisation may volunteer specific financial assistance if they so choose, but if for a particular project it must be formally approved by the Executive Committee or Congress.

ARTICLE VI - Structure

The Structure of the IMO will comprise the following bodies:

        Congress
        Executive Committee
        Bureau
        Secretariat

1.   **Congress**

        A.   The supreme organ of the IMO shall be the Congress which shall meet at least once every four years, the venue and duration to be determined by the Executive Committee.

        B.   Congress will decide on a programme of demands, the orientations and activities of the IMO.

        C.   If necessary, the Executive Committee may convene a special Congress.

        D.   Each affiliated organisation shall have the right to be represented at Congress by a maximum of 10 delegates but a member organisation may also appoint observers to Congress.

        E.   The Executive Committee will be responsible for the preparation of Congress which for normal sessions will include:

                i   Report of credentials and scrutineers.

                ii   General Secretary's report on the activities of the IMO since the previous Congress.

                iii   Election of the leadership; the Executive Committee, Bureau, General Secretary and Secretaries.

                iv   Financial Report.

F.   Voting at Congress shall be either by

i   A show of hands of all delegates present.

ii   Membership vote, which shall always be taken if requested by any delegates present on the following basis:

a.   every affiliated organisation to have one vote.

b.   up to 100,000 members, one additional vote for every 50,000 members or part thereof which is at least 25,000.

c.   when the number of members exceeds 100,000 one additional vote for every 100,000 members or part thereof which is at least 50,000.

d.   no organisation can exceed a maximum of 10 votes.

G.   A two-thirds majority is required for acceptance of a new organisation and for approval of amendments to the Constitution.

2. Executive Committee

The Executive Committee shall manage the affairs of the IMO between the two ordinary Congresses and shall be composed as follows:

A.   The Bureau

B.   One member from each of the following countries, groups of countries or areas:

Europe - Middle East - The Americas - Asia Africa (2 members)

C.   Substitutes shall be appointed for members in (B) who shall attend meetings of the Executive Committee in the absence of the titular member. When the titular member represents more than one country, a substitute member shall be elected from a different country of the group or area.

D.   Congress shall elect the Executive Committee. Each country, group of countries or area shall agree upon the nomination of a member and a substitute member of the Executive Committee.

E.   Meetings of the Executive Committee shall be convened by the Bureau whenever they deem it necessary so to do but there must be at least one meeting per calendar year.

F.   Meetings of the Executive Committee shall also be attended by representatives of special committees by decision of the Executive Committee. Such representatives have no right of vote upon the Executive Committee.

G.   Voting at meetings shall be by a show of hands when adopting a decision, and before passing a vote a consensus shall be sought. In case a consensus is not reached a majority decision will be adopted.

H.   Neither the President nor the General Secretary may vote at meetings of the Executive Committee.

3.   **Bureau**

A.   The Bureau is the management body of the IMO between two sessions of the Executive Committee. It is elected by Congress.

B.   The Bureau comprises the President, the Vice-Presidents, a General Secretary, Secretaries and Chairmen of the Technical Committees. It is responsible to the Executive Committee for executing the orientations and decisions determined by Congress or the Executive Committee. They will meet and communicate each time it is deemed necessary.

C.   The Bureau is elected by Congress.

D.   Each ordinary Congress shall elect a President and Vice-Presidents. Each member organisation shall have the right to nominate one candidate for each of these positions but no country shall hold more than one.

E.   No retired official from an affiliated organisation will be eligible for election.

F.   For the election of a President and Vice-Presidents at all Congresses, subsequent to that at which this Constitution is adopted, the names of nominees must be received by the Secretariat at least sixteen weeks prior to Congress.

4.   **The General Secretary**

The Congress shall elect a full time General Secretary who shall remain in office at the discretion of Congress and whose terms of appointment shall be determined by the Executive Committee. Nominations for the position of full-time General Secretary may be made by any member organisation irrespective of positions held or nominations made by it for President or Vice-Presidents when requests for nominations to this position are specifically required.

ARTICLE VII - Technical Committees

1.   The Executive Committee can establish technical committees for examination and study of particular questions. Such committees shall have advisory status.

2.   At least one official shall be a permanent member of each technical committee.

3.   The Executive Committee shall invite members to attend these special committees.

4.   Standing technical committees shall be Finance and Safety.

ARTICLE VIII - Regional Organisation

1.   Affiliated organisations can be members of regional organisations, providing their objectives do not conflict with the Constitution of the IMO or the decisions of the governing bodies.

ARTICLE IX - Finance and Administration

1.   The IMO shall be responsible for all approved administrative expenses incurred by its activities including Congress and meetings convened.

2.   The IMO shall provide the return fares of:

      A.   two representatives of each member organisation to Congress.

      B.   all members attending an Executive Committee meeting as well as those invited to attend.

      C.   all members invited to attend a special committee.

      D.   the officials when engaged on business of the international or any member to whom such a task has been delegated.

3.   The Executive Committee shall be responsible for the conditions and salaries of the personnel of the International Secretariat.

4.   The accounts of the IMO shall be audited and prepared by the Finance Committee.

ARTICLE X - Dissolution

1.   The IMO can only be dissolved by not less than a two-thirds majority vote at Congress on a motion submitted in accordance with the Constitution. Such a decision to dissolve the IMO must also determine the correct disposal of its assets.

ARTICLE XI - Standing Orders

1. Notices convening Congress shall be issued at least twenty-six weeks prior to the date of Congress.

2. Each affiliated organisation may submit proposals or resolutions for inclusion in the Congress agenda and this must be received at least sixteen weeks prior to the commencement of Congress.

3. The Executive Committee can submit proposals and resolutions for the Congress agenda both prior to and during Congress.

4. The Congress shall be opened and chaired during its first and final sessions by the President and Vice-Presidents. For all other sessions of Congress, a Chairman and Vice-Chairmen shall be elected by Congress.

5. Congress may appoint committees to examine questions on the agenda but reports of such committees must be placed before Plenary Sessions for adoption.

6. Congress shall not commence any discussion of individual agenda items until the report of the Credentials Committee has been approved.

7. The duration of all sessions of Congress shall be determined by the Executive Committee.

8. The languages which constitute the official languages of Congress shall be determined by the Executive Committee.

9. The agenda and any individual proposals or resolutions may be considered by the Executive Committee who can make recommendations to Congress if so decided.

10. During Congress emergency proposals and resolutions may be formulated in writing and are acceptable if presented by at least two member organisations. They must be presented in Plenary Session and immediately a decision has been taken on the item then under discussion, the mover of the emergency proposal or resolution shall be allowed to address Congress for a time not exceeding ten minutes. Without debate Congress will decide whether such emergency proposals or resolutions are admissible and if so, the Chairman and Vice-Chairman presiding over the session shall determine their appropriate place on the agenda.

11. The mover of a motion admitted for debate shall be allowed to address the Congress for a time not exceeding fifteen minutes. All other speakers except committee reporters shall not speak for a time exceeding ten minutes. Delegates wishing to address Congress shall submit their name in writing but no speaker may address Congress twice on any one item. The mover of a motion may reply to points raised in debate but such a reply should not exceed fifteen minutes.

12.   Observers to Congress shall have no right of address.

13.   Motions shall be recorded as carried if more than one half of the votes present are in favour.

14.   A motion for closure of a debate can be carried at any time by a simple majority either on the proposal of a delegate or the suggestion of the Chairman. The motion for closure will be voted without discussion.

15.   A speaker wishing to make a point of order will be automatically given the floor.

16.   The official languages of the IMO will be English, French, Russian and Spanish.

MINUTES OF MEETING OF 7th AND 8th MARCH 1984

Publisher's Note
In the report submitted by Mr Lightman to the National Executive Committee the following document was a photocopy of original material. Because the quality of the photocopy made it unsuitable for photographic reproduction, it has been retyped. The retyped document is a faithful and accurate copy of the original.

FINANCE AND GENERAL PURPOSES COMMITTEE - 7th March 1984

PRESENT: A. Scargill   (President) in the Chair
             M. McGahey   (Vice-President)

             J. Jones
             C. Barlow
             C. T. Bell
             W. Stobbs
             H. Richardson
             O. Briscoe

                 P. E. Heathfield (Secretary)

IN ATTENDANCE: S. Hudson (Finance Officer)
                 R. Windsor (Chief Executive Officer)

APOLOGIES: G. Rees

Following informal discussions with NUM solicitors, Brian Thompson
and Partners, it was agreed that the following decisions be
taken "in camera":

(1) That the Trustees be instructed to consult with Union
     Lawyers with a view to investing the Union's funds
     in the Isle of Man, Jersey and Ireland and/or any
     other location which was deemed appropriate.

(2) That the National Secretary and Trustees be given
     authority to invest the funds of the Union in any
     bank and its subsidiaries.

(3) A brief report should be made on this matter to the
     NEC and a full presentation made to the NEC at a re-
     convened meeting to be held at the Royal Victoria Hotel,
     involving all Area Finance Officers.

(4) That Areas attending this meeting be advised of steps
     to be taken to locate their funds abroad and ensure
     that they were available for use at all times by the
     membership and that a list of solicitors who could
     advise on this question, be made available at the
     meeting.

NATIONAL EXECUTIVE COMMITTEE - 8th March 1984

PRESENT: A. Scargill (President) in the Chair
            M. McGahey (Vice-President)
            P. Heathfield (Secretary)

C. Barlow	E. Clarke	I. Morgan	J. A. Taylor
C. T. Bell	H. C. Hanlon	D. Murphy	K. Toon
O. Briscoe	R. Dunn	J. R. Ottey	S. G. Vincent
G. Butler	J. Jones	G. Rees	J. Weaver
R. Chadburn	E. McKay	H. Richardson	E. Williams
W. Chambers	A. Moffatt	W. Stobbs	

Also present:

A. Eadie MP
R. Ellis MP

A report was made on the various points raised at the F. & G. P.
Committee, which had been discussed "in camera". Following a brief
discussion, the report was accepted.

PRESENT:

A. Scargill (President) in the Chair
M. McGahey (Vice-President)

C. Barlow	E. Clarke	I. Morgan	J. A. Taylor
C. T. Bell	H. C. Hanlon	D. Murphy	K. Toon
O. Briscoe	R. Dunn	J. R. Ottey	S. G. Vincent
G. Butler	J. Jones	G. Rees	J. Weaver
R. Chadburn	E. McKay	H. Richardson	E. Williams
W. Chambers	A. Moffat	W. Stobbs	

P. E. Heathfield (Secretary)

IN ATTENDANCE:
J. Burrows (Derbyshire)
G. Robson (Durham)
B. Griggs (Kent)
C. Gaskell (North West)
J. Colgan (Midlands)
D. Thomas (Midlands)
H. Tilstone (Power Group)
R. Browell (Northumberland)
R. Lynk (Notts)
D. Kennedy (South Wales)
K. Ward (Cokemen)
B. Taylor (COSA)
R. Robertson (Scotland)
K. Homer (Yorkshire)
T. Jones (Yorkshire)
M. Nevin (Durham Mechanics)
G. Whitfield (Northumberland)
A. Crawford (SCEBTA)

NATIONAL OFFICE STAFF IN ATTENDANCE:

R. Windsor
S. Hudson
Y. Fenn
J. Nicholson

The President opened the meeting and invited the Chief Executive
Officer, formerly Finance Officer, Mr. Roger Windsor, to make a
report on what had been discussed and agreed "in camera" at the
Finance and General Purposes Sub-Committee on the 7th March and
NEC earlier today.

Mr. Windsor explained that informal discussions had taken place with the Union's solicitors, Messrs. Brian Thompson and Partners, and also the Union's bankers with regard to the movement of Union monies abroad. It was unclear at this stage what the full impact on Union funds could be of the new Legislation, particularly sections which were not yet enacted dealing with Civil Litigation.

The object of this meeting was to advise how best the Union's funds, both at National and Area level, could at all times be available for the membership's use on a day to day basis, bearing in mind the Union appeared to be entering into a very difficult period, having already been involved in a National Overtime ban from November 1983. Recent developments in Scotland and Yorkshire made it imperative that the Union safeguard the finances in order that they be available for the day to day operations of the Union - for example Common Law damages, Social Insurance and general administrative matters both at National, Area and local level.

It was recommended that initially the Union's finances at National level should be invested in the Isle of Man, Jersey and Ireland, although it may be necessary to invest in other locations following further discussions with bank and legal advisers.

An explanation was given about the Mineworkers' Trust which had initially been agreed between Sheffield City Council, South Yorkshire County Council and the NUM in 1982 and steps instituted in 1983 towards the establishment of such a Trust. Areas were advised that they may also wish to establish similar Trusts and it could be that in the long term, tax advantages, particularly from the point of view of corporation tax, could result to both the National and Area Unions. This was because the Trust would be dealing with educational programmes and welfare matters as well as providing library facilities etc.

It was explained that staff salaries could be paid in advance in any Area where it appeared likely that industrial action was about to take place, and this was another way of ensuring that general administrative matters were kept to a minimum in what could obviously be a very difficult situation.

Following the report by Mr. Windsor, a number of questions were asked by representatives from all the Areas. At the end of the discussion, it was unanimously agreed

    (1) That the report be noted.

    (2) That the funds of the Union be kept available
        for the immediate use of the members and policy
        of the Union.

    (3) That funds be invested, in the first instance,
        in the Isle of Man, Jersey and Ireland.

    (4) That the National Officials be instructed to
        implement these recommendations and decisions
        and to instruct Solicitors as necessary.

(5) To keep all matters under constant review
and to take such action as necessary.

A list of solicitors' names were read out, and it was explained
that the services of the National Finance Officer were available
to any Area who wished to have further discussions on this matter.

It was also explained that at today's meeting the decision could
only apply to the National Union and it was a matter for Areas
to decide individually on the steps that they wish to take following
the report. The President reminded the meeting that this was
a "private" meeting and in line with the decisions of the F and
G P on the 7th March and NEC earlier today, that no minute would
be published because of the confidential nature of this matter.

ANNEXE F

DEED DATED 21.10.84 CONSTITUTING THE MACF

DEED OF TRUST dated 21st October 1984 and made by Arthur Scargill, 2B Yews Lane, Worsbrough Dale, Nr. Barnsley, South Yorkshire, England, and Peter Ernest Heathfield of 262 Newbold Road, Chesterfield, Derbyshire, England (hereinafter called "The Trustees").

(1) A Fund for the purpose of supporting the National Union of Mineworkers' campaign to save pits, jobs and mining communities, preserving the fabric of the NUM itself, alleviating hardship in mining communities and assisting in a general campaign industrially and politically shall be established and be known as the "Miners' Action Committee".

(2) The Trustees should be nominated as the Trustees of the said Fund for all purposes including administration of the same.

The Trustees have consented to act as Trustees of the said Fund and to receive and account for all such remittances, subscriptions, donations and other contributions as may from time to time be made to the Fund or otherwise become subject to the Fund.

The Trust Fund is to be applied for the following purposes:

(a) to assist in the general, industrial and political campaign being conducted by the National Union of Mineworkers in defence of jobs, pits and mining communities;

(b) to provide financial assistance to maintain the fabric of the National Union of Mineworkers, by making available monies from the Fund for the purposes of paying bills, etc., which cannot be met by the Union and its Areas as a result of sequestration and/or receivership;

185

(c) to provide assistance for alleviating hardship
     in mining communities;

(d) to authorise the issue and defence of any legal
     proceedings in relation to the affairs and
     functions of the NUM, its Officials and its members.

3.   In the event of the Trustees appointed being
     incapacitated simultaneously or being unable to act
     simultaneously for any reason whatsoever the Committee
     is requested to appoint two Trustees as replacements.

     In witness whereof the parties hereto have hereinto
     set their hands and affix their seals the day and year
     herein first written.

Signed, sealed and delivered by the said Arthur Scargill
in the presence of
Witness

M. Fellows
21 Poplar Drive
Wath-upon-Dearne
Rotherham

Signed, sealed and delivered by the said Peter Ernest
Heathfield in the presence of
Witness
N. Myers
26 Farringford Road
London
E15

21st October, 1984

186

ANNEXE G

CORK GULLY'S REPORT ON THE NUM AND THE MINERS SOLIDARITY FUND OFFICIAL BANK ACCOUNTS

General

The allegations made by the Daily Mirror and the Cook Report do not appear to relate to the operation of the official bank accounts of the NUM and the Miners Solidarity Fund, i.e. those accounts operated by the NUM and previously disclosed to the auditors, KPMG Peat Marwick, Sheffield. However, in order to obtain comfort in relation to the operation of the official bank accounts, Cork Gully reviewed KPMG Peat Marwick's audit files and various financial records of the NUM.

Seventy-one bank accounts were disclosed to Cork Gully, excluding Colliery Officials and Staff Area accounts, which have been operated by the NUM and the Miners Solidarity Fund since 1984 and are listed in Annexe H. These accounts were brought to Cork Gully's attention with the co-operation of KPMG Peat Marwick and members of the NUM's Finance Department, and have been subject to KPMG Peat Marwick's audit procedures. These bank accounts had been operated in five countries. Four of these countries, being the Isle of Man, Ireland, Switzerland, and Luxembourg, were used to operate bank accounts following the commencement of the miners strike in 1984 when the NUM was advised to move its funds overseas in an attempt to thwart the potential claims of a Sequestrator or Receiver. These overseas bank accounts were disclosed to KPMG Peat Marwick and to the Receiver, Mr Michael Arnold, who ultimately recovered the funds remaining in these accounts for the benefit of the NUM. Cork Gully met Mr Arnold and discussed the operation of these accounts. Cork Gully also obtained documentation from Mr Arnold in support of transactions relating to the overseas accounts.

NUM Audited Accounts

Period of Accounts Examined

- Year ended 31 December 1984
- Year ended 31 December 1985
- Year ended 31 December 1986
- Year ended 31 December 1987
- Year ended 31 December 1988

ANNEXE G

The accounts for the year ended 31 December 1989 were being audited during the enquiry and were not available for review.

The audit report in the NUM's accounts for the year ended 31 December 1984 contained a qualification relating to the transfer of NUM assets to the Mineworkers Trust. This transfer of assets has been considered in paragraph 64 of this report. The audit report contained other qualifications relating to the completeness of contributions from area unions, possible NUM claims to monies received by the Miners Solidarity Fund and Sheffield Womens Action Group, the potential tax position of the NUM and breach of trust action which was taken by the Receiver. Accounts for subsequent periods also contained some of the audit report qualifications that appeared in the 1984 accounts. None of these qualifications are considered to be significant to the terms of reference of this Enquiry.

Cork Gully have reviewed the records and information made available to them relating to the NUM's official bank accounts for the periods referred to above and have found that they do not disclose information relevant to this Enquiry.

Miners Solidarity Fund Audited Accounts

Period of Accounts Examined

- Period 18 March 1984 to 31 December 1984
- Year ended 31 December 1985
- Year ended 31 December 1986

The accounts for the period 1 January 1987 to 31 December 1989 were being audited during the enquiry and were not available for review.

Cork Gully reviewed KPMG Peat Marwick's audit files and the records held by the NUM relating to the Miners Solidarity Fund. The Miners Solidarity Fund received substantial donations during the periods referred to above. The principal source of income was donations in the form of cash and cheques. Given this situation it is not possible to establish that all income received is accounted for. Accounting control commences with the issue of a receipt and a banking of the cash received. It is possible therefore to establish that all income for which a receipt has been issued has been accounted for. It is impossible to state whether all income i.e. donations received are "receipted" and recorded. It is only possible to examine and comment on those monies actually lodged in the Miners Solidarity Fund bank accounts. The audit report in the Miners Solidarity Funds' audited accounts for the periods referred to above was qualified as follows: "we (KPMG Peat Marwick) have been unable to verify independently that all donations have been received and

ANNEXE G

correctly accounted for". Cork Gully understand the audit report qualification to mean that the auditor has been unable to determine whether all monies collected on behalf of, or intended for, the Miners Solidarity Fund have been deposited into bank accounts operated by the Fund and are correctly accounted for. This form of audit qualification is to be expected in an operation of this type given the nature of the income, and is a form which will be seen in the accounts of organisations such as charities and is referred to in the auditing guidelines (3.301 Charities) issued by the Institute of Chartered Accountants in England and Wales.

During the period 18 March 1984 until 30 November 1984 the Miners Solidarity Fund received donations, usually in the form of cheque or bank transfer, which on occasions were made payable to the NUM. The officials of the NUM endorsed such payments in favour of the Miners Solidarity Fund. Following the appointment of the Receiver on 30 November 1984, receipts which were not able to be identified as being meant for the benefit of the Miners Solidarity Fund were held by the Funds' bankers until the Receiver gave authority for the monies to be transferred for the benefit of the Miners Solidarity Fund.

Cork Gully were asked in particular to investigate whether any funds received emanated from Libya or the USSR. In practice it is not possible to state categorically whether or not funds have been received from these sources for the reasons that:-

(a)   There is a question of "completeness of income" as referred to above.

(b)   The theoretical possibility that funds from these sources were received through intermediary sources.

The records presented to Cork Gully do not record donations as being received from Libya or the USSR. However, in the absence of third party verification for the confirmation of all sources of income it is impossible to conclude whether or not monies may have been received from Libya or the USSR through intermediaries. Even if third party verification for the recorded funds was available however, there would still be the question of completeness.

It should be recorded, however, that there is no evidence that the Miners Solidarity Fund received money from Libya or the USSR.

Cork Gully's examination of the records made available to them did not reveal information relevant to the other terms of reference of this Enquiry.

ANNEXE H

NUM AND THE MINERS SOLIDARITY FUND OFFICIAL BANK ACCOUNTS
DISCLOSED TO CORK GULLY

I   Co-Operative Bank plc
    Sheffield Branch
    PO Box 38
    84/86 West Street
    Sheffield S1 3SX

Account Number	Account Number
30103414	NUM GF
30103414-53	NUM GF deposit account
30103427	NUM political fund
30103443	NUM benefits fund
30103443-50	NUM
30103469	NUM building fund
30103469-50	NUM
30103427-53	NUM PF
30103427-50	NUM Political fund deposit account
30103430-50	NUM PF
30103443-00	NUM special benefits fund
30103469-00	NUM building fund
30103469-53	NUM building fund deposit account
30103812	NUM new HQ M Lister clients' account
30103919	NUM (South Africa) strike appeal fund
30103919-50	NUM (South Africa) strike appeal deposit account
30103838	NUM benevolent account and provident welfare scheme
30103838-50	Benevolent and provident call account
30130306	NUM General Fund (held at London branch)
4101688102	NUM new HQ M Lister call account
410627902	NUM general fund call account
4103308402	NUM South Africa strike appeal call account
30000009	Miners' Solidarity Fund
07793.0001	Miners' Solidarity Fund (money market)
30103650	Miners' Solidarity Fund no 2 account
4107793302	Miners' Solidarity Fund call account
04376.0377	NUM BEC convertible

ANNEXE H

II   Midland Bank Trust Corporation (Isle of Man) Limited
PO Box 39
10 Victoria Street
Douglas
Isle of Man

Account Number

00-073177

III   Midland Bank Plc
17 Church Street
Sheffield

Account Number	Account Name
43091244	NUM deposit account

IV   Bank of Ireland Finance Limited
Burlington Road
Dublin 4
Ireland

Account Number	Account Name
2013920011	NUM GF
2013950016	NUM BF
2013940018	NUM PF
2232840011	NUM general fund
2005900015	NUM

V   EBC (Schweiz) AG
Ridenstrasse 22
Zurich
Switzerland

Account Number	Account Name
116.20	Current account
116.22	Current account
116.23	Current account
116.61	Current account
116.60	Deposit account

ANNEXE H

VI   Zurich Cantonel Bank
       Zurich   Funds held in escrow for
       Switzerland   Breach of Trust action

VII   Nobiz Finanz SA
       Luxembourg

          Account Number

          1-3.505

VIII Unity Trust Bank plc
       4 The Square
       111 Broad Street
       Birmingham B15 1AR

Account Number	Account Name
33023753	NUM general fund
33018535/20	NUM no 6 loan
33018548/20	NUM no 7 loan
33018551/20	NUM no 8 loan
33020141/20	NUM no 9 loan
33020251/20	NUM no 10 loan
33015693/20	NUM no 1 loan
33016320/20	NUM no 2 loan
33017303/20	NUM no 4 loan
33017772/20	NUM no 5 loan
33016618/20	NUM no 3 loan
33021975/20	NUM loan 11
33022563/20	NUM loan 12
33023931/20	NUM loan 13
33015693/00	NUM political fund
6110198002	7 days notice account (political fund)

IX   National Westmister Bank plc
      Westminster Branch
      14 Red Lion Square
      London

Account Number	Account Name
01278703	Business Reserve Messrs Sheridans re: NUM sterling money market office account

ANNEXE H

X   Standard Chartered Bank plc
     136 High Street
     Southampton

Receiver's Accounts	Account Name
01.9610049.01	General account
01.9610871.01	General account
01.9617973.01	Current account
01.9617981.10	Current account
01.9619011.01	Suspense account
39610049 01	General account
39610049 02	General account
39610049 03	General account
39610871 01	Miners' contributions
39610871 02	Miners' contributions
39610871 03	Miners' contributions
39619011 01	Suspense account

XI   Barclays Bank plc
     Southwark Branch
     29 Borough High Street
     London

Account Number	Account Name
00565334	NUM in name of Larkins, Barrows, Padmore and Hoult (sequestrators)

ANNEXE I

LIST OF UNOFFICIAL ACCOUNTS DISCLOSED TO CORK GULLY BY MR SCARGILL

	Account Name and Number	Bank	Date Opened and Closed	Signatories
1.	Miners Action Committee Fund	Cash Account	October 1984 - Still Operating	(Trustees) Scargill Heathfield
2.	Sheffield Womens Action Group 50524963	Co-Operative Bank Plc 84/86 West Street Sheffield S1 3SX	January 1985 - Still Open	McCrindle Askham
3.	Jean McCrindle 60430022	Allied Irish Banks Plc 10 Lower O'Connell Street Dublin 1	November 1985 - April 1987	McCrindle
4.	Jean McCrindle 31122054	Allied Irish Banks Plc Albion House Albion Street Leeds LS2 8LE	January 1986 - July 1987	McCrindle
5.	Jean McCrindle 16894020	Bank of Ireland PO Box 419 Lower Baggot Street Dublin 2	April 1987 - July 1989	McCrindle

194

LIST OF UNOFFICIAL ACCOUNTS DISCLOSED TO CORK GULLY BY MR SCARGILL

	Account Name and Number	Bank	Date Opened and Closed	Signatories
6.	Yvonne Fenn 18332896	Co-Operative Bank Plc 84/86 West Street Sheffield S1 3SX	November 1986 - March 1990	Fenn
7.	Yvonne Schneider 10051 029 050	Bank Fur Arbeit Und Wirstchaft AG (BAWAG) 1200 Wien Wallensteinstrasse 1 Austria	November 1986 - October 1989	Schneider
8.	Nell Hyett 7000685/5001	First National Bank of Chicago 44/45 St Stephen's Green Dublin 2	November 1984 - February 1986	Hyett
9.	Nell Hyett 7960023245 6205009000	Chase Bank (Ireland) Ltd Stephen Court 18/21 St Stephen's Green Dublin 2	January 1985 - November 1986	Hyett
10.	Apex Hallam Welfare Assoc 81148575	Midland Bank plc 17 Church Street Sheffield S1 1HH	May 1985 - December 1985	Clapham Ashton
11.	Tom Sibley	Bank of Ireland PO Box 419 Lower Baggot Street Dublin 2	November 1985 - Approx 1988	Sibley

ANNEXE I

LIST OF UNOFFICIAL ACCOUNTS DISCLOSED TO CORK GULLY BY MR SCARGILL

	Account Name and Number	Bank	Date Opened and Closed	Signatories
12.	IMO 10051-029-076	Bank Fur Arbeit Und Wirstchaft AG (BAWAG) 1200 Wien Wallensteinstrasse 1 Austria	November 1986 - Still Open	Simon Scargill
13.	Internationaler Hilfs Und Verteidigungdfond a) 100051 027 154 b) 100051 065 978	Bank Fur Arbeit Und Wirstchaft AG (BAWAG) 1200 Wien Wallensteinstrasse 1 Austria	a) February 1986 - September 1989 b) September 1989 - Still Open	Scargill Simon Scargill
14. a)	Norman West & Alain Simon 84612/81 (MIREDS account)	Irish Intercontinental Bank Limited 91 Merrion Square Dublin 2	January 1985 - Still Open	West Simon
b)	100051 065 560 Opened following receipt of £1m from a/c 84612/81	Bank Fur Arbeit Und Wirstchaft AG (BAWAG) 1200 Wien Wallensteinstrasse 1 Austria	August 1989 - Still open (see note)	West Simon
15.	IMO 30103773	Co-Operative Bank Plc 84/86 West Street Sheffield S1 3SX	May 1986 - Still Open	Scargill

ANNEXE I

LIST OF UNOFFICIAL ACCOUNTS DISCLOSED TO CORK GULLY BY MR SCARGILL

	Account Name and Number	Bank	Date Opened and Closed	Signatories
16.	IMO 13294020	Bank of Ireland PO Box 419 Lower Baggot Street Dublin 2	November 1985 - Still Open	Scargill Simon Swann Srebny
17.	Norman West & Alain Simon 10051-065-579	Bank Fur Arbeit Und Wirstchaft AG (BAWAG) 1200 Wien Wallensteinstrasse 1 Austria	August 1989 - Still open (see note)	West Simon

Note

Documentation relating to the operation of these two accounts,
including bank statements, has not been provided to Cork Gully.

197

REPORT OF CORK GULLY ON THE UNOFFICIAL ACCOUNTS RECORDS AND THEIR INVESTIGATION

Part I - Records

Records Provided to Cork Gully

At the meeting of the NEC on 9 March 1990 Mr Scargill and Mr Heathfield informed the NEC of the existence of fourteen unofficial accounts. Mr Scargill has told Cork Gully that he has provided to them copies of all records in his possession relating to these fourteen accounts in addition to a further three accounts which, for the completeness of the enquiry, he thought should be brought to Mr Lightman's attention.

The records provided to Cork Gully consist of;

I   Summary schedules recording the receipts and payments for eleven accounts. These are the schedules which were prepared with the assistance of Mrs Riley, using documentation held by Mr Scargill, and which were provided to Peats, Leeds;

II   Schedules containing detailed narrative commentary on the receipts and payments for fourteen accounts;

III   Correspondence between the banks and account holders relating to the operation of the account;

IV   Copy bank statements and bank advice notes;

V   Various other documentation, including receipts and correspondence relating to the setting up and operation of the accounts.

Preparation of Summary Receipt and Payments Schedules

Mr Hudson has told Mr Lightman that he was asked by Mr Scargill, towards the end of 1989, for his advice in relation to the preparation of accounts (a form of financial statement) which were to be prepared from information in Mr Scargill's possession pertaining to the unofficial cash and bank accounts. Mr Hudson was shown some of the underlying documentation relating to these accounts. Mr Hudson explained to Mr Scargill the format and layout that he thought should be used to prepare such accounts and suggested that they should also be audited by a professional firm of Accountants. Subsequently, it appears that Mrs Riley was requested by Mr Scargill to assist in the preparation of the accounts in the form suggested by Mr Hudson, during November and December 1989. This work was completed in January 1990.

ANNEXE J

Disclosure to Peats, Leeds

Mr Hudson recommended Mr Scargill contact Mr Richmond of Peats Leeds, to arrange for the accounts to be audited. Mr Hudson told Mr Lightman that he considered it important for the accounts to be examined by the NUM's auditors, Peats, and suggested Mr Richmond because he was known to Mr Scargill, having been responsible for the audit of the NUM Yorkshire area whilst Mr Scargill had been President of NUM Yorkshire. Mr Scargill, Mr Hudson and Mr Richmond met to discuss the work that could be undertaken by Peats, Leeds in relation to these accounts. Mr Hudson told Mr Lightman that at this meeting Mr Scargill told Mr Richmond that he believed Mr Windsor was talking to a national newspaper and that information relating to the unofficial accounts might be published and that it was important to have the records of these accounts examined. Mr Hudson told Mr Lightman that Mr Richmond explained to Mr Scargill that it would be almost impossible for a statutory audit of the accounts to be completed and that the best option was for Peats, Leeds to complete an accountant's review.

Accountant's Reports prepared by Peats, Leeds

The report presented to the NEC dated 9 March 1990 stated that "all of the accounts for which we (Mr Scargill and Mr Heathfield) were signatories or trustees have been examined by Messrs Peat Marwick McLintock (Peats, Leeds) and they have confirmed in relation to each and overall, that every receipt and every payment has been in accordance with the books and records of each individual trust fund". Cork Gully contacted Peats, Leeds who agreed to co-operate with the enquiry and make their files available. It should be noted that Peats, Leeds were only provided with records relating to eleven accounts. The records relating to the APEX account (number 10 in Annexe I), Tom Sibley account (number 11 in Annexe I, which was effectively dormant) and the MIREDS account (number 14(a) in Annexe I) were not examined by Peats, Leeds. In addition, the records of the other three accounts which were brought to Cork Gully's attention by Mr Scargill were also not examined by Peats nor reported to the NEC in the National Official's Report of 9 March 1990.

It is important to understand that Peats, Leeds told Mr Scargill that it was not possible to perform an audit of the eleven accounts. They were not required nor did they attempt to determine whether or not the receipts and payments, as presented in the records provided to them, had occurred. They were not required to express an opinion on the records of each account. Their engagement was a different type of accounting assignment from the annual audit of the NUM's financial records undertaken by Peats, Sheffield and simply required the agreement of the entries appearing on the summary receipts and payments schedules to the supporting records.

ANNEXE J

Incomplete Documentation relating to the Unofficial Accounts of the NUM

The records provided to Cork Gully by Mr Scargill were compared to the records held by Peats, Leeds to ensure that complete copies of all records available had been provided to Cork Gully. What, in practice, Cork Gully assume Mr Richmond was telling Mr Scargill when talking about a statutory audit is that it was not possible to give an unqualified "audit" opinion to confirm the accuracy and completeness of the transactions. Cork Gully consider that it is not possible to give an unqualified opinion, pointing to the following matters inter alia:

(a) **Completeness of Income**

(i) The MACF is a cash fund which appears to have operated without financial controls and for which the records are incomplete. It would be difficult, if not impossible, for an auditor to report on cash transactions undertaken four or five years ago for which the records are incomplete.

(ii) In order to substantiate some entries in the MACF records, reliance on the co-operation of third parties who were involved in the transactions recorded in the MACF, would be required. Some of the parties identified refused to co-operate with this enquiry.

(iii) Some transactions recorded in the bank accounts are not supported by documentation and cannot be substantiated.

(b) **Specific Inaccuracies in records**

(i) Mr Scargill, Mr Heathfield and Mr Hudson have confirmed that some signed documentation, supporting transactions recorded in the MACF's records are falsely dated, which must raise doubts about the accuracy of other entries in the MACF records.

(ii) There are inconsistencies between entries appearing on the detailed narrative schedule and entries appearing on the summary receipts and payments schedule of the MACF. As the purpose of the narrative schedule is simply to provide more detail to the entries appearing on the summary schedule, the monetary amounts appearing in the schedules should be identical. Mr Scargill has told Cork Gully that the narrative schedule is more likely to be correct. If this is the case, the cash balance of £573.96 as reported on the summary schedule provided to Cork Gully would require a net reduction of £3,103.23 resulting in a "negative" cash balance of £2,529.27 (ie cash payments

200

<u>**ANNEXE J**</u>

are greater than the cash that was available to make the payments). The inconsistencies between the summary and narrative schedules demonstrates that the MACF's records are inaccurate

(iii) One entry appearing on the summary schedule of the MACF relates to a receipt of £14.32 reportedly received when account number 6 in Annexe I was closed in October 1989. This account was not in fact closed until April 1990, after the MACF summary and narrative schedules were prepared. The entry in the MACF records is incorrect as the money was not received from account number 6.

(iv) Some entries appearing in the MACF records are not supported by underlying documentation. Other entries in these records are supported by receipts, signed in 1989, relating to transactions which occurred in 1987. A number of other entries in the MACF records can only be supported by Mr Scargill's recollection of events.

(v) A number of transactions recorded on the bank statements, particularly the SWAG account as referred to in Annexe K, were undertaken in order to withdraw cash from the bank accounts. Although Cork Gully are able to agree the closing bank balances, some of the records recording the purposes for which the cash was applied consist of hand written memorandums. These transactions are not supported by third party receipts. In the case of the SWAG account there is an apparent difference of £29,669.73 between the records of the Finance Department and the SWAG account, relating to monies received in cash and recorded by the Finance Department, not recorded in the SWAG account.

Conclusion

Cork Gully consider that the records made available to them in relation to the unofficial accounts are incomplete and contain inaccuracies. These inaccuracies are described in more detail in Part III of this Annexe. The records are such that without placing reliance on a number of third parties and without receiving the co-operation of those third parties, it is impossible to substantiate a number of entries appearing in these records. As a number of these accounts received and paid monies for the benefit of the NUM, it is reasonable to have expected the people involved in the operation of these accounts, to all intents and purposes Mr Scargill, to have maintained complete records which would be to the satisfaction of the NUM. The operation of a simple cash receipts and payments memorandum, recording each transaction as it is undertaken and retaining supporting documentation, would have enabled the account operator to ascertain what had happened to the monies passing through the account. The records provided to Cork Gully do not allow this exercise to be completed.

Mr Scargill has explained that a typed list detailing the receipts and payments of the MACF was stolen in July 1989. Accepting that this list was stolen, Cork Gully confirm that the records relating to the bank accounts did not contain an analysis of receipts and payments which had been prepared on a regular basis.

Part II Loans and Donations

Work undertaken by Cork Gully

Cork Gully considered that for the purposes of this enquiry, it was important to determine the accuracy, as far as possible, of the entries in the records of the seventeen accounts. In order to determine the accuracy, it was first necessary to identify and remove all of the transactions simply moving money from one account to another. Cork Gully then attempted to identify those transactions relating to the movement of funds outside of the pool of accounts and contact those third parties identified as being involved in the payment or receipt of those funds.

As stated in paragraph 56 of the report, during the strike and the receivership period two British trade unions made funds available to the NUM, through NUM Scotland area and other British trade unions advanced monies direct to the National Officials. In addition a number of receipts were recorded as being provided by overseas trade unions.

British Trade Unions

NUM Scotland area provided Cork Gully with detailed documentation relating to the funds it received and paid to the National Officials and three area offices. Cork Gully corresponded with the three area offices and received co-operation from all of them. Monies routed through NUM Scotland area and received by the National Officials were provided by two British trade unions. Cork Gully noted that although there were differences between NUM Scotland areas' records and the NUM records in relation to the dates and amounts of advances it received from NUM Scotland, the total amount advanced was agreed as £363,578.93. The National Officials received these monies out of a total of £1,100,000 paid to the NUM Scotland area by the two trade unions, the balance of which was distributed to the three area offices. One of the trade unions provided documentation to Cork Gully confirming that the monies were advanced to NUM Scotland in the form of interest free loans. The loans were repayable in five equal annual instalments commencing on a date twelve months after the finalisation of the 1984/85 Industrial

ANNEXE J

Dispute. There does not appear to be any documentation detailing the terms on which the NUM Scotland area advanced the monies which were received in the MACF and SWAG accounts. Mr Scargill has explained that the advances from NUM Scotland were in accordance with a "gentleman's agreement". Both of these trade unions confirmed to Cork Gully that the amounts they provided during the period of the miners strike and receivership had been repaid and Cork Gully traced the amounts and dates of repayment to the records of the unofficial accounts. Thus, the monies received through NUM Scotland were repaid direct to these trade unions and not via NUM Scotland. The only amount which could not be traced to the unofficial accounts was a repayment of £523.93 apparently made on 29 November 1989. Mr Scargill has told Cork Gully that he does not know where the monies used to make this repayment came from.

Excluding the monies routed through NUM Scotland area referred to above, a number of loans and donations appeared in the records provided to Cork Gully. As a result of these entries, Cork Gully corresponded with five British trade unions, including one of the two unions referred to in the paragraph above. Three of the unions replied. Two of the unions confirmed that they had provided the monies recorded in the NUM unofficial accounts as being received from them. One of these trade unions, confirmed that the monies made available by them was in the form a of loan. Another of the trade unions confirmed that an amount of £50,000 provided by them was a donation. The other trade union which replied provided information which does not agree with the records of the unofficial accounts and is referred to in detail in Annexe K. The other two unions did not reply to Cork Gully's request for assistance and accordingly the amounts attributed as being received from these two unions could not be verified with their records.

The NUM loan and repayment details as set out in Annexe L confirm that an apparent overpayment of £28,760.63 was made to a trade union in relation to the loans made direct to the NUM.

Overseas Monies

The receipts attributed to overseas trade unions are believed to have been donations. As shown by the table set out in paragraph 114 monies were recorded in the MACF records as being received from the CGT, Bulgarian and Czechoslovakian trade unions. Cork Gully wrote to the three overseas unions concerned but did not receive a reply to their requests for assistance. Without the co-operation of these three trade unions, Cork Gully are unable to substantiate the amounts attributed to these trade unions.

As reported in paragraph 117, Cork Gully identified six receipts totalling £1,404,616 received in the MIREDS account between February 1985 and December 1985. The

ANNEXE J

Irish Intercontinental Bank, at which this account was operated, confirmed to Cork Gully that these lodgements were received from a bank in Austria by order of "Internationale Solidaritaet Prag". Cork Gully wrote to the bank in question requesting confirmation of the source of these monies. The bank replied by letter dated 20 June 1990 and said "by consultation (with) the account holder we have to inform you that we are not allowed to give you any information about the questioned transfers" (Annexe N). Without receiving the co-operation of the account holder, Cork Gully are unable to substantiate the origin of these funds.

Part III - Memorandum on inconsistency in records and monies which do not appear to have been recorded

(a)   Documentation provided to Cork Gully by an NUM area confirmed that the area received a total of £32,000.00 during the period November 1984 to January 1985 from the NUM's offices in Sheffield. Cork Gully have been unable to trace these monies in the records of the unofficial accounts. As noted in paragraph 109 Mr Scargill told Mr Lightman that he believed that monies were paid to area unions from funds which he had collected but which had not been recorded in the records of the MACF. Cork Gully noted that the Finance Department's records detail payments to the area concerned of £38,000.00 in the corresponding period, which does not appear in the MACF records and which may relate to the £32,000.00 apparently received by the area from the NUM.

(b)   Mr Scargill has told Mr Lightman that the IMO account, which is shown as number 13(a) in Annexe I and is operated with a bank in Austria, was opened at the request of the IMO to hold monies for emergency use. On 15 April 1987 £37,116.04 was deposited in cash, into this account. Mr Scargill has told Cork Gully that this deposit included the balance of monies he had received from the APEX account following its closure in December 1985, believed to have been £17,307.30 according to the APEX account records. Mr Scargill has told Cork Gully that part of the APEX account monies he received in December 1985 were used to purchase two cars for area officials in February 1986. Following the discharge of the Receiver in July 1986 a cheque drawn on an NUM bank account was paid to the motor company. The motor company cashed the cheque and returned the cash to Mr Scargill as the cars had previously been paid for in February 1986, using cash taken from the APEX account monies held by Mr Scargill. Approximately eight months elapsed between Mr Scargill receiving cash from the motor company and these monies being deposited into the IMO account in April 1987. Mr Scargill has told Cork Gully that he teemed and laded these monies during the eight month period prior to depositing them into the IMO account. This practice is referred to in paragraph 109. Mr Scargill

ANNEXE J

also told Cork Gully that an amount of £6,035.71, the balance of an £85,000 donation by IMO by the Miners Solidarity Fund, was given to him by the Finance Department on 29 July 1986. This is confirmed by the Finance Departments records. This amount also formed part of the £37,116.04 deposited into the IMO account in April 1987. Cork Gully consider that part of the £37,116.04 deposited into the IMO account on 15 April 1987 belonged to the NUM. Records relating to this deposit are incomplete but Mr Scargill's explanation appears to confirm that it contained NUM monies. It would appear that part of this deposit should be repaid by the IMO to the NUM.

(c)   In addition to the discrepancies referred to under the heading "Specific inaccuracies in records" in part I of this Annexe, the following inconsistencies were also found in the MACF records:

   (i)   A payment of £100,000 is recorded as having been made to the special account (MIREDS) via a trade union on 21 January 1985. This trade union has provided documentation to Cork Gully confirming that it only received £98,500 from Mr Scargill, although Mr Scargill has presented Cork Gully with a hand written receipt confirming that he passed £100,000 to the trade union representative.

   (ii)   As set out in Annex M, it appears that approximately £70,000 was deposited into the MIREDS account which cannot be traced to the records of the unofficial accounts, although it almost certainly originated from monies which should have been held in these accounts.

(d)   As noted in the section titled "British Trade Unions" in this annexe, an amount of £523.93 was received by a trade union but cannot be traced to the records of the unofficial accounts. A total amount of £28,571.63 (Annexe L) cannot be traced to the records of the APEX account although these monies were collected by representatives of the NUM for deposit into this account and have been repaid to the trade union which made the funds available. An amount of £189 (Annexe L) has also been identified as being repaid to a trade union although no record of this advance can be found in the APEX account. A further difference of £523.73 is identified in the APEX account records (Annexe K).

(e)   As noted in Annexe K, there is a difference of £29,669.73 recorded as received by the Finance Department from the SWAG account but which cannot be traced to the SWAG account records. A further difference of £154.64 has been identified relating to monies received from an unknown source.

ANNEXE K

THE SHEFFIELD WOMENS ACTION GROUP AND APEX
HALLAM WELFARE ASSOCIATION ACCOUNTS

Sheffield Womens Action Group Account("SWAG")

Of the total monies agreed as routed to the NUM through NUM Scotland area, being £363,578.93, a total of £193,475.70 was received by SWAG. According to records maintained by the Finance Department, this account provided £211,850.39 to the Finance Department to be used in payment of NUM creditors.

The records relating to this account include a receipt of £5,154.64 attributed to a British trade union. The trade union confirmed to Cork Gully that on approximately the date on which the receipt appeared in the records, a cash payment of £5,000.00 was made to Mr Scargill. According to the trade union, this payment was made to purchase the TUC Congress Bell which had previously been donated to the NUM, but was apparently intended to benefit the striking miners. There remains an unidentified receipt of £154.64.

The source of donations for £1,000.00 and £9,000.00 have not been substantiated although these receipts have been agreed to the bank statements for the SWAG account.

According to the records provided to Cork Gully cheques totalling £737,437.25 were presented to the bank in order to obtain cash. Cork Gully have agreed with the bank statements and other schedules that cheques with a value of £737,437.25 appear to have been cashed during the period 6 February 1985 to 24 October 1989. However, Cork Gully believe that there are other entries which appear on the bank statements which must have been the withdrawal of cash, although these entries are not listed on the schedule provided to them detailing the cash withdrawals according to the cheque book records. As stated above, it appears that £211,850.39 was provided to the Finance Department to be used to pay NUM creditors. Cork Gully have identified £94,606.16 as having been paid from the SWAG account to the Finance Department. This leaves a balance of £117,244.23 (£211,850.39 less £94,606.16) which, according to the Finance Department records was provided to the Finance Department from the SWAG account. These funds were provided to the Finance Department by obtaining cash from the account and passing it to a member of the Finance Department. Cork Gully have identified a total amount of £87,574.50 which would appear to have been provided to a member of the Finance Department in this manner. This would leave an amount of £29,669.73 (£117,244.23 less £87,574.50)which the Finance Department believes it received from the SWAG account but which cannot be accurately identified as originating from this account. In addition, as stated above, there appear to be a number of cash withdrawals from this account for which there is no documentation explaining how the cash was spent.

ANNEXE K

APEX Hallam Welfare Association Account

The account signatories were Mr Clapham and Ms Ashton. The account's main function was to receive monies from one particular trade union in order to pay NUM staff wages, expenses and some creditors. These monies were advanced by the trade union in the form of interest free loans, with repayment to be made in five equal amounts on an annual basis commencing one year after the date on which the monies were loaned. Documentation provided by the trade union to Cork Gully recorded an amount of £125,756.00 as having been made available to the APEX account over a five month period. The bank statements for the APEX account confirm that a total of £97,184.37, received from the trade union, was deposited into the account. The difference is a shortfall of £28,571.63. (Annexe L)

Records maintained by the Finance Department during the period of the strike and receivership show that payments totalling £432,109.47 were made in cash by the Finance Department and that a total of £406,953.62 was received from the MACF (£195,103.23) and SWAG (£211,850.39) to fund these payments. If the records detailing the payments are correct, an amount of £25,155.85 (£432,109.47 less £406,953.62) must have been received in order for sufficient cash to be held to enable the payments to have been made. It is possible that £28,571.63, made available by the trade union referred to above for the APEX account, was spent by the Finance Department but not recorded as being received from the trade union. A further £523.73 is believed to have been deposited into the APEX account from an unknown source.

An amount of £130,000.00 was repaid to the trade union in question on 21 July 1988 (Annexe L). Of this amount, £125,945.00 was in repayment of the monies provided to the APEX account during 1985. This is a difference between the monies received and repaid by the NUM of £189.00 (£125,945 less £125,756) referred to in Annexe L.

207

ANNEXE L

LOAN AND REPAYMENT DETAILS

Receipts

Date £	Trade Union A £	Trade Union B £	Trade Union C £
18.12.84		55,000.00	
22.01.85			200,000.00(b)
23.01.85	5,000.00		
30.01.85	45,000.00		
06.02.85	35,000.00		
13.02.85	58,000.00		
19.02.85	32,000.00		
27.02.85	25,000.00		
06.03.85	23,103.23		
14.03.85	25,000.00		
15.03.85	30,475.70		
04.06.85	30,000.00		
24.07.85	19,189.00		
23.08.85	19,000.00		
25.07.85	19,131.52		
23.11.85	19,248.85		
20.11.85	20,615.00		
29.11.85			
Total Receipts	**£405,763.30**	**£55,000.00**	**£200,000.00**

Analysis

MACF	115,103.23	55,000.00	200,000.00
SWAG	193,475.70		
APEX	97,184.37		
	£405,763.30	**£55,000.00**	**£200,000.00**

ANNEXE L

Payments

Date	Trade Union A £	Trade Union B £	Trade Union C £
20.06.88		10,000.00	
21.07.88		15,000.00	
21.07.88	125,945.00		
21.07.88	4,055.00		
25.07.88		30,000.00	
17.03.89			
24.10.89	1,700.00		
24.10.89	243,300.00		
24.10.89	59,000.00		
20.12.89			200,000.00
Total Payments	434,000.00	55,000.00	200,000.00
Difference	28,236.70(a)	Nil	Nil

Notes

(a) The difference of £28,236.70, representing an apparent over-payment to Trade Union A, consists of:

	£
Funds not deposited in Apex account	28,571.63 (See Annexe K)
Difference in repayment to union in July 1988 of £125,945 less £125,756 received during Receivership	189.00
	28,760.63
Less:	
Repayment recorded by Trade Union A on 28 November 1989 not found in unofficial accounts	(523.93)
	£28,236.70

(b) The trade union purported to have advanced these monies to the NUM did not respond to Cork Gully's request for information.

ANNEXE M

TRANSFER OF MONIES FROM MACF

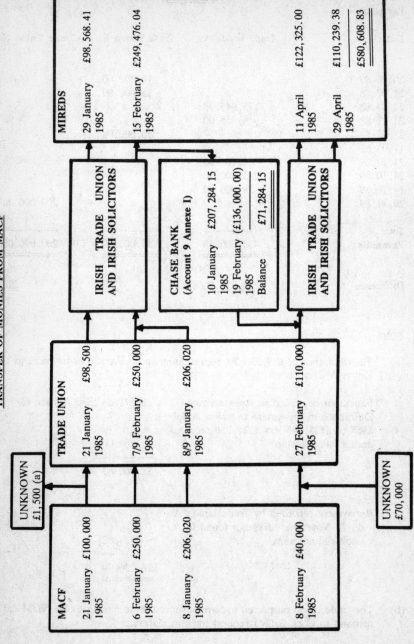

MACF			**MIREDS**
21 January 1985	£100,000	29 January 1985	£98,568.41
6 February 1985	£250,000	15 February 1985	£249,476.04
8 January 1985	£206,020	11 April 1985	£122,325.00
8 February 1985	£40,000	29 April 1985	£110,239.38
			£580,608.83

TRADE UNION
21 January 1985 £98,500
7/9 February 1985 £250,000
8/9 January 1985 £206,020
27 February 1985 £110,000

IRISH TRADE UNION AND IRISH SOLICITORS

CHASE BANK (Account 9 Annexe I)
10 January 1985 £207,284.15
19 February 1985 (£136,000.00)
Balance £71,284.15

UNKNOWN £1,500 (a)

UNKNOWN £70,000

210

ANNEXE M

TRANSFER OF MONIES FROM MACF

Notes:

Monies were withdrawn from the MACF and passed to a British trade union which arranged for the monies to be transferred to a trade union in Ireland. The monies received by the trade union in Ireland were converted from £ sterling to Irish £ and deposited into an Irish solicitors' client account. The solicitor then made arrangements for the monies to be deposited into the MIREDS account. Allowing for exchange differences arising on the currency conversion and bank charges incurred during these transactions, the following discrepancies were noted:

(a) The MACF records show £100,000 was paid to the British trade union on 21 January 1985. The trade unions records show that only £98,500 was received, a difference of £1,500.

(b) The MACF records show that £40,000 was paid by Mr Scargill to Ms Myers on 8 February 1985, for deposit into the MIREDS account presumably via the trade unions and Irish solicitor. This money does not appear in the British trade unions records as being received for deposit into the MIREDS account. Ms Myers was unable to remember details relating to this transaction. However, the trade unions records refer to two amounts being received totalling £111,900.99 in February 1985. The trade union issued a cheque for £110,000.00 which was paid to the trade union in Ireland and appears to have been deposited into the MIREDS account. If the trade unions records are correct and if the deposits into the MIREDS account are to be fully accounted for, it would appear that £110,000 was combined with £136,000, already held by the trade union in Ireland and, after an exchange loss of £13,346 arising from the change in the currency conversion rate between February and April 1985, deposits of £122,325 and £110,239 were made into the MIREDS account in April 1985. Assuming that the British trade union received £111,900.99 as described above, approximately £70,000 must have been added to the £40,000 withdrawn from the MACF on 8 February 1985, and paid to the trade union, resulting in the receipt of £111,900.99 referred to above.

Cork Gully have been unable to trace a withdrawal of £70,000 in the records of the unofficial accounts.

ANNEXE N

LETTER FROM BANK FUR ARBEIT UND WIRTSCHAFT VIENNA

BANK FÜR ARBEIT UND WIRTSCHAFT | BAWAG

AKTIENGESELLSCHAFT
ZWEIGSTELLE WALLENSTEINSTRASSE

Cork Gully

Shelley House 3 Noble Street
London EC2V 7DQ
GREAT BRITAIN

Telefon: (0 22 2) 35 53 83, 35 53 86
Bankleitzahl: 14000
Telegrammadresse: Bawagbank Wien
Nationalbankgirokonto: 1-2140-1
Postsparkassenkonto: 4.318.932
DVR: 0041050

1200 Wien, Wallensteinstraße 1

Ihre Zeichen	Ihre Nachricht vom	Unsere Zeichen	den
David Brookland	1.Juni 1990	Pe/bm	20.6.90

BETREFF:
National Union of Mineworkers
Transfers to the account of Alain Simon
Norman West

Dear Sirs,

We refer to your letter of 1 June 1990. By consultation the account holder
we have to inform you that we are not allowed to give you any informations
about the questioned transfers.

Yours faithfully,

BANK FÜR ARBEIT UND WIRTSCHAFT
AKTIENGESELLSCHAFT
Zweigstelle Wallensteinstraße 1

213

ANNEXE O

MINUTES OF MEETINGS OF NATIONAL EXECUTIVE COMMITTEE AND FINANCE AND GENERAL PURPOSES COMMITTEE

Publisher's Note

In the report submitted by Mr Lightman to the National Executive Committee the following documents were photocopies of original material. Because the quality of the photocopies made them unsuitable for photographic reproduction, they have been retyped. The retyped documents are faithful and accurate copies of the originals.

8. PROVISION FOR NATIONAL OFFICIALS UPON RETIREMENT

Reference was made to the differing procedure in the past in the provisions made for National Officials upon their retirement. The view was expressed that some standard provisions should be made, which would apply to all National Officials irrespective of circumstances or personalities.

It was pointed out that the finding of suitable living accommodation could be a problem, as some National Officials might not wish to continue living in London after their retirement. In addition it was suggested that any ex-gratia payment to be made should have due regard to service to the Union.

It was **agreed**:

"We recommend that upon retirement, National Officials shall be given the option of:-

(i) Remaining in their residence at an annual rental equal to 2% of the capital outlay on the property (exclusive of rates), or

(ii) Living in another property of comparable value (purchased by the Union) at an annual rental equal to 2% of the capital outlay on the property (exclusive of rates), or

(iii) Purchasing his present residence from the Union at the book value of the property at the date of retirement."

Note: In the case of options (i) and (ii), it is intended that whichever is chosen should apply to the widow (during her widowhood) of a National Official."

It was also **agreed**:

"That we recommend that an ex-gratia payment equivalent to two years pension shall be paid to a National Official upon his retirement."

NATIONAL EXECUTIVE COMMITTEE, 12 OCTOBER 1967

5. FINANCE

It was reported that a meeting of the Finance and General Purposes Sub-Committee had been held on the 11th October, 1967. The minutes of the meeting had been circulated for the information of Committee members (see Appendix I).

It was **agreed**:

"That the report be accepted and approved."

(a) Provision for Officials on Retirement

Reference was then made to the provision which had been made for National Officials on retirement (see Appendix I - Minute 8) and it was suggested that an examination should be made into the cost involved in making some provision for all N.U.M. Officials.

1   (d) 21 Eversley Avenue, Wembley
Consideration was given to a request from Mr. A. L. Horner that the Union
should bear the cost, estimated at £29 10s. 0d., of alterations and
replacements to the outside w.c. at the above address.
   It was **agreed**:
      "That this expenditure be approved."

FINANCE SUB-COMMITTEE, [?] OCTOBER 1968 [precise date obscured]

(a) Depreciation
Consideration was given to a suggestion from the Head Office Auditors that
the Committee should review the question of whether the annual charge for
depreciation in the annual Accounts should be discontinued. It was pointed
out that, although property values had risen steadily over the last twenty
years, there was no question of the Accounts being misleading as the cost
prices of property and the total amount written off were clearly set out in
the Balance Sheet and Property schedule attached thereto.
   It was **agreed**:
      "That capital expenditure on Union owned propertoes be depreciated at
      5% per annum on the depreciated value for the first ten years and
      thereafter at 2½% per annum."
   It was also **agreed**:
      "That this decision shall apply retrospectively."

(b) Valuation of Properties
Consideration was given to the question of whether it was necessary to
revalue the Union owned properties in view of the fact that the disposal of
any such property would, in all probability, attract a liability for Capital
Gains Tax and that such tax was payable on the difference between the open
market value at 5th April, 1965 and at the date of sale.
   It was **agreed**:
      "That a professional valuation of all Union owned properties at 5th
      April, 1965 be arranged."

(c) 21, Eversley Avenue, Wembley Park
The National Officials reported they had been informed by the executors
of the late Mr. A. L. Horner, that this property would, in all probability,
be vacated early in November, 1968.
   It was **agreed**:
      "That the National Officials be empowered to act in connection with the
      sale of the property."

(d) 32, Broadfields Avenue, Edgware
It was reported that certain expenditure on repairs and decoration, which
should more correctly have been charged to revenue, had been charged against
the capital cost of the property.
   It was **agreed**:
      "That the necessary adjustment be made in the Head Office accounts."

3. N.U.M. PROPERTIES
   (a) 32 Broadfields Avenue, Edgware
   It was reported that, in accordance with the decision of the National Executive Committee on 12th October, 1967, Mr. W. Paynter had exercised his option to purchase the above property and that the transfer had now been completed.
   It was **agreed**:
   "That the sale of this property be noted."

   (b) 22 Gloucester Drive, Staines
   Consideration was given to a request for the installation of a solid fuel housewarming system in the above property at a cost of £446.
   It was **agreed**:
   "That permission be given and the rent increased by £12 5s. 3d. per annum."
   It was also **agreed**:
   "That immediate attention be given to the drawing up of tenancy agreements in respect of the houses owned by the Union and occupied by staff."

FINANCE SUB-COMMITTEE, 8 JANUARY 1969

2. ACCOMMODATION FOR SECRETARY

   The Secretary reported that he had inspected various properties and had obtained the option to purchase a house at Boxmoor, Hertfordshire.
   It was **agreed**:
   "That this property be purchased, subject to a satisfactory Surveyor's report, at a cost of £11,000 freehold."

FINANCE AND GENERAL PURPOSES SUB-COMMITTEE, 14 MAY 1969

1. STAFF HOUSES

   It was reported that four properties had been purchased for the accommodation of staff members prior to the decision of the National Executive Committee to grant mortgages to employees at an interest rate of 2½ per cent per annum. Three of these properties were let (exclusive of rates) at an annual rental based on a return of 2¾ per cent of the purchase price (including improvements). (See N.E.C. 8th and 9th November, 1946 - Appendix III - Minute (5); N.E.C. 23rd June, 1949 - Appendix XI - Minute (9); N.E.C. 11th June 1959 - Appendix IX - Minute 6(b).)
   The rent of the remaining property (56 Shirlock Road, London N.W.3) was calculated on a higher basis, in view of the age and condition of the property

and the fact that the premises were, in effect, made up into three flats, two of which were sub-let. (See N.E.C. 22nd March, 1956 - Appendix VIII - Minute 10(b).)

On 14th May, 1964 (see N.E.C. 14th May, 1964 - Appendix VI - Minute 4(e)) the National Executive Committee decided to terminate the existing tenancies and that fresh tenancy agreements should be drawn up. Six months' notice to terminate was served on the tenants on 30th June, 1964, but no further action was taken.

It was suggested that the present rentals could apply whilst the staff concerned were still employed by the Union, but that provision should be made for an economic rent to be charged upon leaving the Union's service. Our Solicitors had advised that it would be preferable for agreements to be drawn up for the reduced rent to be payable whilst staff were employed by the Union and that provisions should be made for termination of the agreement when the person concerned left the Union's service. This would remove any question of implied tenancy after this event and it would then be up to the Union to decide whether a fresh agreement should be drawn up or whether the property should be vacated.

Three of the staff members concerned are still in the employ of the Union, but the occupier of 56 Shirlock Road (Mr. W. H. Williams) retired on pension on 18th January, 1965 and he had continued to pay the same rent. It was pointed out that no agreement was in existence as to tenancy should Mr. Williams predecease his wife and also that the Union could be left in the position of becoming landlord to two sitting tenants in the event of the death of both Mr. Williams and his wife. Our Solicitors had advised that Mr. Williams' tenancy was excluded from the Rent Act, whereas the sub-tenants enjoyed the protection of the Act. A small increase in the rent paid by Mr. Williams would give him the protection of the Act. There is no way of contracting out of the Rent Act and upon the death of a tenant, the tenancy can pass to a dependant who lived with the tenant and upon the death of such dependant can pass once again. However, the two sub-tenants are living alone and if this state of affairs continues, their tenancies will come to an end at their deaths.

It was **agreed**:
"That

(a) The Union's Solicitors be instructed to prepare agreements in respect of the houses occupied by existing staff members. Such agreements to provide for the payment of the nominal rentals already approved by the National Executive Committee whilst the persons concerned were in the Union's service but that provision should be made for the fixing of an economic rental when they left the Union's employment.

(b) The employees concerned be given the option to purchase the properties in which they reside at a price calculated on the same basis as that used in a similar case on 15th October, 1963.

(c) The Union's Solicitors be instructed to draw up an agreement for the whole property with the tenant of 56 Shirlock Road restricting his right to re-let unfurnished and that enquiries should be made as to the possibility of selling this property."

3. N.U.M. PROPERTIES
    (a) "Glencraig", Hempstead Lane, Berkhamsted
    It was reported that the purchase of a residence for the Secretary had now been completed.
    It was **agreed**:
    "That the completion be noted and a rent of £91 17s. 4d. per annum be payable as from 1st August, 1969."

    (b) 56 Shirlock Road, London, N.W.3
    Further to the decision of the Committee (see N.E.C. 12th June, 1969 - Appendix VII - Minute 1) it was reported that this property had now been sold to the tenant for £3,300.
    It was **agreed**:
    "That this sale be noted."

FINANCE SUB-COMMITTEE, 8 APRIL 1982

3. NATIONAL PRESIDENT

    Following a detailed discussion, it was **agreed**:
    "That all allowances and facilities accorded to the previous President should apply to the new President as and from 5th April, 1982, and that the arrangements and allowances in respect of his own home in Yorkshire - currently borne by the Yorkshire Area - be paid in future by the National Union."

    In furtherance of Minute 1 of the Finances and General Purposes Sub-Committee held on 21st December, 1981, it was **agreed**:
    "That Mr. Scargill be authorised to rent or to purchase suitable accommodation in Inner London, in consultation with the Vice-President, Secretary and Trustees of the National Union."

    It was also **agreed**:
    "That the President:
    (i) be allowed to purchase equipment and furniture, etc., as and when necessary for the National Office;
    (ii) extend hospitality to any visitors or guests, and this to be a legitimate charge on the General Fund."

7. PRESIDENT'S ACCOMMODATION

The President reported that he had been able to rent a flat owned by the local authority in Central London. The Officials and Trustees had approved the acquisition of this flat on a rental basis subject to an inspection. It was reported that there was no floor covering, etc., and it was **agreed**:
"That the Union would provide basic furnishing."

NATIONAL EXECUTIVE COMMITTEE, 15 JULY 1982

It was **agreed**:
"That the report be noted, the action of the President endorsed, and the correspondence circulated to members of the National Executive Committee for their information."

15. T.U.C. INDUSTRIAL TRAINING CONFERENCE

The Committee had before them an invitation from the T.U.C. to send three delegates to a Conference to be held on the 24th August, 1982 regarding the Manpower Services Commission Youth Task Group Report and to assist the General Council to assess the various options open to Unions regarding the youth training scheme and the new training initiative, i.e., the divergence in the attitudes expressed by the Government in their recent White Paper on youth training and those of the Manpower Services Commission.
It was **agreed**:
"That the Union be represented by Mr. W. Chambers (N.E.C.), Mr. K. Richards, M.I.F. Youth Representative and Mr. R. Austin, Scottish Area Youth Representative."

16. SOUTH AFRICA - FOOTBALL TEAM

Reference was made to the forthcoming tour of South Africa of a football team, and it was **agreed**:
"That the National Executive Committee express its opposition to this tour and condemns all individuals and administrators involved."

17. UNION HEADQUARTERS

The recommendations of the Organisation Sub-Committee and the Finance and General Purposes Sub-Committee relating to Resolution 8 carried by the Annual Conference were put before the meeting (see Appendix II - Minute 2 and Appendix III - Minute 1) and it was **agreed**:

"That the Committee would examine the various proposals contained in the document prepared by the National President and take a decision as to where the new headquarters should be located before the end of the meeting."

After the Committee had examined the document, there was a discussion on the various options, and it was **agreed**:

"(i)   That the Union should build its new National Headquarters in Sheffield and that the offer made by Sheffield City Council be accepted.

(ii)   That the National Officials be given plenary powers to sell the present National Headquarters at 222 Euston Road at the highest price, taking into account the valuation.

(iii)   That the Officials be given authority to rent temporary accommodation (if necessary) in Sheffield, in the event of the Union having to vacate the present premises at 222 Euston Road before our new building is completed."

NATIONAL EXECUTIVE COMMITTEE, 16 SEPTEMBER 1982

3.   POINT OF AYR LIQUEFACTION

Concern was expressed at the apparent failure to make any real progress on this matter, and it was explained that a meeting had been arranged with the Board, but had had to be postponed because of the Day of Action on the 22nd September, 1982. Alternative dates were being sought as a matter of urgency. In the meantime, pressure was being continued both through the Fuel and Power Committee of the T.U.C. and with the Board directly as the previous report had indicated (see N.E.C. 15th July, 1982 - Minute 2); according to the Government the problems were of a technical nature and not financial, whereas the Board were contending that the problem was a financial one.

It was proposed that the Officials should ascertain from the Board whether there were any technical difficulties, and if so were they causing the Board to have second thoughts. Having ascertained the facts, the Union could then raise the question of financial support with the Government.

It was **agreed**:

"That the report be accepted, and an early meeting arranged with the Board."

4.   TRIPLE ALLIANCE

In response to a question arising from the previous minutes (see N.E.C. 15th July, 1982 - Minute 3) the President explained that little progress had been made regarding a meeting under the Triple Alliance. We in fact had asked for such a meeting in May, and were still awaiting a positive reply. However, the National Officials had informally talked to the Secretary of the Iron and Steel Trades Confederation, and in principle it had been agreed that there would be a meeting of the National Officials of the Triple Alliance as soon as a mutually convenient date could be fixed.

It was **agreed**:

"That the report be noted."

5. BRITANNIA COLLIERY, SOUTH WALES AREA

Further to the previous decision (see N.E.C. 15th July, 1982 - Minute 12) it was explained that the Board had been asked for a meeting and had indicated that they would communicate with us when they had made further investigations. As nothing further had been heard from the Board we had again pressed for a meeting.

It was **agreed**:
"That the report be noted."

6. UNION HEADQUARTERS

Reference was made to the previous decision of the Committee (see N.E.C. 15th July, 1982 - Minute 17) when it was suggested that the matter should be referred back to the Finance and General Purposes Sub-Committee for a detailed examination regarding costs. The President pointed out that the decision to move the Office out of London had been taken by the Annual Conference and therefore constitutionally could not now be changed by the N.E.C.

Following the Annual Conference decision to move the Offices out of London, the N.E.C. had unanimously agreed to accept an offer of a prime central city site from Sheffield City Council. The National Officials had been given plenary powers to acquire the site and complete the transaction. They had also been empowered to complete negotiations for the substantial financial grants offered by both Sheffield City Council and South Yorkshire Council. The President explained that an accountant had assured the Union that there would be no problem with capital gains tax, and reminded the N.E.C. that a report had already been given on this matter to a previous N.E.C. meeting....

FINANCE AND GENERAL PURPOSES SUB-COMMITTEE, 12 JANUARY 1983

1. RETIREMENTS

As a result of the Retirement of Mr. R. A. Mansfield and Mr. A. M. Jones (Head Office Staff) and in conformity with Minute 6 of the Finance and General Purposes Sub-Committee held on 10 June, 1977.

It was **agreed**:
"That an ex-gratia payment equivalent to three years' pension be made in each case."

2. MOTOR CARS

In accordance with the agreed procedures (Minute 4 of the Finance and General Purposes Sub-Committee, 8th December, 1976) three applications to exchange vehicles were examined and approved.

3. CAR MILEAGE ALLOWANCE

Consideration was given to the effect of increased prices to present mileage allowance and it was **agreed**:

"That with effect from the 1st January, 1983 the Mileage allowance applicable to certain staff members be increased from 18p to 22p per mile."

4. REPAIRS AND DECORATIONS

"Glencraig", Hempstead Lane, Berkhamsted
It was accepted that certain renovations and repairs (including treatment for dry-rot) were necessary at the Union owned property for which estimates had been obtained in the region of £750, plus V.A.T. It was **agreed**:
"That the necessary work be authorised."

5. GRANTS AND DONATIONS

The Committee considered a number of requests which fell within the definitions of allowable grants and it was **agreed**:

"(a) Amnesty International:	Affiliation fee of £100 be paid when it becomes due.
(b) Anglo Soviet Friendship Society:	£10 affiliation fee be paid.
(c) Bertrand Russell Peace Foundation:	£50 donation to the European Nuclear Disarmament Trade Union Campaign Appeal.
(d) The British Polio Fellowship:	A donation of £100.
(e) Unity Theatre Fund:	A donation of £100."

6. OVERSEAS TRAVEL

Consideration was given to the class of air ticket which should be provided for members travelling abroad on Union business and it was **agreed**:
"That for a flight of under four hours duration an economy class ticket was appropriate, but for all flights of over four hours duration a first class or similar category (e.g. Club Class) be provided."

7. FINANCE DEPARTMENT

It was reported that a Head of Finance Department had been appointed, but he would be unable to take up his post until 1st March, 1983. Due to an acute staff shortage in the Department arrangements had been made for the temporary transfer of an existing staff member to the Department and for the retired Head of Department to work part time for a short period.

8. NATIONAL OFFICE

The President stated that a full report would be made to the National Executive Committee at its meeting tomorrow giving details of the sale of the existing National Offices, the purchase of a site in Sheffield and the acquisition of temporary accommodation.
It was **agreed**:
"That the report be accepted."

9. STAFF REDUNDANCY/TRANSFER TERMS

A full discussion took place on proposals prepared by the Office for redundancy payments and transfer terms to apply to staff when the re-location of the Headquarters took place. A number of amendments were made and it was **agreed**:

> "(i) That no details should be given about the proposals until the N.E.C. had considered the matter and taken a decision:
> (ii) that the tables of the amounts offered should not be circulated; individual members of staff would be made aware of the offer which applied to them individually and the procedure to be followed would be that which was normally observed in the Industry:
> (iii) the general structure and outline of the proposals would be given to C.O.S.A., but not the actual individual offers."

NATIONAL EXECUTIVE COMMITTEE, 13 JANUARY 1983

16. FINANCE

It was reported that a meeting of the Finance and General Purposes Sub-Committee had been held on 12th January, 1983. It was accepted that there was no requirement to increase the car mileage allowance to Officials and, subject to amendments, it was **agreed**:

> "That the report be accepted and approved (for amended Minutes see Appendix VIII)."

17. NATIONAL OFFICE

In keeping with the undertaking given to the Finance and General Purposes Sub-Committee (see Appendix VIII - Minute 8) it was reported that the National Office had been sold in accordance with the previous decision (see N.E.C. 15th July, 1982 - Minute 17(ii)). The National Officials had sold 222 Euston Road for £1,825,000 and the final documents had been signed last night, subject to the Camden Council giving a Certificate of Use from that of Trade Union building to Offices.

The present Head Office must be vacated by June 1983. Therefore temporary accommodation had been arranged in St. James House, Sheffield in keeping with the previous decision of the National Executive Committee (see N.E.C. 15th July, 1982 - Minute 17 (iii)). This was owned by the British Railways Pension Fund and had been occupied by the N.C.B. who had now vacated the premises and the rental was £2.85 per square foot (subject to periodic review).

It was **agreed**:

> "That the report be accepted and approved. That the temporary accommodation in Sheffield be properly fitted out and the move from London be made as soon as the offices are ready."

18. STAFF REDUNDANCY/TRANSFER TERMS

Consideration was given to Minute 9 of the Minutes of the Finance and General Purposes Sub-Committee held on 12th January, 1983 (see Appendix VIII) and to the proposals put forward by the Finance and General Purposes Sub-Committee. Following a full and detailed discussion, it was unanimously **agreed**:

"That:
    (i) Staff who were in employment with the N.U.M. prior to the decision of the Annual Conference (July 1982) to move out of London, be offered transfer terms basically in line with those applicable to Mineworkers:
    (ii) Members of Staff who accepted Redundancy would be paid in strict accordance with the Redundant Mineworkers Payments Scheme:
    (iii) In the case of three members of Staff who on account of age and service were entitled to weekly benefits, they be offered lump sums in lieu of weekly benefits."

19. KINNEIL COLLIERY - SCOTLAND

It was reported that a meeting had been held between representatives of the N.U.M. and the N.C.B. on Tuesday, 14th December, 1982 where the N.U.M. had pressed for the Board to continue development work at the Colliery and to work the extensive coal reserves.

The Board had replied following the meeting, informing the N.U.M. that because of severe geological difficulties, the coal reserves at Kinneil Colliery had proved to be unworkable and for this reason the Colliery should close. Alternative jobs were available for the displaced men.

It was **agreed**:
"That the Board's reply be noted."

FINANCE SUB-COMMITTEE, 13 JULY 1983

4. PROPERTY

(a) The Committee **approved** the internal and external painting of 1 Springfield Grove, Sunbury, subject to satisfactory estimates being received.

(b) Furthermore, it was **agreed** that external painting of Union houses be allowed once every three years and internal painting and decorations once every two years.

(c) **Approval** was given for Mr. A. Bulmer's (Senior Mining Engineer) residence to be converted from gas central heating to solid fuel heating, subject to satisfactory estimates being received.

7.   REPLACEMENT BUILT-IN EQUIPMENT, 1 SPRINGFIELD GROVE

It was **agreed:**
"To authorise expenditure to replace built-in equipment at the N.U.M.
property at 1 Springfield Grove, Sunbury on Thames."

FINANCE SUB-COMMITTEE, 8 FEBRUARY 1984

10. PURCHASE OF PROPERTY

It was **agreed:**
"That the National Union purchase, at sitting tenant rates, the house
occupied by Mr. Heathfield from the North Derbyshire Area."

FINANCE SUB-COMMITTEE, 7 MARCH 1984

6.   NATIONAL OFFICIALS

In accordance with the normal practice of the Uniuon, it was **agreed:**
"That the Union purchase property to provide accommodation for the
National Officials."

DELEGATION OF AUTHORITY WITH REGARD TO THE EXPENDITURE OF THE UNION

This code of authority supersedes all previous decisions and resolutions of the N.E.C. with regard to the authority to approve expenditures of the Union. Any subsequent changes in these matters shall be tabled as amendments to this code.

(a) Annual Budget of Expenditures
1. The Finance and General Purposes Sub-Committee shall approve an annual budget of expenditures of the Union in which is detailed an analysis of projected expenditures at both National and Area level. This annual budget shall include all normal recurring expenditures relating to the administration of the Union, together with other foreseeable expenditures.
2. The National Executive Committee shall adopt the Annual Budget of expenditures as recommended by the Finance and General Purposes Committee.
3. The Finance and General Purposes Sub-Committee shall receive regular reports comparing expenditure actually incurred with the adopted Annual Budget and shall bring to the attention of the National Executive Committee any major deviations.

(b) Purchase of Union Property
1. The Finance and General Purposes Sub-Committee shall approve all expenditures relating to the possible purchase of property save that the National Officials shall authorise all reasonable expenditures when any delay would be detrimental to the interests of the Union.
2. The National Executive Committee shall approve by specific resolution the purchase and disposal of any property or land.

(c) Repairs, Alterations and Improvements to Property
1. The National Officials shall approve all expenditures relating to repairs, alterations and improvements to property that is included in the Annual Budget and such other similar expenditures which arise and where any delay would be detrimental to the interests of the Union.
2. The Finance and General Purposes Sub-Committee shall approve all expenditures relating to repairs, alterations and improvements to property that have not been included in the Annual Budget subject to the provisions of paragraph C.1.

(d) Ex-gratia Payments to Staff on Retirement
1. The National Executive Committee shall approve any and all ex-gratia payments to staff employed by the Union on the occasion of their retirement and shall approve any transfer of title in a Union motor vehicle on the retirement or death of any Official.

(e) Amendment to Staff Establishment
1. The National Officials shall approve the appointment of a replacement employee to any casual vacancy.
2. The Finance and General Purposes Sub-Committee shall approve:
   (i) The creation of any new posts;
   (ii) The change of remunerative grade of any existing post;
   (iii) Any amendment of the scales of pay;
   (iv) Any changes in the terms and conditions of service.

(f) Union Motor Vehicles
1. The National Executive Committee shall determine the procedures under which Union motor vehicles shall be provided for the personal use of Officials and employees.
2. The Finance and General Purposes Committee shall approve such posts that shall attract the benefit of a Union vehicle.
3. The Finance and General Purposes Sub-Committee shall approve the replacement of any vehicle in accordance with the procedures under F.1.

(g) Donations and Grants
The Finance and General Purposes Sub-Committee shall approve all payments of grants or donations to external persons or bodies.

(h) Representation of the Union on Overseas Delegations or Visits
1. The National Executive Committee shall approve payment of expenditure to reimburse travel overseas in accordance with the procedures of the T.U.C.
2. The Finance and General Purposes Committee shall approve all amendments to that procedure as advised by the T.U.C.
3. The National Executive Committee shall approve the inclusion of individual members of an overseas delegation or visit on behalf of the Union, whether in a delegate, observer, advisory or other capacity.

(i) Guests at Annual Conference
The National Executive Committee shall approve the issue of invitations to persons to attend Annual Conference as guests of the Union.

(j) Claims for Damages at Common Law
1. All cases relating to claims for damages at Common Law shall be approved by the appropriate Area Official in accordance with the Model Rules for Areas of the N.U.M. and shall be notified to the National Office in a manner as directed.
2. The National Executive Committee shall approve all decisions to appeal against unfavourable decisions in such cases.

ANNEXE P

BANK ACCOUNT DETAILS PROVIDED BY MR SCARGILL

	Bank	Account Name	Account Number	Period for which Details Obtained
1.	Co-operative Bank Peel Street Barnsley	A Scargill	19006118	20 December 1983 - 17 February 1986
2.	Jyske Bank Foreign Department Vesterbrogade-9 Post Box 298 DK-1501 Copenhagen V Denmark	A Pickering (alias A Scargill)	5005-953-338-5 5005-953-339-3 5005-953-340-1	28 August 1984 - 31 December 1984 28 August 1984 - 31 December 1984 28 August 1984 - 31 December 1984 (Account closed during December 1984)
3.	Leeds Permanent B.S. 42 Cheapside	A Scargill A Scargill	6P/2209210 6S/470899	15 August 1978 - 8 October 1984 30 July 1976 - 2 January 1985
4.	Nationwide B.S. 4 Eldon Street Barnsley	A Scargill	820/18/608/499	14 August 1978 - 20 August 1984
5.	Bradford & Bingley B.S. 22 May Day Green Barnsley	A Scargill	46/P/385/188N	6 January 1971 - 8 October 1984
6.	Yorkshire B.S. 10 Eldon Street Barnsley	A Scargill	2075641150	19 August 1978 - 7 August 1986

ANNEXE Q

RECEIPTS FOR REPAYMENT OF MONEY IN RESPECT OF THE HOMES OF MR SCARGILL, MR HEATHFIELD AND MR WINDSOR

NATIONAL UNION OF MINEWORKERS

ST. JAMES' HOUSE, VICAR LANE,
SHEFFIELD, SOUTH YORKSHIRE S1 2EX

President A. SCARGILL   *Secretary* P. E. HEATHFIELD

Telephone: 0742 700388

Please quote our reference in reply:

Your Ref:

Our Ref:

Mr. S. Hudson,
Finance Officer,
National Union of Mineworkers,
St. James' House,
Vicar Lane,
SHEFFIELD S1   27th October, 1984

Dear Mr. Hudson,

2B, Yews Lane, Worsbrough Dale, Barnsley

On the 8th March, 1984, the NEC agreed to purchase the above property
to provide accommodation for me as National President. The terms
and conditions were to be along the same lines as those applicable
to my predecessor.

The matter was put into the hands of Messrs. Raley & Pratt, solicitors
and on the 8th August I redeemed my mortgage with the NUM Yorkshire
Area and paid the National Union of Mineworkers £22,255.45.

The matter has remained in the hands of our solicitors since that time
and to date the transaction has not been completed. On the basis
of legal advice, it is clear that at this stage it would not be practical
to complete the transaction/conveyance.

From the time of the agreement between the NEC and myself £6,118
was spent on improvements to the property and £742.58 on general
and water rates, and electricity, a total of £6,860.58.

In view of the time being taken to complete this transaction, I feel
I should pay the £6,860.58 covering the above items until such times
as the conveyance is complete and the ownership of the above property
transferred from me to the NUM. I enclose £6,860.58.

When the sale has been completed and the necessary approval obtained
for this Union property, it is my understanding that the Union will
complete the transaction and pay the amount stated in your letter
dated 9th August, 1984, plus the £6,860.58 referred to above.

Could you please confirm this.

Yours sincerely,

A. Scargill
PRESIDENT

Dear Mr. Scargill,

2B Yews Lane, Worsbrough Dale, Barnsley

Thank you for your letter of the 27th October, 1984.

I acknowledge receipt of £6,860.66 from you, to reimburse expenses incurred by the General Fund for improvements to property (£6,118) and rates/electricity (£742.58).

I confirm that once conveyance has been completed and approved, the Union will repay to you the amounts stated above and the amount as agreed in my letter of 9th August, 1984.

Yours sincerely,

S. HUDSON
Head of Finance

Mr. A. Scargill,
2b Yews Lane,
Worsbrough Dale,
BARNSLEY.

NATIONAL UNION OF MINEWORKERS

ST. JAMES' HOUSE, VICAR LANE,
SHEFFIELD, SOUTH YORKSHIRE S1 2EX

President A. SCARGILL   Secretary P. E HEATHFIELD

Telephone: 0742 700388

Please quote our reference in reply:

Your Ref:

Our Ref: PEH/EA

Mr. S. Hudson,
Finance Officer,
National Union of Mineworkers,
St. James' House,
Vicar Lane
SHEFFIELD S1 2EX   16th November, 1984

Dear Mr. Hudson,

262, Newbold Road, Chesterfield

The National Executive Committee agreed on the 8th March, 1984, to
purchase the above property and provide accommodation for me as
Secretary of the National Union of Mineworkers.   The terms and conditions
were to be the same as those applied to my predecessors.

This matter was put into the hands of our solicitors and arrangements
made to purchase the property from the NUM Derbyshire Area.

Unfortunately this matter has not yet been completed due to the situation
in the industry, although £13,511.21 has been paid for renovations/re-
building of the garage referred to in the valuer's report.

Until the property has been purchased by the National Union of Mineworkers,
I feel I should pay the amounts referred to above and I enclose £13,511.21

It is my understanding that when the sale has been completed, the
Union will repay to me £13,511.21 in accordance with the agreement
reached on the 8th March, 1984

Yours sincerely,

P.E Heathfield

P.E. Heathfield
SECRETARY

Dear Mr. Heathfield,

262 Newbold Road, Chesterfield

Thank you for your letter of the 16th November.

I acknowledge receipt of £13,511.21 in respect of renovations/
rebuilding of the above property. I confirm that once conveyance
has been completed and approved, the Union will repay to you the
amount stated above in accordance with the agreement reached on
8th March, 1984.

Yours sincerely,

S. HUDSON
Head Of Finance

Mr. P. E. Heathfield,
262 Newbold Road,
CHESTERFIELD.

12, MONCRIEFFE ROAD

NETHER EDGE

SHEFFIELD

29th November 1984

Dear Mr. Heathfield,

Temporary Bridging Loan

You will recall that the Union made available to me a bridging loan in connection with my transfer from London and to assist in the purchase of my house in Sheffield, in accordance with the Staff Agreement relating to relocation.

As agreed the bridging loan was to be repaid before the end of December 1984 and I have pleasure in remitting the sum of £29,500 (TWENTY-NINE THOUSAND AND FIVE HUNDRED POUNDS) in full repayment in respect of which I shall appreciate your receipt below in confirmation of full discharge.

Yours sincerely,

Roger Windsor

30th November, 1984

Dear Mr. Windsor,

TEMPORARY BRIDGING LOAN

I have pleasure in acknowledging receipt of £29,500 on the
29th November 1984 to clear the Bridging Loan granted to you by
the Union, in accordance with the staff agreement relating to
relocation.

Yours sincerely,

S. HUDSON
Head of Finance

Mr. R. Windsor
12 Moncrieffe Road,
Nether Edge,
Sheffield, 7.

NATIONAL UNION OF MINEWORKERS

HOLLY STREET,
SHEFFIELD, SOUTH YORKSHIRE S1 2GT

President: A. SCARGILL   *Secretary:* P. E. HEATHFIELD

Telephone: 0742 766900   *Fax:* 0742 766400

Please quote our reference in reply:

Your ref:

Our ref:
　　　NO81/IW/HH/90

9 April 1990

Ms E Jones
13 Old Square
Lincoln's Inn
London
WC2A 3UA

Dear Ms Jones

Please find enclosed all relevant documentation with regard to
Mr Scargill's mortgage, Mr Heathfield's renovation/repair costs
and Mr Windsor's bridging loan.

With regards to the union's bank accounts, I will be sorting
these out with Mr Brookland this afternoon.

Yours sincerely

I White
Finance Officer

Encs

9th March, 1984

Dear Mr. Homer,

In accordance with Minute 6 of the Finance and General
Purposes Sub-Committee of the 7th March, 1984, we have
pleasure in enclosing our cheque for £22,255.45.

Yours sincerely,

P   E   HEATHFIELD
Secretary

Mr. K. Homer,
National Union of Mineworkers,
Miners' Offices,
BARNSLEY.
S70 2LS

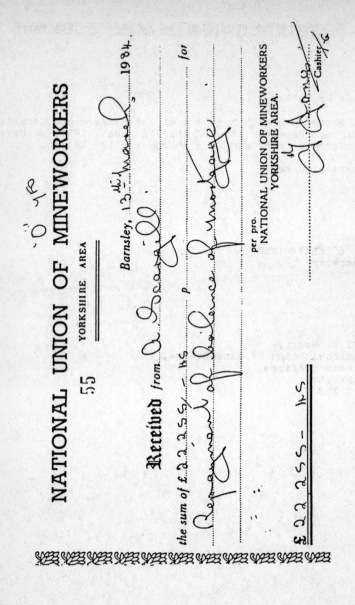

NATIONAL UNION OF MINEWORKERS

YORKSHIRE AREA

55

No. 0.45.

Barnsley, 13th March 1984.

Received from A. Scargill

the sum of £2,255. ... 45. ... p.

for

Repayment of balance of mortgage

per pro.
NATIONAL UNION OF MINEWORKERS
YORKSHIRE AREA.

Cashier

£2,255 - 45

NATIONAL UNION OF MINEWORKERS

ST. JAMES' HOUSE, VICAR LANE,
SHEFFIELD, SOUTH YORKSHIRE S1 2EX

President A. SCARGILL

Secretary P. E. HEATHFIELD

Telephone: 0742 700388

Please quote our reference in reply:

Your Ref:

Our Ref: AS/NM

8 August, 1984

Steven Hudson
Finance Officer
NATIONAL UNION OF MINEWORKERS
St. James House
Vicar Lane
Sheffield S1 2EX

Dear Mr. Hudson:

MORTGAGE REPAYMENT

Please find enclosed two cheques for the sum of
£22,255.45, representing the repayment of my mortgage
to the National Union of Mineworkers.

Could you please confirm that this mortgage has now
been redeemed?

Yours sincerely

Arthur Scargill
President

NATIONAL UNION OF MINEWORKERS

**ST. JAMES' HOUSE, VICAR LANE,
SHEFFIELD, SOUTH YORKSHIRE S1 2EX**

President A. SCARGILL   *Secretary* P. E. HEATHFIELD

Telephone: 0742 700388

Please quote our reference in reply:

Your Ref:

Our Ref: SH/NM

9 August, 1984

Arthur Scargill
President
NATIONAL UNION OF MINEWORKERS
St. James House
Vicar Lane
Sheffield S1 2EX

Dear Mr. Scargill:

Redemption of Mortgage: 2B Yews Lane, Worsborough

Thank you for your letter of 8th August, 1984. I
confirm receipt of £22,255.45 in respect of the redemption of the above mortgage.

Following final clearance of the conveyance of the
above property, the National Union will pay to you the
agreed capital sum of £50,250 (Re: Valuation per Holroyd,
Sons & Pickersgill) and accrued interest at the UK Clearing
Banks Average Base Rate for the period.

Yours sincerely,

Steven Hudson
Finance Officer

NATIONAL UNION OF MINEWORKERS

ST. JAMES' HOUSE, VICAR LANE,
SHEFFIELD, SOUTH YORKSHIRE S1 2EX

President A. SCARGILL   Secretary P. E. HEATHFIELD

Telephone: 0742 700388

Please quote our reference in reply:

Your Ref:

Our Ref:

Mr. S. Hudson,
Finance Officer,
National Union of Mineworkers,
St. James' House,
Vicar Lane,
SHEFFIELD S1   27th October, 1984

Dear Mr. Hudson,

2B, Yews Lane, Worsbrough Dale, Barnsley

On the 8th March, 1984, the NEC agreed to purchase the above property
to provide accommodation for me as National President.   The terms
and conditions were to be along the same lines as those applicable
to my predecessor.

The matter was put into the hands of Messrs. Raley & Pratt, solicitors
and on the 8th August I redeemed my mortgage with the NUM Yorkshire
Area and paid the National Union of Mineworkers £22,255.45.

The matter has remained in the hands of our solicitors since that time
and to date the transaction has not been completed.   On the basis
of legal advice, it is clear that at this stage it would not be practical
to complete the transaction/conveyance.

From the time of the agreement between the NEC and myself £6,118
was spent on improvements to the property and £742.58 on general
and water rates, and electricity, a total of £6,860.58.

In view of the time being taken to complete this transaction, I feel
I should pay the £6,860.58 covering the above items until such times
as the conveyance is complete and the ownership of the above property
transferred from me to the NUM.   I enclose £6,860.58.

When the sale has been completed and the necessary approval obtained
for this Union property, it is my understanding that the Union will
complete the transaction and pay the amount stated in your letter
dated 9th August, 1984, plus the £6,860.58 referred to above.

Could you please confirm this.

Yours sincerely,

A. Scargill
PRESIDENT

241

Dear Mr. Scargill,

2B Yews Lane, Worsbrough Dale, Barnsley

Thank you for your letter of the 27th October, 1984.

I acknowledge receipt of £6,860.66 from you, to reimburse expenses incurred by the General Fund for improvements to property (£6,118) and rates/electricity (£742.58).

I confirm that once conveyance has been completed and approved, the Union will repay to you the amounts stated above and the amount as agreed in my letter of 9th August, 1984.

Yours sincerely,

S. HUDSON
Head of Finance

Mr. A. Scargill,
2b Yews Lane,
Worsbrough Dale,
BARNSLEY.

NATIONAL UNION OF MINEWORKERS

ST. JAMES' HOUSE, VICAR LANE,
SHEFFIELD, SOUTH YORKSHIRE S1 2EX

President A. SCARGILL   Secretary P. E HEATHFIELD

Telephone: 0742 700388

Please quote our reference in reply:

Your Ref:

Our Ref: PEH/EA

Mr. S. Hudson,
Finance Officer,
National Union of Mineworkers,
St. James' House,
Vicar Lane
SHEFFIELD S1 2EX   16th November, 1984

Dear Mr. Hudson,

262, Newbold Road, Chesterfield

The National Executive Committee agreed on the 8th March, 1984, to
purchase the above property and provide accommodation for me as
Secretary of the National Union of Mineworkers.   The terms and conditions
were to be the same as those applied to my predecessors.

This matter was put into the hands of our solicitors and arrangements
made to purchase the property from the NUM Derbyshire Area.

Unfortunately this matter has not yet been completed due to the situation
in the industry, although £13,511.21 has been paid for renovations/re-
building of the garage referred to in the valuer's report.

Until the property has been purchased by the National Union of Mineworkers,
I feel I should pay the amounts referred to above and I enclose £13,511.21

It is my understanding that when the sale has been completed, the
Union will repay to me £13,511.21 in accordance with the agreement
reached on the 8th March, 1984

Yours sincerely,

P.E.Heathfield

P.E. Heathfield
SECRETARY

Dear Mr. Heathfield,

262 Newbold Road, Chesterfield

Thank you for your letter of the 16th November.

I acknowledge receipt of £13,511.21 in respect of renovations/
rebuilding of the above property. I confirm that once conveyance
has been completed and approved, the Union will repay to you the
amount stated above in accordance with the agreement reached on
8th March, 1984.

Yours sincerely,

S. HUDSON
Head Of Finance

Mr. P. E. Heathfield,
262 Newbold Road,
CHESTERFIELD.

Steve Hudson.

Bridging Loan

I have experienced certain difficulties with the purchase of my new house in Sheffield and the National Officials have agreed to make bridging facilities available.

The amount required in the first instance is £29.500.

I should be pleased thus if you could make a cheque payable to
        'Leeds Permanent Building Society'
for that sum in order that this matter is kept confidential and will not attract attention outside the union.

Roger Windsor

NATIONAL UNION OF MINEWORKERS

ST. JAMES' HOUSE, VICAR LANE,
SHEFFIELD, SOUTH YORKSHIRE S1 2EX

President A. SCARGILL   Secretary P. E. HEATHFIELD

Telephone: 0742 700388

Please quote our reference in reply:

Your Ref:

Our Ref: NO2/PEH/EA   25 May 1984

Mr R. E. Windsor
Melbourne House
Lower Street
STROUD
Glos.

Dear Mr Windsor,

Assistance with House Purchase

In accordance with the arrangements made for your predecessor whereby the Union provided him with financial assistance with a house purchase, and in line with the undertakings made in respect of the relocation of National Office Staff to Sheffield from London as indicated to you at the time of your appointment, I approve your application for a bridging loan in connection with your purchase of a family home in Sheffield.

The Union has given assistance to key personnel who transferred to Sheffield by way of temporary accommodation whilst locating a permanent residence and I understand that in order to effect a purchase within the near future you require temporary financial assistance.

Such an advance would have to be repaid as soon as possible and not later than the 31 December 1984 or further approval from the Finance and General Purposes Committee may be required.

Yours sincerely,

P. E. Heathfield
SECRETARY

1 2 , M O N C R I E F F E   R O A D

N E T H E R   E D G E

S H E F F I E L D

29th November 1984

Dear Mr. Heathfield,

<u>Temporary Bridging Loan</u>

You will recall that the Union made available to me a bridging loan in connection with my transfer from London and to assist in the purchase of my house in Sheffield, in accordance with the Staff Agreement relating to relocation.

As agreed the bridging loan was to be repaid before the end of December 1984 and I have pleasure in remitting the sum of £29,500 (TWENTY-NINE THOUSAND AND FIVE HUNDRED POUNDS) in full repayment in respect of which I shall appreciate your receipt below in confirmation of full discharge.

Yours sincerely,

Roger Windsor

NO81/SH/ST

30th November, 1984

Dear Mr. Windsor,

TEMPORARY BRIDGING LOAN

I have pleasure in acknowledging receipt of £29,500 on the
29th November 1984 to clear the Bridging Loan granted to you by
the Union, in accordance with the staff agreement relating to
relocation.

Yours sincerely,

S. HUDSON
Head of Finance

Mr. R. Windsor
12 Moncrieffe Road,
Nether Edge,
Sheffield, 7.

ANNEXE R

MR SCARGILL'S PERSONAL MONIES

Part I

Deposit of Mr Scargill's Personal Monies into an NUM Bank Account

One additional matter which I consider requires clarification relates to Mr Scargill's personal funds, the NUM official bank accounts and the payment of £29,100 from the NUM's Bank of Ireland Finance Limited account into an account in the name of A Pickering at the Jyske Bank in Denmark. A Pickering was the maiden name of Mr Scargill's mother. Mr Scargill has satisfied me that he kept and invested personal funds in the name of "Pickering" to place them beyond the reach of any Sequestrator or Receiver. KPMG Peat Marwick, Sheffield, reviewed the deposit of Mr Scargill's funds with the NUM during the audit of the NUM's financial statements for the year ended 31 December 1984. KPMG Peat Marwick, Sheffield were satisfied that the monies were Mr Scargill's personal funds and did not belong to the NUM.

Cork Gully have examined various financial records and documentation relating to the account operated with Jyske Bank. Mr Scargill deposited £30,100 into an NUM account held with the Cooperative Bank, Sheffield. This deposit was made in two tranches. One deposit was of £17,000 drawn by cheque from Mr Scargill's account operated with the Leeds Permanent Building Society and deposited into the NUM bank account on 20 August 1984. The second deposit consisted of three cheques drawn on Mr Scargill's accounts at Nationwide Building Society, Yorkshire Building Society and Leeds Permanent Building Society totalling £13,100, which were deposited in the account on 24 August 1984.

Two of the four accounts used to deposit £30,100 had been operated by Mr Scargill since at least 1978, one had been operated since 1982 and one once since 1976. The NUM, having received £30,100 from Mr Scargill, repaid £1,000 from its

ANNEXE R

Cooperative Bank account to Mr Scargill's Cooperative Bank account in Barnsley. The NUM then obtained a bank draft, payable to the Jyske Bank, for £29,100. This bank draft was drawn from the NUM bank account held with the Bank of Ireland Finance Limited, Dublin. The request for a bank draft to be drawn from this NUM account was made by Mr Heathfield in a letter to Bank of Ireland Finance Limited, dated 24 August 1984. The bank draft was provided to Mr Scargill who made arrangements to deposit the draft into three accounts in the name of A Pickering with Jyske Bank.

There is therefore no doubt that the £29,100 paid to Mr Scargill from the NUM's Bank of Ireland Finance Limited account was matched by an equivalent amount deposited into the NUM Cooperative Bank in Sheffield, the source of which was Mr Scargill's personal funds.

ANNEXE R

Part II

**Personal Cash Received by Mr Scargill between December 1984 and August 1987
out of which interest repayments were made to the MTUI/IMO
in respect of the bridging loan/mortgage**

Date	Description	Amount
		£
14 December 1984	National Savings Certificate (Note 2)	£13,155.00
07 September 1985	A Pickering Account (Note 3)	£9,000.00
1984 - August 1985	Rent received in cash from H Scargill (father)	£4,700.00
1984 - August 1987	TV Fees	£5,889.00
1984 - August 1987	Expenses (including N Myers) paid by credit card and reimbursed in cash	£4,193.00
04 February 1987	National Savings Certificate redeemed and cashed	£16,921.24
	TOTAL	£53,858.24

Notes:

(1) The above information was provided to Cork Gully by Mr Scargill on 12 June 1990. Cork Gully have not undertaken any work to substantiate the details shown above.

(2) Mr Scargill provided Cork Gully with a copy of a National Savings Certificate repayment confirmation dated 14 December 1984 in the amount of £13,155.00

(3) Mr Scargill explained that these monies arose from:

251

ANNEXE R

	£
IMO Loans	100,000.00
Jyske Bank Funds	34,000.00
	134,000.00
less	
House Purchase	(125,000.00)
Balance	£9,000.00

ANNEXE S

DOCUMENTS RELATING TO REPAYMENT
OF MR WINDSOR'S £29,500 LOAN TO THE IMO

DATED 1st September 1987

MR. & MRS. R. E. WINDSOR

SECOND CHARGE

RALEY & PRATT,
BARNSLEY.

254

Land Registration Acts 1925-1971

County and District: SOUTH YORKSHIRE - SHEFFIELD

Title Number:

Property: *19 KENBOURNE ROAD SHEFFIELD. S7 INT SOUTH YORKSHIRE*

DATED the   *1 ST*   day of   *SEPTEMBER*   1987

IN CONSIDERATION of Twenty nine thousand five hundred pounds (£29500.00)
(the receipt whereof is hereby acknowledged) **WE ROGER EDWARD WINDSOR** and
ANGELA CHRISTINE WINDSOR of the above property (hereinafter called "the
Borrowers") hereby as Beneficial Owners charge the land comprised in the
title above referred to with payment to **ARTHUR SCARGILL** of Treelands
Cottage Hound Hill Lane Worsbrough Bridge Barnsley South Yorkshire
ALAIN SIMON of 119 rue Pierre Sémard 93000 Bobigny France and **PETER ERNEST
HEATHFIELD** of 262 Newbold Road Chesterfield Derbyshire as Trustees on
behalf of the International Miners Organisation (otherwise known as the
Organisation Internationale Des Mineurs) of 119 rue Pierre Sémard
93000 Bobigny France (hereinafter called "the Lenders") on the First day
of September One thousand nine hundred and ninety seven of the principal
sum of Twenty nine thousand five hundred pounds with interest thereon
per annum at the minimum lending rate from time to time of Co-operative
Bank PLC (of 1 Balloon Street Manchester M60 4EP).

The Borrowers hereby covenant with the Lenders that so long as any
money remains owing on this security they will maintain the insurance
of the premises hereby charged as required by a prior Charge in favour
of the said Co-operative Bank PLC dated the   *25 TH*   day of
SEPTEMBER 1986 and registered on the *13 TH*   day of
OCTOBER 1986   (hereinafter called "the Prior Charge") and will keep

the said premises in good and sufficient repair in accordance with the covenant in that regard contained in the Prior Charge.

If the Borrowers shall fail to perform any of their obligations under this clause the Lenders may effect such insurance as aforesaid and may enter upon the premises hereby charged and execute such repairs as in the opinion of the Lenders may be necessary or proper without thereby becoming liable as a mortgagee in possession and the Borrowers will on demand repay to the Lenders all expenses so incurred by the Lenders and will pay interest thereon at the said rate from the date of demand until repayment and all such expenses and interest shall be charged on the property hereby charged

PROVIDED ALWAYS

1.   No statutory or other powers of leasing or accepting surrenders of leases shall be exercisable by the Borrowers without the consent in writing of the Lenders

2.   In the event of any proceeding or step being taken to exercise or enforce any powers or remedies conferred by the Prior Charge against the property hereby charged the Lenders may redeem the Prior Charge or procure the transfer thereof to themselves and may settle and pass accounts of the Chargee under the Prior Charge and any accounts so settled or passed shall be conclusive and binding on the Borrowers and all the principal money interest costs charges and expenses of and incident to such redemption or transfer shall be paid by the Borrowers to the Lenders on demand with interest at the said rate from the time or respective times of the same having been paid or incurred and until payment the property hereby charged shall stand charged with the amount so to be paid with interest as aforesaid.

In this Charge the terms "the Borrowers" and "the Lenders" shall where the context so admits include the persons deriving title under the Borrowers and the Lenders respectively.

SIGNED SEALED AND DELIVERED by the said)
)

ROGER EDWARD WINDSOR in the presence)
)

of:-

    Roy Hyde
    42 Penderel Crescent
    Stroud. Gloucestershire

    Engineer

SIGNED SEALED AND DELIVERED by the said)
)

ANGELA CHRISTINE WINDSOR in the presence)
)

of:-

    Meryl Hyde
    42 Penderel Crescent
    Stroud. Gloucestershire

    Nurse.

12 Moncrieffe Road,
Nether Edge,
Sheffield, 7.

22nd July 1986

Mr. A. Scargill,
President,
National Union of Mineworkers,
St. James's House,
Vicar Lane,
Sheffield.

Dear Mr. Scargill,

Personal Loan/Bridging Loan

I acknowledge receipt of your letter dated the 21st July 1986,
and also acknowledge receipt of £29,500 cash, representing
an interest-free, personal loan/bridging loan, to be repaid
in full on or before the 21st July 1987 to the International
Miners' Organisation.

Yours sincerely,

R. Windsor

AS/NM

Mr. R. Windsor,
12 Moncrieffe Road,
Nether Edge,
Sheffield 7.

21st July 1986

Dear Mr. Windsor,

Personal Loan/Bridging Loan

I am writing on behalf of the International Miners' Organisation (IMO) to confirm that we are prepared to give you an interest-free personal loan/bridging loan for a period of 12 months from the date of this letter.

The loan will be in the sum of £29,500 (which I enclose with this letter) repayable, on or before the 21st July 1987. Could you please confirm receipt of this loan and also acceptance of the conditions in connection with same.

Yours sincerely,

A. Scargill
PRESIDENT

ANNEXE T

ACKNOWLEDGEMENTS BY IMO

Président :
Arthur Scargill

Secrétaire Général :
Alain Simon

119 rue Pierre Sémard
93000 Bobigny
FRANCE

Tél. : 48.95.96.87
Telex : 233419
Télécopieur : 48.95.96.88

The International Miners' Organisation of 119 Pierre Semard 93000
Bobigny, Paris, France, hereby recognises and declares that the
properties known as and situate at 12 Carver Lane, Sheffield and
62 Alexandra Road, Swadlincote, Burton-on-Trent which are
registered at HM Land Registry in the name of the International
Miners' Organisation under title numbers SYK 218634 and DY 148498
are held by the International Miners' Organisation for the National
Union of Mineworkers absolutely and that the said properties or
the proceeds of sale will be transferred to the National Union of
Mineworkers on request.

Signed the .... day of June 1990
For and on behalf of the
International Miners' Organisation
by Alain Simon

In the presence of

CHERIKA Hadjid, Collaborateur de l'OIM
119 rue Pierre Semard 93000 Bobigny

[   ]
In the presence of   elestakov
CHESTAKOV VALERI, secrétaire de l'OIM

ORGANISATION INTERNATIONALE DES MINEURS

Président :
Arthur Scargill

Secrétaire Général :
Alain Simon

119 rue Pierre Sémard
93000 Bobigny
FRANCE

Tél. : 48.95.96.87
Telex : 233419
Télécopieur : 48.95.96.88

The National Executive Committee
The National Union of Mineworkers
Holly Street
Sheffield
South Yorkshire

Dear Sirs,

On 1st September 1987, Mr. Roger Windsor signed a second legal charge agreeing to pay £29,500 plus interest at the minimum lending rate from time to time of the Co-operative Bank plc to the International Miners' Organisation.

It has always been the intention of the International Miners' Organisation ("the IMO") that when recovered from Mr. Windsor, the sum of £29,500 plus interest would be paid to the National Union of Mineworkers ("the NUM"). The IMO hereby declares that it is content for the said money to be paid by Mr. Windsor to the NUM or to the Miners' Solidarity Fund as the National Executive Committee of the NUM chooses.

The IMO will, once the National Executive Committee has decided whether it requires the funds to be paid to the NUM or the Miners' Solidarity Fund, direct Mr. Windsor so to pay the money. If Mr. Windsor refuses to pay the money, then the IMO will at the choice of the National Executive Committee either take steps to assign all its right and interest in the debt due from Mr. Windsor pursuant to the deed of 1st September 1987 to the NUM or to the Miners' Solidarity Fund as the NEC directs, to enable the relevant body to take legal action to recover the money, or continue the legal action already commenced in France for the benefit of the NUM or the Miners' Solidarity Fund.

INTERNATIONAL
MINERS'
ORGANISATION
ORGANIZACIÓN
INTERNACIONAL DE
MINEROS
МЕЖДУНАРОДНАЯ
ОРГАНИЗАЦИЯ
ГОРНЯКОВ

Signed [   ]

for and on behalf of the IMO

ANNEXE U

SUMMARY RECEIPTS AND PAYMENTS OF BANK ACCOUNT INTO WHICH NUR LOAN £300,00 WAS DEPOSITED

ANNEXE U

SUMMARY RECEIPTS AND PAYMENTS OF BANK ACCOUNT (ACCOUNT NUMBER 16 IN ANNEXE I) INTO WHICH NUR LOAN OF £300,000 DEPOSITED

Receipts	£	Payments	£
Australian Miners	2,591.05	Purchase of 62, Alexander Road, Swadlingcote	16,000.00
NUR (including Interest earned from Mineworkers Trust account)	310,379.20	Loan to Printing Co-op	1,013.10
Bank Interest	97,642.02	NUR	300,000.00
NUM Affiliation Fees	105,200.00	Professor Allen	8,000.00
Alain Simon (repayment of Mr Scargill's bridging loan)	50,000.00	Bank Charges	55.61
NUM South Africa Appeal Fund	48,150.00	IMO Expenditure	75,703.58
Donation for NUM South Africa	58,181.92	British Telecom Mobile Phone Charges	4,891.92
Grant from Mineworkers' Trust	32,000.00	American Express Chargecard Expenses	6,612.20
Repayment of advance to NUM South Africa	25,000.00	London Conference on Unemployment	6,528.61
Balance from closure of Mineworkers' Trust Account	1,733.53	IMO Australian Conference	4,710.65
Miscellaneous Receipts	998.65	Advance to NUM South Africa	25,032.02
Repayment of Advance to Architect	25,000.00	Onward Payment of Donation for NUM South Africa	50,052.48
		Transfer to another IMO Bank Account	46,004.61
		Transfer to other IMO "Pool" Accounts	105,998.82
		Purchase of Carver Lane From Mineworkers' Trust	25,000.00
		Soviet Miners	7,351.46
		Advance to Architect	25,000.00
		Balance as at 30 March 1990	48,921.31
	£756.876.37		**£756,876.37**

ANNEXE V

INTEREST CALCULATION ON MONEY RECEIVED FROM THE MINEWORKERS' TRUST

<u>ANNEXE V</u>

<u>ATTRIBUTABLE INTEREST CALCULATION ON NUR LOAN</u>

Date	Interest Rate/%	No of Days	Deposit/ (Withdrawal) £	Attributable Interest £
19.03.86			310,379.20 (c)	
31.03.86	11.00	12		1,122.47
30.06.86	10.50	91		8,154.52
30.09.86	9.12	92		7,348.06
31.12.86	9.70	92		7,995.03
31.03.87	9.81	90		8,103.31
30.06.87	8.45	91		7,228.18
30.09.87	8.44	92		7,452.74
31.12.87	8.43	92		7,602.26
31.03.88	7.72	90		6,955.34
30.06.88	6.71	91		6,228.91
30.09.88	9.18	93		8,854.80
31.12.88	11.38	92		11,112.83
17.03.89	11.57	76	(300,000.00)(d)	9,601.15
31.03.89	11.57	14		479.90
30.06.89	10.00	91		2,708.03
30.09.89	11.54	92		3,238.17
05.10.89	12.34	5		193.66
31.12.89	12.34	87		3,375.41
31.03.90	12.21	90		3,556.64

TOTAL INTEREST ATTRIBUTED   <u>£111,311.41</u>

<u>ATTRIBUTABLE INTEREST CALCULATION ON MONIES RECEIVED FROM MINEWORKERS' TRUST</u>

Date	Interest Rate/%	No of Days	Deposits £	Attributable Interest £
16.03.89			32,000.00	
31.03.89	11.57	15		152.15
30.06.89	10.00	91		801.60
30.09.89	11.54	92		958.53
05.10.89	12.34	5	1,733.53	57.33
31.12.89	12.34	87		1,050.14
31.03.90	12.21	90		1,106.53

TOTAL INTEREST ATTRIBUTED

<u>£4,126.28</u>

ANNEXE V

Notes:

(a) The interest rates used have been calculated by estimating the average interest rate applied to the account balance on a quarterly basis.

(b) As the ownership of the funds received from the Mineworkers Trust is uncertain, no allowance has been made in the above calculation for withdrawals from the funds. As a result the interest calculated above is greater than the total actual interest earned on all of the funds held in the bank account into which the NUR loan was deposited.

(c) The deposit of £310,379.20 consisted of:

	£
Loan from NUR	300,000.00
Interest earned in Mineworkers Trust bank account	10,411.70
	310,411.70
Less bank charges	(32.50)
	£310,379.20

(d) The capital sum of £300,000 was re-paid to the NUR on 17 March 1989.

(e) The total amount of Mineworkers' Trust monies, including attributable interest, considered to have been held in this bank account are:

	£
Interest earned in Mineworkers' Trust bank account	10,379.20
Interest on NUR loan	111,311.41
Mineworkers' Trust deposits	33,733.53
Interest on Mineworkers' Trust deposits	4,126.28
	159,550.42

267

Part I

ATTRIBUTABLE INTEREST CALCULATION ON NUM DEPOSITS IN MTUI/IMO TRUST FUND ALLOWING FOR WITHDRAWALS MADE FROM "THE POOL OF IMO ACCOUNTS"

Date	Interest Rate/%	No of Days	Deposit/ (Withdrawal) £	Interest Attributable £
30.01.85			98,568.41	
15.02.85	13.00	16	249,476.04	561.70
04.04.85	13.00	48		5,959.73
11.04.85	12.75	7	122,325.00	866.99
25.04.85	12.75	14		2,336.43
29.04.85	12.00	4	110,239.38	631.36
07.05.85	12.00	8		1,554.32
16.05.85	12.50	9		1,826.26
03.07.85	12.63	48		9,871.67
19.07.85	12.00	16		3,178.35
08.08.85	11.00	20		3,661.01
16.09.85	10.00	39		6,529.10
27.11.85	9.50	72		11,573.39
22.03.86	10.00	115	(4,500.00)	19,822.82
10.04.86	10.00	19		3,354.84
04.05.86	9.50	24	(25,000.00)	4,046.76
16.05.86	9.50	12	(16,000.00)	1,957.84
23.05.86	9.50	7	(1,700.00)	1,116.55
08.09.86	9.50	108		17,210.32
15.10.86	9.00	37		5,742.82
08.12.86	10.00	54	(81,988.00)	9,397.65
16.03.87	10.00	98		15,105.98
31.03.87	9.50	15		2,255.51
09.04.87	9.31	9		1,331.42
03.11.87	9.00	208		29,814.23
04.12.87	8.13	31		4,219.80
12.04.88	8.00	129		17,398.33
18.05.88	7.75	36		4,836.61
16.06.88	7.25	29		3,672.65
20.06.88	6.75	4	(178,800.00)	474.35
25.07.88	6.75	35	(30,000.00)	2,996.36
26.08.88	6.75	32		2,579.73
11.10.88	11.00	46		6,079.01
09.03.89	10.00	149	(25,000.00)	18,148.80

ANNEXE W

17.03.89	10.00	8		959.42
02.06.89	10.00	77		9,254.62
07.08.89	11.00	66	(243,300.00)	8,909.86
11.09.89	11.00	34		2,188.23
18.09.89	12.00	7		496.51
10.10.89	13.00	22		1,694.39
24.10.89	14.00	14	(59,000.00)	1,170.29
08.12.89	14.00	45	(200,000.00)	2,763.49

TOTAL INTEREST ATTRIBUTED   £247,549.50

Note:

1) The interest rates used are those applicable to the account as applied by the Irish Intercontinental Bank.

2) The total amount of NUM funds deposited into the MTUI/IMO trust fund and into other IMO accounts and the interest earned or attributed to these funds is as follows:

	£	£
NUM funds paid into MIREDS account	580,608.83	
Attributable interest	247,549.50	828,158.33
NUM funds paid into account with		
Chase Bank	71,284.15	
Interest earned	16,401.80	87,685.95
NUM funds paid into account with		
First Chicago Bank		800.00(a)
NUM Funds paid into account with		
Co-operative Bank	10,000.00	
Attributable interest	17.53	10,017.53(b)
		£926,661.81

ANNEXE W

(a)   The $1,000 deposited into the First Chicago Bank account on 12 November 1984, was converted to £800 using the exchange rate of $1.25/£1.00. An attributable interest calculation has not been prepared for thisdeposit because any notional interest earned would simply be offset against an exchange loss of £115.23 which arose when the $1,000 was converted to Sterling in February 1986.

(b)   This deposit was a transfer of £10,000 from SWAG account on 1 August 1988 to an IMO pool account for eight days, earning interest of approximately £17.53.

3) The withdrawals represent monies originating in the MTUI/IMO trust fund and other IMO accounts ("The pool of IMO accounts") which have been identified as being for NUM benefit. These withdrawals total £865,288 (See Annexe W Part II).

ANNEXE W

Part II

Payments from pool of IMO accounts which are accepted as being for the benefit of the NUM

	£
Architects Fees	29,500.00
Purchase of 62 Alexander Road, Swadlingcote	16,000.00
Total Loan Repayments (Annexe L)	689,000.00
Legal Fees	81,988.00 (a)
NUM Notts Area re Severance Payment	23,800.00
Purchase of 12 Carver Lane, Sheffield	25,000.00
TOTAL	**£865,288.00**

Note:

(a)　These legal fees are in respect of Mr Scargill's action against the Chief Constable of South Yorkshire police, seeking damages for false imprisonment. This payment has been accepted as being for the benefit of the NUM because of a minute, recording an NEC decision that Mr Scargill be empowered to bring such an action, a copy of which was given to the Enquiry by Mr Scargill. It is difficult to understand why this payment was not made from the official bank accounts of the NUM, unless it was considered by Mr Scargill to be embarrassing to do so.

271

ANNEXE W

Part III

Payments from pool of IMO accounts which Mr Scargill claims were made for the benefit of the NUM

	£
Miners Solidarity Fund	135,000.00
IMO London Conference	30,000.00
Plane Hire	12,000.00
Various Air Fares	27,606.00
NUM South Africa Air Fares	23,700.00
London Conference on Unemployment	6,528.61
IMO Australian Conference	4,710.65
IMO Cairo Conference	2,265.00
American Express Charge Card Expenses of Mr Scargill and Mr Heathfield	6,612.20
British Telecom Mobile Phone Charges of Mr Scargill and Mr Heathfield	4,891.92
TOTAL	**£253,314.38**

ANNEXE W

PART IV

Some of the payments made from pool of IMO accounts for IMO benefit

	£
Bank Charges	1,594.50
Loan to Mr Heathfield	60,000.00
French Miners	20,000.00
Moroccan Miners	8,000.00
Philippine Miners	10,000.00
Professor Allen	20,000.00
Interest Paid	2,149.59
Expenses for IMO Delegates	3,664.58
Mr Simon	35,000.00
Transfer to IMO Bank Account	63,075.65
IMO Conference Costs	48,593.45
Air Tickets	20,178.75
International Delegation	900.00
Exchange Loss	308.00
Unidentified Payments	2,707.86
Monies Transferred to MACF and SWAG and used for Various IMO Expenses	79,142.41
TOTAL	**£375,314,79**

ANNEXE X

LIST OF ABBREVIATIONS

MACF   -   **Miners Action Committee Fund**

SWAG   -   **Sheffield Women's Action Group**

IMO   -   **International Miners Organisation**

President: Mr A Scargill
Gen Secretary: Alain Simon

MTUI   -   **Miners Trades Union International**

WFTU   -   **World Federation of Trades Unions**

MSF   -   **Miners Solidarity Fund**

Trustees: David Blunkett
               Bill Michie
               Richard Caborn

NUR   -   **National Union of Railwaymen**

MIREDS   -   **The Miners International Research
Education Defence and Support Fund**

Trustees: Alain Simon
               Norman West M.E.P.

CEU   -   **Coal Employees Union (in the USSR)**

CGT   -   **French equivalent of the TUC**

ANNEXE X

LIST OF PRINCIPAL CHARACTERS

Mr A Scargill

President of the NUM
President of the IMO

Mr P Heathfield

General Secretary of the NUM
Chairman of Business and Policy Committee
(otherwise General Political Committee) of the
IMO

Mr R Windsor

Chief Executive Officer of NUM from 1983 to
1989

Mr Abbasi

Pakistani businessman living in England. Alleged
to have been involved in procuring financial
assistance for the NUM from Libya during 1984

Ms N Myers

Press Officer of the NUM and personal assistant
to Mr Scargill

Mr Alain Simon

General Secretary of the IMO
Trustee of the Miners International Research
Education Defence and Support Fund

Mr M Srebny

Former President of the Coal Employees Union
of the USSR

Mr S Hudson

Former Finance Officer of the NUM

Mr N West M.E.P

Trustee of the Miners International Research
Education Defence and Support Fund